Rationales for Teaching Young Adult Literature

Rationales for Teaching Young Adult Literature

Edited by

Louann Reid

with Jamie Hayes Neufeld

Boynton/Cook Publishers
HEINEMANN
Portsmouth, NH

Boynton/Cook Publishers, Inc.
361 Hanover Street
Portsmouth, NH 03801–3912
www.boyntoncook.com
First published by Calendar Islands Publishers 1999

Offices and agents throughout the world

ISBN 0-86709-599-7

Library of Congress Cataloging-in-Publication Data

Rationales for teaching young adult literature / [edited by] Louann Reid with Jamie Neufeld.

p. cm

Originally published: Portland, ME. : Calendar Islands Publishers, 1999

Includes bibliographical references.

1. Young adult literature—Study and teaching (Secondary). 2. Teenagers—Books and reading. I. Reid, Louann. II. Neufeld, Jamie.

PN59.R33 1999

809'.89283—dc21 99-32781

Design by Darci Mehall

Printed in the United States of America on acid-free paper

13 12 11 10 09 OPI 3 4 5 6 7

CONTENTS

ACKNOWLEDGMENTS

We are indebted to the contributors to this volume, who patiently wrote and rewrote as we editors refined our vision of the collection. We appreciate the assistance of Connie Cushman and Jean Wyrick, who enlisted teenagers to read books that might be challenged and discuss them with us. The teens and their parents graciously offered their time and homes for the interviews that are included in the Afterword. The College of Liberal Arts and the English Department at Colorado State University provided generous financial support for this project. We especially value working with Peter Stillman and John Watson, who are supportive, patient, and skillful editors and publishers.

Credits for reprinted material appear at the end of the book.

INTRODUCTION

One complaint is often sufficient. Books get pulled from library shelves, department book rooms, and even the hands of students. Teachers decide that no book is worth the trouble that this one has caused and select only "safe" titles in the future. School levies are defeated; administrators and board members are removed. Publishers become more cautious about what they will print, and writers are forced to rethink every word and scene they include in their works. On rare occasions, violence disrupts communities such as the ones James Moffett describes in *Storm in the Mountains*, an account of the 1974–1975 controversy in Kanawha County, West Virginia, surrounding *Communicating*, an innovative set of language arts materials.

It is a paradox, if true, that it takes a village to raise a child, but it takes only one complaint to raze a curriculum.

If you think these statements are extreme, you need this book. If you are all too familiar with aspects of the scenario we have described, you need this book. If you just want recommendations for powerful books to use with teenagers, you will find them here, along with objectives and considerations for teaching the material.

Every detail in that first paragraph comes from what teachers have said to us personally, from reading other teachers' accounts of their experiences, or from reports distributed by People for the American Way or the Office for Intellectual Freedom of the American Library Association. Everything has happened to people we know or know about.

The authors of the rationales in this volume are taking a risk—and asking you to join them. These teachers recommend titles that they know someone will object to. Yet, they strongly believe that adolescents should be allowed to read the books in spite of potential objections. Some of the twenty-two titles are best-suited for individuals or small groups to read; others are suitable for the whole class to discuss. Most of the books in this collection have won recognition and awards. Few are commonly challenged, yet all have the potential to invite censorship.

The relatively small number of challenges may reflect the status of these books as required reading. So far, the titles in this collection are not used as widely as the more challenged books, with which we are probably very familiar. Howard Foerstal's "The Most Frequently Banned Books in the 1990s"

(135–213) lists only two of the titles that are in *Rationales for Teaching Young Adult Literature. Fallen Angels* is number 21; *Annie on My Mind* is number 42. Why? They are not taught as often as titles in the top 5: *Impressions*, a literature-based K–6 reading series; *Of Mice and Men*; *The Catcher in the Rye*; *The Adventures of Huckleberry Finn*; and *The Chocolate War*.

We who are most familiar with the value of reading good literature need to protect the right to teach it. "The Student's Right to Read" from NCTE urges teachers to be sure that the school district has a selection and reconsideration policy—and that everyone follows it. Another important step is collecting and preparing rationales for the books you teach. Writing a rationale lets you articulate the values of a particular work and explain your objectives in using it *before* you are called on to defend it. You can use the rationales in this book to supplement those you write or as models for your own rationales for other books. You may also find a recommendation in here for the perfect book to supplement or replace the titles you currently teach. Annotations for dozens of titles have been included.

Rationales

Exactly what *is* a rationale, anyway? According to Jean E. Brown and Elaine C. Stephens, a "rationale is the articulation of reasons for using a particular literary work, film, or teaching method" ("Rationales" 1). Teachers are advised to have rationales for all of the works they teach, but that is seldom realistic or possible. Given the social and political climate in the United States in recent years, though, teachers would be wise to have clearly articulated reasons and support for materials and methods. Collections of rationales like this one and the ones mentioned in the Works Consulted list can serve as models and resources, but your own words and ideas will probably be the most persuasive if you are challenged. Besides, you know your students, school, and community well.

Following the advice of Brown and Stephens, we asked authors of these rationales to include certain information, using a specified format. Thus, you will find that each rationale begins with a brief excerpt from the book followed by complete bibliographic information and the intended audience. A plot summary and the ways in which the work will meet program objectives follow. Realizing that English language arts programs vary, we asked authors of rationales to rely on their teaching experience and professional reading as they selected goals that could apply to many programs. You may want to add, delete, or adapt these goals to fit your own program when you write your rationales. Authors also suggest the potential impact of the work on the reader, along with possible problems and ways to address them. References provide biographical and critical information about the writer of the featured book. A works cited list directs readers to the sources quoted in the rationale.

Most teachers now include an assurance in their course descriptions or in a letter home to parents that if a student or the parents object to reading a particular work, the teacher will provide an alternative selection. Yet it is often difficult to find a true alternative, one that has all of the qualities and deals with the problems and issues for which you chose the required reading in the first place. An alternative reading selection raises many other problems: Who chooses it? Where will the student go when you are having class discussions? How will you ensure that the student's learning is equivalent to that of others in the class? How do students request an alternative without placing a spotlight on their issues, feeling different, or opening themselves to criticism from peers? There are no easy answers for these questions, but having an alternative title in mind is a good start. Teachers will need to address the other practical matters sensitively with knowledge of the students and the community. A foundation of mutual respect often helps minimize difficulties that could arise around required reading. In addition, because so many teachers are using literature circles or are asking students to read related works, the authors of the rationales offer several other titles that connect to the featured title.

Young Adult Literature

Although the terms "young adult literature" or "adolescent literature" are at least thirty years old, the definitions still vary widely. We used a broad definition of young adult literature for the initial selection of possible titles for this collection, settling on "books that adolescents would probably like and be able to relate to." Certainly the comments of young readers in our classes, on the Internet, and in the interviews later in this book support the selection. If pressed for a more precise definition, we would say that all except four of the titles fit all of Robert Small's characteristics that are unique to young adult literature. He says that:

- the main character is a teenager
- events and problems in the plot are related to teenagers
- the main character is the center of the plot
- dialogue reflects teenage speech, including slang

- the point of view presents an adolescent's interpretation of events and people
- the teenage main character is usually perceptive, sensitive, intelligent, mature, and independent
- the novel is short, rarely more than 200 pages
- the actions and decisions of the main characters are major factors in the outcome of the conflict (qtd. in Herz and Gallo 8–9)

The remaining four titles were written for adults, with adult main characters. However, young readers like them, and many of the characteristics Small lists apply to these books, too.

Defining the genre, of course, was not enough. We wanted to give authors of rationales some idea about the titles deemed appropriate for this volume, but we also wanted them to write about a book that they really wanted to defend. First, we prepared a list of suggested titles by looking for recommended books that had a good probability of being taught in secondary schools *and* of being challenged. Jamie scanned titles of best books from the American Library Association's various lists for the 1990s. She looked at the study guides offered by companies such as Troll, Sundance, and The Writing Company, assuming that study guides would be offered for books that had a high probability of being taught. She also checked lists of frequently challenged books as reported to People for the American Way and consulted the American Library Association's *Banned Books Guide* for 1997. This guide indexes complaints for 1281 titles going back to 387 B.C. that people have banned or considered controversial; not all challenged titles are young adult literature.

People for the American Way reports that most objections to materials and methods are based on sexual content, objectionable language, and religion. Authors of the rationales identified other possibly objectionable elements such as violence, defiance of authority, or certain portrayals of groups or individuals.

A final step in preparing our list was to check for available rationales. We wanted to include contemporary works for which rationales were not readily available. We had decided to recommend books that were either published since 1980 or were more commonly used since then, such as *Their Eyes Were Watching God*, because most of the collections of rationales had been published in the 1980s for books copyrighted earlier (American Library Association 1989; Karolides and Burress 1985; and Shugert 1983). *Censored Books: Critical Viewpoints* by Karolides et al. was published in 1993 and includes three titles published in the 1980s, but only

Annie on My Mind is reviewed in both that volume and this one. *Statement*, the journal of the Colorado Language Arts Society, published a collection of fifteen rationales for books and films in 1997, including *Annie on My Mind* and *Their Eyes Were Watching God.* After authors had written their rationales for this collection, an excellent CD-ROM came from NCTE: *Rationales for Challenged Books.* It contains rationales for eight of the books reviewed in this volume.

Having done our homework, we sent out a call for manuscripts, contacted experts in young adult literature, and hoped there would be enough interest from good writers and teachers to compile a collection of rationales. We were delighted with the results.

After all of the rationales were written, we contacted parents of adolescents who had agreed to read one of the books. We gave them an annotated list of titles and the teens chose one. Our interviews with those who completed the reading are in the Afterword. Read what these adolescents said about *The Crazy Horse Electric Game; The Ear, the Eye, and the Arm; A Lesson Before Dying; Shizuko's Daughter; Fallen Angels;* and *If I Should Die Before I Wake.*

Challenges, Censorship, and Selection

Throughout this book, we refer primarily to book challenges rather than censorship. Censorship, the removal and/or destruction of material that someone objects to, may indeed be the result of a challenge. Those who challenge books see their goal as protecting their children and the children of others from harmful influences. Few people claim to be censors; the term is usually applied to someone else.

Informed selection must occur in classrooms and libraries. Some books suit particular educational purposes better than others. Money is not available to buy *all* books. Yet selection seeks to include all viewpoints in a library or classroom collection rather than exclude ones that may be objectionable.

A number of sources can help teachers select books. Publications such as *Booklist, The Bulletin of the Center for Children's Books, The Horn Book Magazine* and *The Horn Book Guide, Kirkus Reviews, Publishers Weekly, School Library Journal,* and *Voice of Youth Advocates* regularly review new books for children and young adults. Major newspapers often contain reviews, too. Reference books available in major libraries also direct readers to sources of reviews. One excellent recent publication is the two-volume

What Do Young Adults Read Next? A Reader's Guide to Fiction for Young Adults compiled by Pam Spencer. Each of the titles in these volumes is annotated with plot summary, sources of reviews, and related books. If students like a particular book and are looking for one like it, you may be able to find a suggestion here. Titles from 1988–1995 are listed in these two volumes.

Because we believe that multiple points of view enrich a democracy, we fear censorship. Those who wish to have their children read alternate works have every right to make that request. But they should not be allowed to make a decision to keep a work from other young readers. Presumably, there were sound reasons for the selection of the controversial work in the first place, and those reasons should not be ignored just because of a complaint.

Censorship threatens education. If teaching were confined to the transmission of facts, skills, and the literal interpretations of texts, as many challengers would like, students would be denied the opportunity to use their critical and creative faculties. James Moffett wrote, "To ban fantasy, zaniness, and absurdity is to cancel the uniquely human powers of transforming world in mind, of envisioning from what one has seen, and is hence to reduce people to animals, whose solemn adherence to things as they are prevents them from understanding how things might be . . . and may be already" (178). But using one's imagination and "transforming [the] world" are not valued by everyone. Vicki Frost, a Tennessee mother who initiated the challenge that led to *Mozert v. Hawkins County Public Schools* in 1983, said in a 1986 deposition, "The imagination or [sic] the thoughts of a child, and the thoughts are to be captive to the obedience of Christ. Their thoughts are not to go outside the realm of scriptural authority. There are several scriptures that deal with man walking after the imagination of his own heart, and a man's imagination can lead him away from God" (qtd. in DelFattore 48). And this is one of many available examples. We believe that students must be encouraged to explore alternatives and be allowed access to ideas, topics, and viewpoints that reinforce and challenge their own. A democratic society depends on such an education.

Perhaps the greatest threat, however, comes from within. The chilling effects of challenges are difficult to quantify. Yet some kind of second-guessing or possible self-censorship is evident. Writers and publishers must consider the readers who purchase books. While they do not shy away from all controversy, writers certainly consider consequences now in ways they did not previously. Katherine Paterson, author of *Bridge to Terabithia*, a frequently challenged and greatly loved book, said in response to Mark West's question about the influence of censorship on her writing: "Now, when I put a word in a book that I think might offend somebody, I take a second look at it. I no longer write as naively as I once did. . . . I usually keep what I wrote, but I can no longer be naive about the possible consequences of using certain words or including certain scenes" (West 8).

Teachers and education officials are often less brave than Paterson, possibly because they would be in the direct line of attack. People for the American Way reported in *Attacks on the Freedom to Learn 1996*: "An alarming finding in this year's report is that large numbers of those seeking to impose political, religious or ideological pressures on the public schools are education officials themselves: teachers, administrators, librarians, and school board members" (27). A teacher in Kentucky blacked out a phrase in Cormier's *The Chocolate War*, hoping to avoid controversy. Instead, her action just called attention to the book. A parent challenged *The Chocolate War*, and Cormier's *I Am the Cheese* and attempted to file a lawsuit against the teacher (27). Knowing what to do isn't simple, but trying to avoid controversy is neither effective nor educationally wise. It is better to be prepared to meet objections with sound reasons and a solid understanding of possible issues.

More and more educators may have recognized the need to act. Recently, reports of book challenges have declined (Suhor 1). Explanations include teachers choosing "safe" material or the limiting effects of standards-based education accompanied by book lists. On the positive side, Charles Suhor, NCTE/SLATE Field Representative, points out that "book-banners (and film/video-banners) are in an extremely weak position when districts have established fair-minded policies for assignment of substitute works and for review of challenges to instructional materials. Protesters are further confounded when teachers can point to a well-articulated process for selecting materials, refuting the oft-advanced claim that the works under study were chosen capriciously" (2).

To ensure that students may read high-quality, interesting literature we must prepare for the objections that some people will raise. With *Rationales for Teaching Young Adult Literature,* we hope to entice you and your students with outstanding works of literature and provide support for your use of these works—and others like them—in class.

Works Consulted

A number of excellent resources exist. Several can help us understand the worldview of people who would limit what young adults read. Others assist us in preparing for and responding to a challenge. A selected list that includes references for quotations in this chapter follows. Referring to any one of them will lead you to additional resources.

Organizations

The American Library Association, Office for Intellectual Freedom. 50 E. Huron St., Chicago, IL 60611-2795. http://www.ala.org/oif.html

International Reading Association. 800 Barksdale Road, P.O. Box 8139, Newark, DE 19714-8139. http://www.reading.org

National Coalition Against Censorship. 275 7th Ave., New York, NY 10001. http://www.ncac.org

National Council of Teachers of English. 1111 W. Kenyon Road, Urbana, IL 61801-1096. http://www.ncte.org

People for the American Way. 2000 M St., N.W., Suite 400, Washington, DC 20036. http://www.pfaw.org

Publications

American Library Association. *Hit List: Frequently Challenged Young Adult Titles: References to Defend Them.* Chicago: American Library Association, 1989.

Brown, Jean E., and Elaine C. Stephens. "Rationales for Teaching Challenged Books." *Slate Starter Sheet.* Urbana: NCTE, 1994.

———, eds. *Preserving Intellectual Freedom.* Urbana: NCTE, 1994.

DelFattore, Joan. *What Johnny Shouldn't Read: Textbook Censorship in America.* New Haven: Yale UP, 1992.

Edwards, June. *Opposing Censorship in the Public Schools: Religion, Morality, and Literature.* Mahwah: Lawrence Erlbaum Associates, 1998.

Foerstel, Howard. *Banned in the U.S.A.: A Reference Guide to Book Censorship in Schools and Public Libraries.* Westport: Greenwood, 1994.

Herz, Sarah K., with Donald R. Gallo. *From Hinton to Hamlet: Building Bridges Between Young Adult Literature and the Classics.* Westport: Greenwood, 1996.

Karolides, Nicholas, and Lee Burress, eds. *Celebrating Censored Books!* Racine: Wisconsin Council of Teachers of English, 1985.

Karolides, Nicholas, Lee Burress, and John Kean, eds. *Censored Books: Critical Viewpoints.* Lanham: Scarecrow, 1993.

Moffett, James. *Storm in the Mountains: A Case Study in Censorship, Conflict, and Consciousness.* Carbondale: Southern Illinois UP, 1988.

People for the American Way. *Attacks on the Freedom to Learn 1996.* Washington, DC: People for the American Way, 1996.

Rationales for Challenged Books. CD-ROM. Urbana: NCTE, in partnership with the International Reading Association, 1998.

Reichman, Henry. *Censorship and Selection: Issues and Answers for Schools.* Arlington: American Association of School Administrators, 1993; Chicago: American Library Association, 1993.

Reid, Louann, ed. *Rationales for Challenged Materials.* Fort Collins, CO: The Colorado Language Arts Society, 1997. Available for $8 directly from Louann Reid, English Department, Colorado State University, Fort Collins, CO 80523-1773.

Shugert, Diane P., ed. *Rationales for Commonly Taught Challenged Books.* Enfield: Connecticut Council of Teachers of English, 1983.

Spencer, Pam, comp. *What Do Young Adults Read Next? A Reader's Guide to Fiction for Young Adults.* 2 vols. Detroit: Gale Research, 1994, 1997.

The Student's Right to Read. Urbana: NCTE, 1982.

Suhor, Charles. "Censorship Cases Down, Various Organizations Report." *Slate* 24.2 (May 1999):1–2.

West, Mark. *Trust Your Children: Voices Against Censorship in Children's Literature.* 2nd ed. New York: Neal-Schuman, 1997.

AM I BLUE? COMING OUT FROM THE SILENCE

Edited by Marion Dane Bauer

". . . I was just pointing out that it's harder spotting potential partners when you're gay. If a guy asks a girl for a date, about the worst that can happen is that she laughs at him. If he asks another guy, he might get his face pounded in."

That thought had crossed my mind more than once as I was trying to figure myself out over the last year—and not only with regard to dating. I would have been happy just to have someone I felt safe *talking* to about this.

"Is this gaydar something you can learn?" I asked.

He furrowed his brow for a moment, then said, "I don't think so."

"It must be lonely," I muttered, more to myself than to him.

"It doesn't have to be," he replied sharply. "If gay people hadn't been forced to hide for so long, if we could just openly identify ourselves, there would be plenty of people you knew that you could ask for advice. Everybody knows gay people; they just think they don't."

"What do you mean?"

"Listen, honey, the world is crawling with faggots. But most of them are in hiding because they're afraid they'll get treated the way you did about an hour ago."

I took in my breath sharply. Melvin must have seen the look of shock on my face, because he looked puzzled for a moment. Then he laughed. "That word bother you?"

"I was taught that it was impolite."

"It is. But if you live in a world that keeps trying to grind you down, you either start thumbing your nose at it or end up very, very short. Taking back the language is one way to jam the grinder. My friends and I called each other 'faggot' and 'queer' for the same reason so many black folks call each other 'nigger'—to take the words away from the people who want to use them to hurt us." (Bruce Coville 9–10)

Bauer, Marion Dane, ed. *Am I Blue? Coming Out from the Silence.* New York: HarperCollins Children's Books, 1994.

Intended Audience

Students in language arts and sociology courses, grades 9–12. When used as full-class reading material, these fictional stories will establish a low-risk environment in which to explore concerns, perceptions, stereotypes, and personal viewpoints related to gay and lesbian issues. Teachers may prefer to select single stories to read aloud and begin a discussion.

Summary

This book is an anthology of sixteen powerful short stories written specifically for this collection by well-respected and prolific authors of young adult novels—six male, ten female, a few gay or lesbian, most straight. In each story, the featured characters must deal with the fact that they, or someone they care about, is gay or lesbian. Two themes center the collection: none of us is alone in our experience, and adolescents must seek someone with whom to discuss their problems when they are worried about their sexual identity. In most of the stories, the adolescent characters are just discovering that they are gay after experiencing a period of uncertainty about their sexual identity or a general feeling of not fitting in with their peers. Part of their coming to terms with being gay is making the decision to come out to friends or family members, while remaining hopeful that their friends and family will still love and support them.

The majority of the stories are realistic fiction, and the characters are depicted as typical teenagers who display intelligence, a multitude of talents and athletic abilities, and the ever-present need for acceptance by peers and families. Each character is presented as multidimensional, rather than solely as a gay or lesbian, thus avoiding negative stereotyping. The settings for these stories revolve around school and home. Three stories are of literary genres other than realistic: one a fantasy, one a science fiction dystopia, and one mythological. These stories are more complex to read, as the setting must be detected along with the purpose.

Relationship of *Am I Blue?* to the Program

These stories are well-written, model the range of sensitive and insensitive attitudes gay and lesbian teens are likely to encounter within the family circle and within American society, and provide mature high school students with the opportunity to explore (and perhaps to assess) these prevailing attitudes while in the safe environment of the classroom.

Students may never have taken the opportunity to read literature that depicts this marginalized group, because society's homophobia makes checking out and being seen with such a book taboo. A growing number of young adult novels deal with the issue and consequences of heterosexual sex, notably pregnancy, but few portray a gay or lesbian character who is an adolescent. Helping students find these books provides another avenue toward studying the realism of contemporary fiction.

In electing to use this collection, teachers should not feel the need to create a lengthy unit on sexuality in order to use a favorite story or two that would add to the diversity of the reading list. Just as one literary work dealing with racism might be included on a reading list without causing teachers to feel compelled to explore the history of racism in our society, they may also select a favorite work that deals with homosexual teens without creating the need for full exploration of homosexuality in our society.

Read together, the sixteen stories cover different aspects of gay and lesbian relationships, with most of the stories using teen protagonists. Because of the short story format, which is less able to create a full resolution of the internal conflict these characters face, readers are often left to read between the lines to detect the decisions and potential actions of characters. A number of the stories show adolescents making mature decisions and taking steps toward coming to terms with their sexual orientation. In "Parents' Night" by Nancy Garden, Karen and her friend Roxy are beginning a lesbian relationship and make the decision to join a gay, lesbian, bisexual teen organization sponsored by their school. On Parents' Night they work at the club's information booth as a means of coming out to their peers and demonstrating their commitment. In "Slipping Away" by Jacqueline Woodson, intolerance toward the lesbian lifestyle of residents of a resort town causes a rift between teen friends. In M. E. Kerr's "We Might as Well All Be Strangers," a girl's grandmother is the family member who best understands the prejudice Alison is experiencing as a lesbian, because of her childhood experiences as a Jew in pre-WWII Europe.

In language arts class, I begin by reading aloud the fantasy title story "Am I Blue?" by Bruce Coville. On the surface, this is a light-hearted story with a stereotypic "swishy" gay man. Vincent has just been beaten up and called a faggot when his fairy godfather Melvin arrives to grant his wishes. We discover that Melvin died after being beaten by homophobes. Just sitting in a restaurant with Melvin causes the teen a great deal of distress, as Melvin walks funny and persists in winking at a boy he says "wasn't offended. He's one of the gang" (8). Melvin provides "gaydar" for Vincent so he can see that a number of people he knows and admires are gay. Then with a playful wish, everyone in the country with gay tendencies is turned blue for the day, including the bully, as a way of proving that we all know gay people and that gay teens are not as alone as they sometimes feel. The fairy godfather states, "everybody knows gay people; they just think they don't" (9).

This story works to get students thinking. Because it is so obviously fantasy, teens are able to deal with the characters. They can discuss the overt gay behaviors of Melvin that make him appear swishy, then relate his actions to the media's portrayal of gay men. The exaggerated condition of turning blue elicits the concept that people can't be judged solely on their physical mannerisms and appearance, whether they are gay, disabled, or members of some other marginalized group. We go on to create a list of what we understand to be "true" of homosexuals, discussing what facts we have to support these perceptions, and we begin to investigate how we might have learned these perceptions.

We then pair the stories in this collection with informational pieces on the statistics of gay and lesbian teens within our general population; the increasing number of gay and lesbian teens who are part of the homeless population; the statistics of teen suicides attributed to struggles with sexual identity and acceptance; community resources for teens and their families; and the educational efforts of national organizations such as the Gay, Lesbian, and Straight Education Network.

Impact of the Material on Readers

Teenagers need to learn how to come to terms with their own sexuality and gender; develop self-acceptance and acceptance of others; recognize society's influence on our behavior toward marginalized groups; recognize the media's negative and stereotyped portrayal of homosexuals; and learn to adjust personal behavior to be more tolerant toward those unlike themselves. To achieve these lofty goals, teachers have an obligation to introduce their students to good literature that depicts the experiences of all students.

Our students need to fully understand that our differences are many; none of us should be labeled "bad" just for being different. Yet exhibiting prejudicial behavior and language against gays and lesbians is the last vestige of prejudice our society permits. Many people have stopped using language that evidences prejudice against racial groups by placing them in the position of "other," but in many circles it's still okay to gay-bash. Legislation meant to protect basic human rights of gays is still not universal, nor is it always accepted even when passed. Gay and lesbian couples have no legal rights of inheritance or parenthood, and they rarely qualify for health insurance benefits through their partner.

Any of the stories in *Am I Blue?* might encourage readers to be more open about their sexuality and literally "come out of the silence" that can cause teens to feel so alone and friendless. This book belongs on the curricular reading list as the best resource I know for assisting readers to encounter diverse peoples, cultures, and lives both like and unlike their own. Using literature's unique ability to act both as a mirror of the reader's life events and a window to view the lives of others, classroom teachers may use these stories to open the eyes and minds of readers.

Potential Problems with *Am I Blue?* and Ways to Address Them

Homosexuality

The main problem, of course, is the topic. Our current society is unable to deal rationally with the outing of gay and lesbian teens, often choosing to ignore this segment of our population. Statistics suggest that one in ten adolescents is either homosexual or living with a homosexual family member, so teens DO need to be aware of the issue, develop workable social strategies, and develop tolerance for the diverse lifestyles of peers. By including the literature of marginalized groups within our regular curriculum, we can help teens begin to see their life situations as normal, rather than outside the norm presented in mainstream literature.

When censors object to books on diverse lifestyles, they are viewing literature as a how-to manual. They may disapprove of *Am I Blue?* on the false assumption that vulnerable teens will decide that a homosexual relationship sounds intriguing and begin to experiment sexually. What censors need to understand is that the transaction between the reader and a fictional character is indirect; readers can understand the life situation of a character, empathize with the character, and predict the actions of the character without taking on the life of the character as their own.

Other censors may wish that the problem of teen sexuality and raging hormones would be less distressing—in fact, that it would disappear altogether. Of course, this attitude is never helpful with difficult issues, and teens will be better served if issues of sexuality are discussed openly, rather than secretively or not at all. This book may spur open discussion and model strategies for talking through problems and concerns, rather than keeping them bottled up inside.

Graphic language

Collectively, these stories include a number of vernacular terms to represent homosexuals, which presents a potential problem of graphic language. As readers encounter them, teachers will need to define or distinguish between such terms as *faggot, fruit, queer, fag, fairy, homo, dyke*. Because these terms are often used in a derogatory manner and are liberally applied and misused by our society, teen readers need the opportunity to defuse the potentially damaging implications through accurate use. As the character Melvin states in "Am I Blue?" taking back the language by using the terms yourself is one form of empowerment for people in any group against which others are openly prejudiced. Melvin says, "if you live in a world that keeps trying to grind you down . . . taking back the language is one way to jam the grinder. My friends and I called each other 'faggot' and 'queer' for the same reason so many black folks call each other 'nigger'—to take the words away from the people who want to use them to hurt us" (10).

The shock value of these words will be negated if students are mature enough to distinguish appropriate uses from hurtful ones. They will need to develop enough familiarity with the terms to use them accurately, yet not use them to harm the feelings of peers. Most of the stories include at least one of these name-calling terms, but none of the stories use the terms to describe a sexual act in progress. In fact, except for the implication of masturbation in one story, no words for sexual acts are used.

Unrealistic expectations

The stories in this book depict families and peers as willing to accept the coming out disclosures of the teen characters, a fact that presents a somewhat unrealistic portrayal of potential events. In only one story has a character been sent from home and told never to darken the doorstep again. None of the characters mention the possibility of suicide. In the reality of our society, a large number of teens who disclose are either sent from home or elect to leave when tensions run high, thus becoming a part of the growing population of homeless teens. In order to support themselves without having finished their education, these adolescents often turn to alternative lifestyles such as prostitution and drug trafficking. For these teens, medical and dental care and health information are almost nonexistent, so contracting HIV or other STDs or becoming pregnant are very real possibilities. None of the adult or teen characters in the book have experienced these problems, so the stories do not attempt to handle the potential implications of living a gay lifestyle after disclosure.

Also, in reality when adolescents feel that they do not fit in, one way of leaving an unpleasant situation is to commit suicide. Statistics on teen suicides usually cite multiple factors for the suicide attempt, with being homosexual or having a homosexual experience high on the list of factors. When considering the implications of homelessness and suicide, these stories seem very mild, informing teens of the necessity of coming to terms with sexuality but without conjecturing on the potential long-term results.

The role of the language arts teacher is not to offer family and sexual counseling but to offer resources if they are requested. Nor does the classroom teacher want to be placed in the role of moral judge for the behavior of students. The danger here is that if the topic looks daunting, the classroom teacher will not select extracurricular materials that are controversial because of her or his own limited knowledge. Before beginning discussions related to the topic of homosexuality, teachers should investigate local people and organizations that would serve as potential resources for information, speaking, and counseling.

Absence of adults as major characters

As is typical with young adult works, adults are absent in most of these stories. While this absence may be interpreted as adults ignoring their parental role and failing to intervene to soften the resolution of the story, teen readers do not expect teen characters to be "saved" by the intervention of adults in literature. Adolescent readers enjoy reading literature in which a character of their age and gender is the protagonist, and they often identify with the character enough to weigh possible courses of action for themselves based on the actions of that protagonist. In this way, readers experience a life event vicariously and are able to gain valuable practice with a variety of encounters.

Although none of the stories directly address adult homosexuality, in four stories adults who are minor characters are gay. "Holding" by Lois Lowry depicts a gay parent. In this story, the death of Chris, the long-term sexual partner of the character's father, provides the teen with the courage to confront his best friend's misconception that Chris was his father's wife, rather than his male lover. Two stories with adult characters might be perceived as "racy." In James Cross Giblin's "Three Mondays in July," a teenage boy exhibits voyeuristic tendencies as he fantasizes about being with a nude man he views on the beach. "The Honorary Shepherds" by Gregory Maguire begins with the lines "to satisfy that particular curiosity first: Yes, this is a story about two boys who sleep together. Eventually. Not genitally" (65). In contrast, the remaining fourteen stories are less sexually overt and none are sensual.

Although teachers should always read materials before using them in the classroom and select appropriate materials based on curricular mandates and student developmental needs, they should not classify this book as inappropriate because of the topic of homosexuality. The stories include a wide range of teen characters who are struggling successfully with matters of sexual and gender identity—for themselves, in relation to their peers, and in relation to their family members.

References

Marion Dane Bauer is the editor and a contributing author to this collection of short stories. Her young adult book *On My Honor* was a 1987 Newbery Award honor book. *Am I Blue? Coming Out from the Silence* was named an ALA Best Book for Young Adults (1995) as well as a Recommended Book for Reluctant Young Adult Readers (ALA 1995). It was also on the *Horn Book's* Fanfare Honor List (1995) and won the Lesbian and Gay Children's/YA Award given by Lambda Book Report (1994).

Alternative Works

There are other good collections of short stories that use gay and lesbian teens as characters, as well as some young adult novels. Because of the homosexuality topic, all of the listed books are subject to censorship as well.

Related Works

Because there are no true alternative works that would meet the objectives for selecting *Am I Blue?,* it is more accurate to think of the following titles as related works. Teachers should take care to select more recent works, as older books often exhibit a judgmental attitude toward homosexuals, portraying the teen characters as isolated and adults as predatory.

Collections of short stories

Grima, Tony, ed. *Not the Only One: Lesbian and Gay Fiction for Teens.* Boston: Alyson, 1995.

Heron, Ann, ed. *One Teenager in Ten: Short Stories from a New Generation of Gay and Lesbian Youth.* Boston: Alyson, 1983.

———, ed. *Two Teenagers in Twenty: Writings by Lesbian and Gay Youth.* Boston: Alyson, 1994.

Singer, Bennett L., ed. *Growing Up Gay/Growing Up Lesbian: A Literary Anthology.* New York: The New Press, 1993.

Novels with homosexual characters by authors who contributed short stories to *Am I Blue?*

Garden, Nancy. *Annie on My Mind.* New York: Farrar, 1982. This is a coming-out book in which a college freshman recalls her high school romance with a young woman.

———. *Lark in the Morning.* New York: Farrar, 1991. *Lark* is a detective novel with lesbian main characters.

Newman, Leslea. Leslea Newman has a number of adult books about lesbian issues, as well as two classic picture books for younger readers that address lesbian family issues from the child's point of view. High school students might use these picture books as a discussion starting point: *Heather Has Two Mommies* (Northampton: In Other Words, 1989) and *Gloria Goes to Gay Pride* (Boston: Alyson Wonderland, 1991).

Woodson, Jacqueline. *The Dear One.* New York: Dell, 1991; *From the Notebooks of Melanin Sun.* New York: Scholastic, 1995; *The House You Pass on the Way.* New York: Delacorte, 1997. Jacqueline Woodson has three novels in which the teen characters live with or encounter adult lesbian characters. Each novel shows the concerns of a teen when peers make comments and each depicts the adults as accessible for discussions when the teens question their own sexuality.

Nonfiction

Bass, Ellen, and Kate Kaufman. *Free Your Mind: The Book For Gay, Lesbian, and Bisexual Youth and Their Allies.* New York: HarperPerennial, 1996.

Berzon, Betty. *Setting Them Straight: You Can Do Something About Bigotry and Homophobia in Your Life.* New York: Penguin, 1996.

Due, Linnea. *Joining the Tribe: Growing Up Gay and Lesbian in the 1990's.* New York: Anchor, 1995.

About Nancy Prosenjak

Nancy Prosenjak, an assistant professor of English at The Metropolitan State College of Denver, teaches courses in children's and young adult literature and was formerly a middle school language arts teacher. She participates in curricular development projects with Denver-area middle school faculty.

WEETZIE BAT

by Francesca Lia Block

"I am the genie of the lamp, and I am here to grant you three wishes," the man said.

Weetzie began to laugh, maybe a little hysterically.

"Really, I don't see what is so amusing," the genie said with a sniff.

"Never mind. Okay, I wish for world peace," Weetzie said.

"I'm sorry," the genie said. "I can't grant that wish. It's out of my league. Besides, one of your world leaders would screw it up immediately."

"Okay," Weetzie said. "Then I wish for an infinite number of wishes!" As a kid she had vowed to wish for wishes if she ever encountered a genie or a fairy or one of those things. Those people in fairy tales never thought of that.

"People in fairy tales wish for that all the time," the genie said. "They aren't stupid. It just isn't in the records because I can't grant that type of wish."

"Well," Weetzie said, a little perturbed, "if this is my trip I think at least you could say I could have one of these wishes come true!"

"You get three wishes," the genie said.

"I wish for a Duck for Dirk, and My Secret Agent Lover Man for me, and a beautiful little house for us to live in happily ever after."

"Your wishes are granted. Mostly," said the genie. "And now I must be off." (23–24)

Block, Francesca Lia. *Weetzie Bat.* New York: HarperCollins, 1989.

Intended Audience

Students in grades 9–12. Some topics demand maturity, but the reading is fast and easy. This would be a good book for students hesitant or skeptical toward mainstream reading assignments and a choice book for students studying fairy tales.

Summary

Weetzie, a spunky punk, feels she is the only one in her school who appreciates and understands the glam, glitter, and fantastical surroundings of L.A., until she meets Dirk, the most handsome boy in school. Weetzie, with her white flattop and Dirk with his "shoe-polish-black Mohawk"(4) and "dark smudged eyes"(6) find themselves in empty, self-sacrificing relationships while searching for soul mates they can't seem to find. Dirk's grandmother, Fifi, realizes their need for love and companionship and uses her canaries as examples of two "who are in love, but even before they were in love they knew they were going to be happy . . . they trusted . . . they have always loved themselves and they would never hurt themselves" (22). She then gives Weetzie a magical vase from which a genie emerges and grants Weetzie her three wishes of finding a soul mate for her, one for Dirk, and a place they can all share. An unexpected death takes Fifi and grants Weetzie's third wish by leaving Dirk and Weetzie her cottage. They soon find soul mates to share it with—Duck, a surfer boy, for Dirk and My Secret Agent Lover Man for Weetzie. All four now play in the fantastical city of L.A. and share the cottage.

The four friends face many difficulties but are ultimately brought together by love. Weetzie compares love and disease to electricity, both always there, offering the option to "plug into the love current . . ." (88).

Relationship of *Weetzie Bat* to the Program

Fantasy can be a form of escapism, both for the reader and the writer. Fantasy also serves a serious purpose in that it allows readers to re-create or reimagine life from another perspective. There are two important issues that *Weetzie Bat* can raise for readers. First is the need to be aware of what is real, what really matters, while developing the wisdom to know what isn't real and doesn't matter. Weetzie's wisdom stems from the view that she is aware of the falseness of L.A., and this perceptiveness allows her to enjoy it. Her parents' lives mirror the man-made fantasy city of L.A., with their self-made reality of alcohol and drugs. Like Weetzie and Dirk in the beginning of the story, they are hurting, not loving themselves.

Second, the story plays with love as an element of both reality and fantasy. Self-love allows Weetzie and Dirk to find their soul mates, while the somewhat fantastical idea of unconditional love allows significant betrayals to be easily forgiven. Discussion of the story could reflect upon the positive attributes of self-love while comparing the ideal of unconditional love with the reality of unconditional love.

The story takes the reader into the special existence of Weetzie's vividly animated life in Shangri-L.A. (Los Angeles). There are fountains of tropical soda-pop colors; Jetson-style restaurants with roller-skating waitresses; and a replica of Venice, complete with canals and columns "but cooler because there are surfers in it" (4). Magically, colors are brighter, smells are more vivid, and scenery is intensified. The dramatic attention given to Weetzie's surroundings takes the reader on a tour through fantastical qualities of real life.

Impact of the Material on Readers

The story is a magically funny yet truthfully sad social commentary on the falseness and surrealism of today's society. In the book, the glam and glitz of L.A. are monstrously magnified. Real-life people—Marilyn Monroe, Jim Morrison—are turned into gods and goddesses through Hollywood and the fans who admire them. The wisdom of Weetzie, reflected in Fifi, lies in the ability to place herself beyond the fakeness and still enjoy it. Teens in fact and fiction often struggle with the tension between the ideal and real worlds. (Holden Caulfield comes to mind.) Through reading *Weetzie Bat*, students will be able to discuss this tension in terms of the world that they know.

The novel also provides readers with provocative ideas about love. Love serves as the intersection between reality and fantasy, but it also falls into both categories. Without love the characters are drifting and self-disparaging, as Weetzie and Dirk were before they met their soul mates. With love they are happy, given God-like abilities of unconditional love and absolute forgiveness. The capacity for self-love transcends the trappings of L.A., and only in conjunction with self-love are healthy relationships shown. But the absolute unconditional love, as displayed in the book, seems to fall more into the realm of fantasy in that the characters are able to completely accept and forgive each other, no matter how they are betrayed.

Potential Problems with *Weetzie Bat* and Ways to Address Them

The most controversial issues include sex without marriage, Dirk's sexual orientation (he is gay), and adult drug and alcohol use. In addition, some people may object to Block's use of fantasy. The issues and style are thematically necessary. First, Dirk's and Weetzie's search for soul mates, which involves sleeping with people who do not respect them, is essentially self-hurting. This behavior is not condoned. When the two are sad and think they will not find love, Fifi tells them they must first love themselves and have faith that they will find love—and they do.

Second, Dirk's gay relationships are parallel to Weetzie's heterosexual relationships—they both search for love. The need for love is not dependent on sexual orientation, and the story makes a strong point of the acceptance and unconditional love exhibited by all four friends.

The drug and alcohol use of Weetzie's parents is shown negatively; Weetzie's parents are trapped in their man-made fantasy world. Brandy-Lynn is a "bleach-blonde [actress] sparkling with fake jewels" (17). Charlie Bat is an artificial scenery maker, a creator of the unreal. Charlie falls in love with Brandy-Lynn's beauty and Brandy-Lynn falls in love with the romance. Similar to Dirk and Weetzie's initial unhealthy search for love, Brandy Lynn and Charlie Bat's relationship is shallow and destructive. Their relationship was not based on self-love. Alcohol and drug use reinforce their destructive behavior.

Some people object to asking children and young adults to use their imagination. Joan DelFattore describes the objections of the Tennessee plaintiffs in *Mozert v. Hawkins County:*

> They rejected all fairy tales and folk tales on the grounds that anything involving magic castles, enchanted forests, dragons, spells, unicorns, wizards, trolls, and the like promotes witchcraft and encourages children to create worlds inside their own minds instead of concentrating on the Word of God. Apart from the specific content of any particular fantasy, thinking imaginatively is wrong in itself because it tempts people to substitute their own ideas for God's. (48)

Most people will understand the fantasy in *Weetzie Bat* as a necessary technique for coping with reality. Block establishes a dichotomy between the negative aspects of daily life and the positive joys of fantasy life. Yet it is through fantasy that the characters learn the importance of acceptance and unconditional love in the real world.

If parents or community members object to fantasy in general, the teacher needs to respect the sincerity of those beliefs. The student may need to be excused from any units that include works of fantasy. Teachers would offer an unrelated novel or work of nonfiction in that case. However, these students will not meet the objectives described earlier in this rationale.

References

Born in 1962, Francesca Lia Block is the award-winning author of eight novels read by young adults. Written in a blend of delightful magic and harsh reality, the novels speak about issues of importance to teens today—love and loss, power and powerlessness, phoniness and truth. Publisher Wendy Mass writes of the worlds Block creates: "Magic is always around the next corner and love is the axis around which the stories spin. These books blur the line between reality and fairy tales, and once you find yourself there, you'll never want to leave."

Block majored in English at UCLA and Berkeley, where she took creative writing and poetry classes. Her family background also influences the worlds she creates in her novels. She told *Writes of Passage*, a literary journal for teenagers, "As the daughter of a filmmaker turned painter, I learned to see the world through my senses; when I was growing up everything was about color and feeling, emotion and creative expression." Irene Lacher of the *Los Angeles Times* notes, "Weetzie was born as Block was edging into adulthood in a dazzling but uncertain L.A." (E1). In the same *Times* story, Lacher quotes from an essay Block wrote for the *Times* two years before: "While Los Angeles was full of fairy-tale magic and possibility for me, there was also a sense of encroaching darkness. My friends and I found ourselves confronted with punks wearing swastikas as fashion statements. People were beaten at concerts. There was the personal pain I was experiencing due to my father's illness. And there were the first terrifying signs of the disease that would later be named AIDS. I wrote *Weetzie Bat* as a celebration of the beauty and sparkle I had seen and as a way to deal with the suffering" (E1).

Weetzie Bat was named an ALA Best Book for Young Adults and an ALA Recommended Book for Reluctant Readers. Critics praise Block's style and the topics she addresses:

> Like liquid poetry, these books will melt into your consciousness, turning your world a little more like Weetzie's, where seeing through rose-colored glasses will show you everything you need to find. (Mass)

> The book is full of magic, from the genie who grants Weetzie's wishes to the malevolent witch Vixanne, who visits the family three times. There are beauties and beasts and roses, castles and Cinderella transformations. . . . The language is inventive Californian hip, but the patterns are compactly folkloristic and the theme is transcendant. (Hearne 47)

Alternative Work

An alternative work that contains elements of fantasy but not much social realism is Robin McKinley's *Beauty*, a retelling of the story of Beauty and the Beast. Of course, those who object to fantasy may object to this story, too.

Related Works

Other titles by Block with characters from *Weetzie Bat*

Baby Be-Bop. New York: HarperCollins, 1995. Dirk comes to terms with being gay in this prequel to *Weetzie Bat*.

Cherokee Bat and the Goat Guys. New York: HarperCollins, 1992. Four children form a rock band while their parents are away.

Missing Angel Juan. New York: HarperCollins, 1993. Witch Baby follows Angel Juan to New York City.

Witch Baby. New York: HarperCollins, 1991. Witch Baby comes to live with Weetzie and My Secret Agent Lover Man.

Other fantasies

Block, Francesca Lia. *Girl Goddess #9: Nine Stories*. New York: HarperCollins, 1996. These nine short stories feature other characters but display Block's magic realism style.

Geras, Adele. *Pictures of the Night*. San Diego: Harcourt, 1992, 1998. In this modern version of Snow White, eighteen-year-old Bella suspects her stepmother of causing a series of accidents while Bella is singing with a band in London and Paris.

Works Cited

DelFattore, Joan. *What Johnny Shouldn't Read: TextBook Censorship in America*. New Haven: Yale UP, 1992.

Hearne, Betsy. "Pretty in Punk." *New York Times Book Reviews* 21 May 1989, sec. 7:47.

Lacher, Irene. "'Weetzie Bat' Proves Someone Understands." *Los Angeles Times* 25 Jan. 1994, home ed.: E1.

Mass, Wendy. "The Cool Block." *Writes of Passage, The Literary Journal for Teenagers* 1.2 (1995): n. pag. Online. Internet. 23 Mar. 1999. Available www.writes.org.

About Karen Williams

Karen Williams has done extensive practicum work at Centennial High School, Fort Collins, Colorado. She has completed her B.A. in English and the teaching licensure program and is interested in alternative education.

THE MOVES MAKE THE MAN

by Bruce Brooks

That is when and why I decided to write this story of Bix. Of Bix and me, mostly, I guess it has to be. I may not understand it all yet myself, but I got all summer ahead of me, and a room to myself, cool up under the eaves, because my brother Henri is off to camp. My momma wanted to send me first, but I told her I wouldn't go on account of I knew I could use the summer better writing this out. So it's Henri gets to make the wallets and lanyards and sing the national anthem while the flag is raised every morning and swim in a lake warm as blood.

It's me gets to tell the truth. (5)

Brooks, Bruce. *The Moves Make the Man*. New York: HarperCollins, 1984.

Intended Audience

Students grades 9–12. This book can be read at different levels; more mature and sophisticated readers will find the text challenging enough to engage them, but even less-skilled readers will enjoy and benefit from the novel's main story line. This novel could be used effectively in a survey of contemporary American literature. It would work well also as assigned reading for a psychology course or as parallel reading with American history of the 1960s, particularly the civil rights movement. Because of its detailed scenes of basketball technique, it might even be used as supplemental reading in a sports or P.E. course.

Summary

Jerome Foxworthy, a precocious thirteen-year-old African American, tells the story of his friendship with a white boy, the troubled and enigmatic

Braxton Rivers III, a.k.a. Bix. Jerome meets Bix when Jerome becomes the first and only student to integrate an all-white junior high in Wilmington, North Carolina, in 1961. The boys have much in common. Both are fatherless, both have an incapacitated mother, and both are exceptionally talented in one sport: basketball for Jerome, baseball for Bix. Jerome's troubles with the racist school system and his mother's recent accident fade into the background as he tries to help Bix overcome emotional problems—some of which Bix probably inherited from his "crazy" mother—that have been compounded by the death of his father. Jerome learns that Bix's mother has been committed to a mental institution and that his stepfather will not allow Bix to visit her. Eventually, Bix gets his stepfather to agree to allow him to visit his mother if he can beat his stepfather in a game of one-on-one. Bix enlists the aid of Jerome to teach him to play basketball and manages, by overcoming his obsession with "truth" and resorting to "moves," to defeat his stepfather. The experience makes Bix increasingly unstable in the days leading to his visit to his mother, a visit that ultimately proves tragic for Bix, his mother, and his friend Jerome.

Relationship of *The Moves Make the Man* to the Program

The Moves Make the Man, a 1985 Newbery Honor book, stands out in the young adult literature field as an enduring work of high literary quality. This novel effectively blends sophistication with accessibility; the story of interracial friendship, emotional illness, and sports appeals even to reluctant readers, but experienced readers will also enjoy the complexities of Brooks' narrative style and the novel's layered themes. *The Moves Makes the Man* is certainly a "high end" example of young adult literature, one that can help students recognize and appreciate the range and quality of the field. Teachers can use it to reinforce essential objectives in their courses, including helping students understand writing style, literary structure, and some of the complexities of racism and family relationships.

The Moves Make the Man is often labeled a sports novel, and although it does have a strong thread of sports woven into it, it is much more than a sports story. When it's paired with sports books like John Tunis' *The All-American* or Robert Lipsyte's *The Contender*, students can see that Brooks' novel is less about sports than it is about a young man dealing with the painful and difficult problems of his good friend. In this respect, *The Moves Make the Man* is closer to the novels of Chris Crutcher, which feature an athlete protagonist who must deal with conflicts that transcend the sports arena. After reading books like this and discussing their essential themes and plots, students will realize that *The Moves Make the Man* is a coming-of-age story, not a sports story.

Students may also study the novel's portrayal of mental illness through Bix's mother and, especially, through Bix's obsessive nature. Throughout the novel Bix is obsessed with the truth, so obsessed that he cannot abide the mock apple pie of his home economics class, the mild jokes of Jerome, or the moves and fakes of basketball. In sports, he prefers baseball because of its purity, its truthfulness—and it is Bix's aversion to sports fakery that finally pushes him over the edge of sanity.

Though portrayed subtly throughout the novel, the scenes of racism will be recognizable to students: how Jerome is forced to integrate a white school, his abuse and rejection by the white basketball coach, the reaction of a prejudiced gas station owner. The events are painful to Jerome, but as the narrator he downplays them in order to focus his narrative on Bix. Students can be asked why Jerome includes these scenes without describing the pain he felt in them. While discussing elements of racism, it is also useful to point out to students that Brooks, a white author, uses an African American voice to tell his story. There has been considerable debate over whether or not it is fair or accurate for authors to write about cultures outside of their own. After reading *The Moves Make the Man* students can discuss how effective—or fair—Brooks was in writing from an African American perspective.

The Moves Make the Man can also be used as a literary model for students. They can examine Brooks' adroit use of dialect, his development of character, his structuring of plot, his use of figurative language. Students can learn from Brooks' example that some talented and careful writers can effectively write outside of their race. Students can also study how Brooks violates standard conventions of writing in ways that benefit the overall work.

The Moves Make the Man offers many opportunities to discuss narrative technique and literary form. For example, the entire novel is told without use of quotation marks, even in dialogue. Why? Is it effective? How? Does it detract from or enhance the reading experience? Jerome, the narrator, is not entirely reliable. For example, he says that his book is the story of Bix, but in many ways, it is really Jerome's story. In the beginning of his narrative, he also says, "this is the truth," but by the end of the novel, especially after observing Bix's obsession with "truth," readers may be left wondering about the relative merits of "truth." Students might also consider the structural technique of creating parallel characters and families. Bix and Jerome both have lost their fathers and have incapacitated mothers. Both boys must be more independent than they would like to be; both excel in a single sport, etc. Teachers can ask students why Brooks creates such parallels. How do they affect the text? What do they add to plot and character?

Impact of the Material on Readers

Most students who read *The Moves Make the Man* come away with greater sympathy for victims of emotional and mental illness. Brooks' sensitive yet painful portrayal of Bix helps readers gain a better understanding of the suffering that often accompanies mental illness and how these kinds of maladies are beyond the control of those afflicted. After seeing how intensely Bix suffers, students will be unlikely to expect victims of emotional or mental illness to "just get over it." Brooks makes it clear that there are some things that cannot be "gotten over."

Students will also come away with a heightened sense of racial stereotyping and the evils of racism. Jerome is a bright and admirable character, much brighter than the stereotypical dumb jock or ghetto kid. For him, basketball is not a game; it is a science, an art, something that must be studied and practiced diligently. Contrary to the contemporary media stereotypes of African American athletes, basketball is not the be-all and end-all for Jerome. He loves the sport, but he also realizes and values the importance of family and education; in short, Jerome is a good role model for any student—male or female, athlete or nonathlete, black or white.

Brooks' novel contains some scenes of raw and ugly racism. Jerome's narration almost downplays the pain involved in these scenes, but most readers will see through Jerome's cover and recognize the deep hurt he feels when he is forced to be a token integrated student in an all-white school; when the racist basketball coach insults, cheats, and humiliates him; when he's taunted by the white men on the train; and when he must endure the slurs and verbal assault of a racist café owner. Students today have little understanding of the blatant racism of the 1960s, but after reading these scenes, they will feel defensive and indignant about how Jerome is treated and how he seems to accept it. These reactions will provide an opportunity for class discussion about Jim Crow laws and the conditions African Americans had to endure in the early days of the civil rights movement. After reading the novel and participating in such discussions, students will come away with a better and more personal understanding of the evils of racism.

Potential Problems with *The Moves Make the Man* and Ways to Address Them

This book may be challenged for several reasons, most specifically for its portrayal of racism and emotional illness. In general, readers should also be reminded that issues like these are often exacerbated by society's reluctance to talk about them. This novel provides an opportunity for thoughtful discussion of these and other social issues.

A white author exploiting or misrepresenting African American culture

Usually the complaint about inaccurate portrayals of culture is based on evidence that the author has been careless in presenting a culture or that the author has presented a culture from a white perspective. Brooks has been very careful to avoid stereotypes; indeed, Jerome and his family have many realistic and admirable characteristics. Brooks does not exploit race in this novel. Jerome's race is essential to the story because it creates added tension in his friendship with Bix. It also allows Brooks to expose some of the problems that resulted from segregation and that still result from racism. In his defense, Brooks has said that he does not pretend to represent or understand all African American culture, but he does know and thoroughly understand his character Jerome Foxworthy, and this novel is simply Jerome's story.

Teachers can point out to students that talented and dedicated writers are able to write outside both their gender and their culture. It is not easy to overcome one's own experience and perspective—nor is it easy to avoid the easy use of racial stereotypes—but careful and determined writers can do so. Teachers can also point out that even stories about a culture written by someone within that culture may present only that person's perspective and experience. Others within the same ethnic group may have experiences completely unlike those presented by their racial peers in books and stories.

The representation of mental and emotional illness

The scenes that show Bix and his mother when they are disabled by their illnesses are painful and unpleasant, but they are essential to the plot because they reveal both Bix's tragic flaws and his motivation. Brooks does not demean either character; he merely shows how powerless they are against their afflictions. Although Bix is not as engaging as Jerome, readers do feel empathy for him. Brooks understands this pain well; his own mother was crippled by emotional illness, and much of the reality in this novel comes from his own childhood experience. *The Moves Make the Man* has even been praised by mental health professionals for its portrayal of mental illness.

In today's society, many people suffer from emotional and mental illnesses; after reading Brooks' novel, students will be less judgmental of those who are disabled by flaws not visible to the naked eye. All students need to learn tolerance, but too often students are least tolerant of those who appear healthy but act "strangely." Readers of this novel cannot help but share Jerome's concern for—and frustration with—Bix, and perhaps they will transfer those feelings into their own lives.

Language

Negative racial labels and slang terms appear occasionally in the novel. These are used appropriately within the context of both the setting and the characters. Teachers can help students see that these words are not meant to injure anyone; they are simply the language used by the kinds of people that are portrayed in this novel. Characters who use racial epithets are shown in a very negative light, suggesting that the author does not endorse the use of such language.

Racial epithets are a shameful but undeniable fact of American history. To leave them out of a story set in the South in the 1960s would be to misrepresent the society of that time. In addition to being faithful to historical realities, Brooks uses these powerful words to help readers gain some idea of how much these expressions sting whether they are heard or read. Their negative force is made clear each time they are used, helping readers sense how such words have been used to exclude and marginalize others.

Poor role models

Bix's mother is a troubled character. Brooks makes it clear that she loves her son dearly and that she has good intentions; unfortunately, her illness makes it impossible for her to act on her good intentions. Bix's stepfather is quite harsh, but careful readers will see that he is more fair-minded than Bix thinks he is and that often he is working with the best interests of Bix and his mother in mind. Brooks is careful to show that even though Bix's parents are flawed, they are still motivated by genuine concern for their son. Their portrayal is essentially realistic: as with most parents, their intentions are good but their performances are sometimes limited by their circumstances or personal weaknesses. Brooks balances Bix's dysfunctional parents with Jerome's mother; she is an effective counterbalance to the negative adult characters in the novel. Loving, kind, and wise, she is a model mother whose good qualities are accentuated by comparison to the weaknesses of Bix's parents.

Students and parents should be encouraged to look for the good in this novel. Brooks has written a powerful story of friendship and love, but he has placed it within a painful reality. To do anything less would have weakened the novel by sugarcoating some of the harsh realities many families face.

References

Bruce Brooks is a widely praised author of fiction and nonfiction for children and young adults. Born in Washington, D.C., and raised there and in North Carolina, Brooks graduated from the University of North Carolina and later earned an M.F.A. from the University of Iowa. Two of his novels, *The Moves Make the Man* and *What Hearts* have been named Newbery Honor books. He has won many other awards for his books, including several ALA Best Books for Young Adults notations.

Brooks has always maintained that he doesn't write for teenagers or children; he writes for intelligent readers. His refusal to condescend to a younger audience has earned him a reputation for quality and sophistication.

Reviews of *The Moves Make the Man* have been very favorable:

> *The Moves Make the Man* is an excellent novel about values and the way people relate to one another. It is entertaining and accessible. (Watkins 54)

> This is a difficult story to read, but better readers will enjoy its humor, electric tension and great characters, and their efforts will be well rewarded. The description of the basketball action is simply excellent, but all the writing is top rank. (Unsworth 103)

> The novel is memorable for its successful experimentation with language and for the shrewd exposition that grows out of complex characterization. (Wilms 783)

For more information about Brooks and his work, consult the following sources:

Brooks, Bruce. *Speaking for Ourselves*. Ed. Donald R. Gallo. Urbana: NCTE, 1990: 33–35.

"Bruce Brooks." *Something about the Author.* Ed. Anne Commire. Vol. 72. Detroit: Gale, 1993: 22–26.

Cart, Michael. "Brooks, Bruce." *Twentieth-Century Young Adult Writers.* Eds. Laura Standley Berger, et al. Detroit: St. James, 1994: 78–80.

Crowe, Chris. "Bruce Brooks." *Writers for Young Adults.* Ed. Ted Hipple. Vol. 1. New York: Scribner's, 1997: 173–182.

Herc, Karen. "Bruce Brooks." *Writers of Multicultural Fiction for Young Adults.* Ed. M. Daphne Kutzer. Westport: Greenwood, 1996: 59–64.

McDonnell, Christine. "New Voices, New Visions: Bruce Brooks." *Writers on Writing for Young Adults.* Eds. Patricia E. Feehan and Pamela Petrick Barron. Detroit: Omnigraphics, 1991: 367–370.

Telsen, Diane. "Bruce Brooks." *Something about the Author.* Vol. 72. Detroit: Gale, 1993: 22–26.

Alternative Works

Oneal, Zibby. *A Formal Feeling.* New York: Viking, 1982. Still depressed by her mother's death, sixteen-year-old Anne is home from boarding school for the winter holidays. Her father has recently remarried, and the presence of the new stepmother has made Anne's home seem alien to her. The Christmas season seems empty to Anne, and her depression only grows worse. Gradually, though, she works through the stages of mourning and begins to accept her loss and her new stepmother.

Taylor, Theodore. *The Cay.* Garden City: Doubleday, 1969. When the freighter on which he is traveling is torpedoed by a German submarine during World War II, Phillip, a twelve-year-old white boy who has been raised in a racist environment, is blinded by a blow on the head. He is rescued by an old black ship hand, Timothy, and together they are stranded on a small desert island in the Caribbean. Timothy's courage, wisdom, and love help Phillip survive and overcome his racist prejudices.

Related Works

Books about interracial friendship

Cannon, A. E. *Shadow Brothers.* New York: Delacorte, 1990. A Native American high school student who has lived his teenage years in a supportive white foster home begins to question both his identity and his friends after he returns from a visit to his reservation.

Hughes, Dean. *The End of the Race.* New York: Atheneum, 1993. Two boys, one white, one African American, find their friendship at risk when they compete against one another in track.

Klass, David. *Danger Zone.* New York: Scholastic, 1996. A talented white high school basketball player is invited to join an all-star team playing in an international tournament. As the only white player on the team, he must learn to overcome the inherent animosity of his teammates.

Taylor, Mildred D. *The Friendship.* New York: Dial Books for Young Readers, 1975. An old African American man insists on holding a white man to a promise made when both were young. In the presence of his racist peers, the white man denies the promise and the friendship and shoots the African American man for being "uppity."

Books about dealing with emotionally or mentally disturbed parents

Brooks, Bruce. *What Hearts.* New York: HarperCollins, 1992. These four stories present different episodes in a young boy's life. Saddled with an alcoholic and emotionally unstable mother, he tries to find security and safety by himself.

Cannon, A. E. *Amazing Gracie.* New York: Delacorte, 1991. A high school girl must deal with the difficulties resulting from her move to a new city, which are compounded by having to care for her mentally unstable mother.

Marino, Jan. *Searching for Atticus.* New York: Simon, 1997. The horrors of the Vietnam war have created severe emotional damage to the father of a shy high school girl, and she must work desperately to save him from his illness.

Books about adolescent mental and emotional illness

Anonymous. *Go Ask Alice.* New York: Prentice-Hall, 1971. This book, based on the diary of a high school girl, reveals both the pain and the mental/emotional confusion caused by drug abuse.

Guest, Judith. *Ordinary People.* New York: Ballantine, 1976. Greatly disturbed by the death of his older brother, a high school boy battles depression and contemplates suicide while his parents struggle with problems of their own.

Neufeld, John. *Lisa Bright and Dark.* New York: New American Library, 1969. A high school girl cannot convince her parents that she is teetering on the brink of sanity. Their refusal to recognize her problems nearly leads to disaster.

Works Cited

Unsworth, Robert E. Rev. of *The Moves Make the Man*, by Bruce Brooks. *School Library Journal* 31.4 (Dec. 1984): 103.

Watkins, Mel. "A Trickster and His Upright Friend." *New York Times Book Review* 11 Nov. 1984, sec. 7: 54.

Wilms, Denise M. Rev. of *The Moves Make the Man*, by Bruce Brooks. *Booklist* 81: 782–783.

About Chris Crowe

Chris Crowe, a high school English teacher for ten years, is now a Professor of English at Brigham Young University. He has served on the Board of Directors of ALAN and as editor of the Young Adult Literature column for *English Journal*. He recently completed a critical biography, *Presenting Mildred D. Taylor*, for the Twayne Young Adult Authors Series. He lives in Provo, Utah, with his wife, Elizabeth, and their four teenage children.

LAKOTA WOMAN

by Mary Crow Dog and Richard Erdoes

> When I heard the words "Wounded Knee" I became very, very serious. Wounded Knee—Cankpe Opi in our language—has a special meaning for our people. There is the long ditch into which the frozen bodies of almost three hundred of our people, mostly women and children, were thrown like so much cordwood. And the bodies are still there in their mass grave, unmarked except for a cement border. Next to the ditch, on a hill, stands the white-painted Catholic church, gleaming in the sunlight, the monument of an alien faith imposed upon the landscape. And below it flows Cankpe Opi Wakpala, the creek along which the women and children were hunted down like animals by Custer's old Seventh, out to avenge themselves for their defeat by butchering the helpless ones. That happened long ago, but no Sioux ever forgot it. (124)

Crow Dog, Mary, and Richard Erdoes. *Lakota Woman*. New York: HarperPerennial, 1990.

Intended Audience

Students in grades 9–12. Mature students would readily explore the issues raised in the book about identity, gender, and racism with the assistance of the teacher. This book would work particularly well with a diverse group of students, though its effectiveness is not limited to such a population.

Summary

Lakota Woman begins with the story of the Sioux and their "reining in" onto the barely arable reservation lands in the 1870s and 1880s. It also touches on the massacre at Wounded Knee in 1890, the result of those actions. More than anything else, however, the book follows the autobiographical story of Mary Brave Bird, a half-blood Lakota who grew up in a one-room cabin without running water or electricity on a South Dakota reservation. Mary tells of her difficult childhood, of her stay at a brutal missionary school, and of the forced tearing-apart of her family by the white control over Native American lives. After Mary marries Leonard Crow Dog, she decides to join the tribal pride movement AIM (American Indian Movement), which Leonard leads. Together they survive the second siege on Wounded Knee in 1973, although Mary delivers her baby as bullets are flying outside. Leonard revives the sacred and outlawed Ghost Dance with Mary's help, as both struggle to keep their tribal heritage alive and meaningful. Although Leonard is imprisoned and several close friends are killed or thrown into jail, Mary learns from Leonard the ways of the medicine man's wife and embraces the "old" ways of her people with pride and remarkable strength.

Relationship of *Lakota Woman* to the Program

Lakota Woman provides a rich tapestry of issues for exploration in an English classroom. Not only does it address issues of the treatment of Native Americans throughout our history and in the recent past, but it also exposes readers to the infinitely complex questions of identity, stereotypes, and racism. In addition, *Lakota Woman* cannot be clearly placed within a specific genre. Although it reads like an autobiography, a factual account of a person's life, it seems to coexist in the realm of memoir, since sections seem to have been fictionalized to "fill in spaces" in Mary Crow Dog's life. For all of these reasons, it provides a dynamic landscape for literary and historical investigation.

This book is ideal for the exploration of issues of identity as connected with race and gender within and without literary texts. Several parts of *Lakota Woman* introduce aspects of these issues with particular poignancy. As a half-blood and a woman, Mary is marginalized several times and on several levels. She finds that she is constantly struggling against a white society that desires to label and identify her in ways contrary to how she sees herself as a partial outsider to the Lakota world as well.

This book, above all others, sets in concrete the notions of bidialectalism that students grapple with daily, both inside and outside of classrooms. It provides students the opportunity to explore their own experiences of feeling apart and feeling part of the larger tapestries of their social lives. Students identify with Mary Crow Dog as she suffers because she does not have a distinct "world" she can call her own. She has experienced the discrimination and violence typically unleashed on Native Americans in the 1960s and 1970s, and yet she cannot turn to the pure-bloods of her own people. Her blood is "tainted." At times, she seems almost desperate for acceptance into a world, any world, that will accept her unconditionally. Adolescents identify with these issues personally when I use this book. Some express concerns of peer acceptance. Others describe the differences in school and community or peer culture. From Mary Crow Dog's situation, students raise issues of their own bidialectic or bilingual marginalization. Many share their questions: Are they accepted by their peers? Is the culture of their school similar to the culture of their neighborhoods, or do they have to find ways to live and survive in very different worlds? Many students must embrace discourse compatible with school half the day and a street discourse the other half of the day.

Because this book works so well for investigations of identity, most of the issues the students raise fall into the larger category of "who am I?" Working with tenth graders in a racially diverse inner-city school, I began an initial exploration of *Lakota Woman* by having students work with the notion of identity—what the word meant to them, how they defined themselves, how others sought to define them, and what words and images the world uses to identify people. Students were asked to construct boxes roughly six inches square, with the top left open. On the outside, they were asked to paste or write words or use visual text such as photographs or drawings that defined how the outside world (friends, parents, teachers, caregivers) saw them—how they felt the outside world "defined" them. In the inside of the box, students pasted ways in which they defined themselves. The outside world interpretations often proved to be a complex collection of racial and gender stereotypes, while the inside interpretations tended to reject social labeling and concentrated on the wonderfully authentic ways these students saw themselves. No other book I have used has resulted in such deep and meaningful explorations of the self.

Ultimately, this book allowed students to consider the relevance of Mary Crow Dog's story and how it might relate to their own lives. Students readily identified with the problems they struggled with on a seemingly daily basis, issues of how they are defined or identified by external forces. Vibrant conversations grew out of students' personal experiences with others who made assumptions about them due to their race, ethnicity, gender, dialect, first language, or socioeconomic position. Several young African American males remembered being followed by Korean owners of convenience stores in Brooklyn as they shopped for groceries. An Asian student recalled being spoken to as if he were a young child who didn't understand

English, despite the fact that he is a fluent speaker. Several young women told of times they were advised not to take on tasks that were meant for young men. One young man wrote that many adults outside his family told him not to waste his time trying to go to college since he was from such a poor family. Again, Mary Crow Dog's experiences with bias and oppression touch students deeply.

I've found it effective to begin with a quote by Mary Crow Dog from the end of Chapter One: "But you can't live forever off the deeds of Sitting Bull or Crazy Horse. You can't wear their eagle feathers, freeload off their legends. You have to make your own legends now. It isn't easy" (11). Notions of legends and myths pervade *Lakota Woman*, and students work in remarkable depth as they explore Native legends and myths they have identified during individual research. Students often find creation mythology, Mother Earth mythology, or the legend of Crazy Horse particularly interesting. They create a "story plate" from their myth or legend, illustrating one side of a paper plate with a scene from the story, and marking the other side with story mnemonics to help the storyteller in the oral rendering of the myth or legend.

Through such study, students are exposed to creation mythology and stories in which the importance of the land to the Lakota people is clear, particularly the references to the sacred Sun and Moon dances. Later, students work in small groups of three or four to conduct an in-depth investigation of one or two related myths for presentation to the rest of the class. This is more useful than trying to tackle two dozen legends or myths at a superficial level, and the references to Native myths and legends in *Lakota Woman* help students make connections with the book and with Native culture that would otherwise be impossible.

This book so clearly delineates gender roles and biases that students find they can identify with Mary Crow Dog and make connections between her experiences and their own lives. Chapter One begins with a Cheyenne proverb:

> A nation is not conquered until
> the hearts of its women
> are on the ground.
> Then it is done, no matter
> how brave its warriors
> nor how strong their weapons. (3)

This proverb provides an opportunity for students to reflect on the role that gender will play in the novel. Do they agree with the quote? Why would

Mary Crow Dog choose to begin her piece this way? I ask students to chart the ways in which the Lakota treat women and juxtapose this with the ways in which the Lakota women are treated off the reservation by the often violent white culture. We compare these experiences with those that the students see in contemporary society and their own lives. Possibly because Mary's life is distant in some respects from their own, her situation seems to help students discuss gender stereotype and objectification in mature and valuable ways. Oftentimes, the young men in my classroom address this quote as passionately as do the young women. One way or the other, lively debate ensues.

This book also lends itself to the exploration of the power of language. Its candor and lyricism give students the springboard from which to look more closely at the author's craft and the message she wishes to leave with the reader. One way to explore the language while examining the themes is to have students keep a quote book as they read. Students include quotes from the text that resonate for them, perhaps for reasons only they can explain. Occasionally, students use these quotes to shape found poetic responses to the novel. We layer this poetry into the work students have done on their identity boxes, weaving ways they see themselves with lines and phrases from the book. How much of the book do they see in their own lives? These poetic pieces, made up of words and phrases from the novel, not only serve as ways of interpreting the text but also show the unique and meaningful ways in which the students are connecting with the text. As a final reflective step, students are asked to explain their choices in writing and, in this way, reveal their decision-making process.

On more than one occasion, Mary mentions the difficulties she experiences as a half-blood Lakota. Since she is neither full-blood nor white, she is shunned by both groups. This ties in nicely with Faulkner's *Absalom, Absalom*, and provides fertile territory for conversation about the importance of fitting in. Students' recollections of times when they felt they didn't fit in invariably bring stories of awkward social moments and teenage angst. Again, students will better appreciate the depth of Mary Crow Dog's plight as they personalize their stories with hers.

Impact of the Material on Readers

Through reading and discussing this book, students become curious about the history of the relationships that have existed between the white people and the Native peoples of America. Much of what students know (or think they know) about the experiences of Native Americans comes from various media they have absorbed throughout their lives. *Lakota Woman* provides a new lens through which to challenge these images and assumptions. Since much of what happens in the novel takes place at Wounded Knee in the recent past, the novel provides an invitation to investigate the history of the massacre at Wounded Knee in 1890 in greater detail. Additionally, other broken treaties between Native tribes and the United States government can be researched and discussed. Many students have found the AIM movement of the 1970s particularly interesting, and have researched the debates over reservation casinos that are raging today.

Students have come to appreciate that Native Americans have been treated with remarkable disdain and hostility in the short history of our country. This novel offers myriad possibilities to investigate these national values, even as students make sense of the personal ethics that they embrace in these debates. This book addresses social responsibility, and students will begin to think about ways in which we can, individually and collectively, inform ourselves in order to be an educated and thoughtful citizenry.

The systematic destruction of the Native American extended family unit is detailed in chilling narrative in this novel. Men are separated from women, and children are removed from homes deemed "unfit" for them. Unlike history textbooks, which often gloss over details of how Native American tribes were treated in America, *Lakota Woman* provides the voice of a strong, determined woman who chose to fight for what she believed was important for herself, her child, her husband, and her people. Students will better appreciate the struggle of an often overlooked, disenfranchised people, while making personal connections to the relevant struggles Mary Crow Dog attempts to overcome. As Native Americans are pushed ever closer to the fringes of a livable landscape, Mary Crow Dog provides a character of strength, pride, spirit, and faith.

As one student wrote in response to a found poem she had added to her journal several days earlier:

> So. I can't? Just
> because I don't look
> like you or
> talk like you—
> or pray to your
> pale gods—I can't? Why
> do I have to wait until
> you can see not differences,

but just
me?

Tonya (12th Grade)

Potential Problems with *Lakota Woman* and Ways to Address Them

In one class, when we explored issues of racism and ethnic bias through the use of identity boxes and ongoing class conversations, several students appropriated Mary Crow Dog's criticism of white culture. In other words, a type of reverse racism settled over my students as they investigated Mary's encounters with white racism directed at the Lakota tribe. Many students remembered their own encounters with racism and chose to rail against their oppression, effectively choosing the path of an eye for an eye. This caught me off guard, and in retrospect, it could perhaps have been avoided if the conversations about Mary Crow Dog's experiences and the students' work with their identity boxes, had been prefaced more effectively. It seems important to take a step back and speak candidly with students about what racism is and what it means to them before engaging in the exploration of the novel and the many real and painful memories it may arouse in students. An overarching discussion of racism and bias in this context could serve to distance them enough from their potentially visceral anger and allow them to engage in a more thoughtful approach to the issues they identify as important to them in the book.

The book contains a number of very mature themes, such as sexuality, abuse (both physical and emotional), and oppression. Students should be provided a safe space in which to candidly discuss these weighty topics. Why teach a book with such topics? The reality is that these issues exist, and the best way to demystify and come to terms with controversial issues is to do so in the relatively controlled space of the classroom, with a teacher willing to guide and facilitate students' investigations. Many people do not wish to talk about the institutional racism that has existed in this country since its inception; indeed, they object to such a conversation. Many people do not want to face the fact that political and economic systems we have created have also created oppression. Our nation has to deal with these issues, so shouldn't our youth begin tackling them as well? A dialogic journal has worked best for me while exploring these topics; it affords the teacher an opportunity to address issues of personal impact to individual students in an ongoing conversation that takes place in the relative privacy of the journal.

Students may be confused by some of the historical references made in the book, and some background information, particularly about Wounded Knee, AIM (American Indian Movement), and the BIA (Bureau of Indian Affairs) should be provided as context to facilitate students' interactions with and understanding of the text.

References

Mary Crow Dog has written two books, *Lakota Woman* and *Ohitika Woman*. Her insight into the marginalized culture of Native Americans is piercing, and she brings a powerful voice to the story of Native American women in particular. She grew up in the misery of a South Dakota reservation and became very active in the 1960s and 1970s in the American Indian Movement in an attempt to bring about much needed change for her peoples.

Lakota Woman has received several positive reviews:

> . . . this narrative flows from the oral tradition, especially in the deeply moving first chapter in which Mary recites the devastating losses she experienced before even reaching midlife. (Monaghan 1260)

> Short, choppy sentences impart a sense that Mary Crow Dog is speaking directly to readers, and her story is startling in its intensity of feeling and its directness about the Indians' reliance on their heritage and religion. . . . By no means a pretty account . . . the book is an important bridge to cultural understanding. (Addison 269)

> The story of [Mary Crow Dog's] coming of age in the Indian civil rights movement is simply told and, at times, simply horrifying. Throughout the book, Ms. Crow Dog's recollections seem to exemplify the Cheyenne proverb that introduces her story: "A nation is not conquered until the hearts of its women are on the ground." (Guthrie 15)

Alternative Work

One book that could serve as an alternative to *Lakota Woman* would be *The Way to Rainy Mountain,* by N. Scott Momaday (U of New Mexico P, 1969). In it, Momaday presents multiple perspectives and combines myriad viewpoints for retelling the history and traditions of the Kiowa tribe in the Northern Plains. Using personal stories, tribal stories, and historical interpretations, Momaday paints a rich picture of the Kiowa history without controversy and with a straightforward approach.

Related Works

By Mary Crow Dog and Leonard Crow Dog

Brave Bird, Mary [Mary Crow Dog]. *Ohitika Woman.* New York: Grove Press, 1993.

Crow Dog, Leonard, and Richard Erdoes. *Crow Dog: Four Generations of Sioux Medicine Men.* New York: HarperCollins, 1995.

Native American myths and legends

Bruchac, Joseph. *Native Plant Stories.* Golden: Fulcrum, 1995.

Geronimo et al. *Geronimo: His Own Story.* New York: Dutton, 1970.

Hitakonanu'laxk. *The Grandfathers Speak, Native American Folk Tales of the Lenape People.* New York: Interlink, 1994.

Sandoz, Mari. *Crazy Horse: The Strange Man of the Oglalas.* New York: Knopf, 1942.

Van Camp, Richard. *A Man Called Raven.* San Francisco: Children's Book Press, 1997.

Autobiographies of Native Americans

Allen, Charles Wesley. *The Autobiography of Red Cloud: War Leader of the Oglalas.* Ed. by R. Eli Paul. Helena: Montana Historical Society Press, 1997.

Krupat, Arnold, ed. *Native American Autobiography: An Anthology.* Madison: U of Wisconsin P, 1994.

Books about growing up Native American

Larson, Sidner J. *Catch Colt (American Indian Lives).* Lincoln: U of Nebraska P, 1995.

Red Shirt, Delphine. *Bead on an Anthill: A Lakota Childhood.* Lincoln: U of Nebraska P, 1998.

Life of the Lakota

Flood, Renee Sansom. *Lost Bird of Wounded Knee: Spirit of the Lakota.* New York: Scribner's, 1995.

Grobsmith, Elizabeth S. *Lakota of the Rosebud: A Contemporary Ethnography.* New York: Holt, 1981.

St. Pierre, Mark. *Madonna Swan: A Lakota Woman's Story.* Norman: U of Oklahoma P, 1991.

Works Cited

Addison, Dorothy. Rev. of *Lakota Woman,* by Mary Crow Dog and Richard Erdoes. *School Library Journal* 36.9 (1990): 269.

Guthrie, Patricia. *New York Times Book Review* 1 July 1990, sec. 7: 15.

Monaghan, Pat. *Booklist* 1 Mar. 1990: 1260.

About Rene Schillinger

Rene Schillinger is currently a doctoral candidate in English at Columbia University's Teachers College. In addition, he is an instructor in the English Education Program and the Liaison across Programs for the Department of Arts and Humanities. He taught middle school (grades 6 through 8) for six years, and is presently teaching an adolescent literature class at Teachers College.

THE CRAZY HORSE ELECTRIC GAME

by Chris Crutcher

"This school," he says, "saved my life. I don't mean it made me a better person, or picked me up when I was really down, or taught me the true meaning of anything. I mean it saved my life; because when I came here I was to the end of me. My family was wrecked and I thought I'd wrecked it. My brain didn't work right and the physical skills I had always depended on were shot completely to Hell." He looks out to Lacey. "My friend Mr. Casteel picked me up off the street and gave me a home; his home. I have to admit I haven't always been the perfect roommate, and I would have to say our lifestyles are somewhat different, but old Lacey's stuck with me, and in his way he's a wise man, and I owe him a lot."

Lacey looks around the crowd, smiling, a bit embarrassed.

Willie goes on. "Nobody here preached at me. Nobody told me everything would be okay, or that I should go back home to my parents and work things out when I knew the time for that wasn't here yet. They let me figure it out for myself; demanded that I figure it out for myself; but they never deserted me. And now, I'm ready to go back home. I don't know what will happen there; whether I can stay and make it or not, but at least I'm strong enough to give it a try." (200–201)

Crutcher, Chris. *The Crazy Horse Electric Game.* New York: Bantam Doubleday Dell Books for Young Readers, 1987.

Intended Audience

Students in grades 9–12. Teachers may use the novel with groups of students identified as "at risk," as a stand-alone text, or as a bridge to reading classical literature with related themes. Students may read it as a whole-class novel or choose it as individual reading.

Summary

Eighteen-year-old Willie Weaver from Coho, Montana, recalls the past two years of his life, which were dramatically changed by a treacherous waterskiing accident. Only weeks before the accident, Willie was on top of the world, having successfully pitched his Samson Floral team to victory over arch-rival summer league team Crazy Horse Electric. School had started, and he expected to continue his star student and athlete reputation in the classroom and on the football field. Everything changed, however, on his last weekend at the lake, when he pushed the edge of safety while waterskiing and suffered speech and physical damage. Willie now has to deal not only with his feelings about the unexpected death of his infant sister twelve years ago, but also with his fall from stardom and the collapse of his family and friendships. Willie runs away to California and spends the next two years trying to reclaim his life at the "One More Last Chance" School, where he teaches his body and his brain to deal with their new limitations.

Relationship of *The Crazy Horse Electric Game* to the Program

The very fact that this novel deals with challenging themes substantiates that it should be taught. Part of a teacher's mission is to prepare students for success in life as adults, and this novel exposes students to elements they may have to face throughout their lives. The main character, Willie Weaver, is a high school student himself; therefore, students can readily identify with this age and maturity level, making it easier for them to connect with the story on a personal level. This novel helps students discover who they are and how they define themselves.

By incorporating study of this novel as part of a unit on self-discovery, teachers can help freshman and sophomore students research issues; apply critical thinking skills; see themselves in literature; gain insight into family relationships, handicaps, teenage suicide, and drug abuse; understand style and literary structure; understand problem solving and decision making; and gain research skills. Students can answer questions such as Who am I? How do I define myself? What impact do my friends have on what I do and say? Teachers can provide hypothetical situations and ask students to roleplay their interactions with friends and family as they solve the predicaments.

Students can keep dialectical journals and create theme posters that recognize ideas presented in the novel related to family relationships and communication, to creation of self-esteem and identity through perseverance, to learning to love oneself, to forgiveness, to overcoming adversity, to setting and achieving goals (including willingness to sacrifice), and to maturation. These posters will define themes, present examples from the text that support the themes, offer visual representations of the themes, and show connections from the novel to everyday life scenarios. Students can also be introduced to literary elements of simile, symbolism, and allusion.

Furthermore, Socratic seminar discussions can be held in which students discuss possible solutions to Willie's problems. Students can learn research skills by investigating nonfiction accounts of some of the topics in the novel—physical and mental disabilities, teenage suicide, runaways, divorce, prejudice, and Tai Chi. Finally, students can examine the realistic use of language based on the age and education levels of the characters.

Other activities and forms of assessment might include writing the next chapter in the text; writing a synopsis for a new Crutcher novel; mapping events of the novel; designing a graphic representation of the symbols, structure, characters, or stylistic elements of the novel; writing a research paper; and presenting factual information and solutions to various real-life problems as addressed in the novel. At the end of the unit students can answer the questions from the beginning of the unit again. What have they learned about what it takes to define themselves? What can they do when they run into adversity? Another culminating activity can be the creation of personal mandalas using ideas from Fran Claggett's *Drawing Your Own Conclusions.*

Additionally, this novel connects to other literature typically studied at the freshman or sophomore level: *To Kill A Mockingbird* and *Romeo and Juliet.* Willie must deal with being an outcast because he is no longer the star ball player. Instead he walks with a cane and has no control of his left hand (his former pitching hand). Scout must deal with her father's treatment as an outcast, a "nigger lover," when he decides to defend a black man accused of raping a white woman. She also learns not to believe all the rumors about Arthur "Boo" Radley, who was isolated from civilization by his father.

Willie makes decisions without thinking about the consequences and reacts emotionally, as Romeo and Juliet do. Willie constantly pushes the edge of disaster by not wearing his helmet when motorcycling and by pushing the G-force to the extreme while waterskiing. Ultimately, his rash behavior ends in disaster, leaving him physically incapacitated. Afterward, when he sees his girlfriend looking at another boy, Willie reacts violently, causing Jenny Blackburn to retreat from him entirely. Romeo and Juliet fall in love at first sight and choose to disregard their family's "ancient grudge" and romance each other sub rosa. This decision leads to other tragedies. Romeo hastily avenges Benvolio's death, which banishes him from Verona, and then he carelessly races to Mantua upon word of Juliet's "death" instead of waiting for word from the Friar. As a result, both Romeo's and Juliet's lives come to an unnecessarily abrupt end. Ultimately, then, another goal students can achieve is to gain insight into the relationships that exist among a variety of literary works and the relationships that exist between literature and life.

A similar unit can be used with junior and senior students to achieve the same goals and to connect to classical literature such as *Hamlet* and *Julius Caesar*. Betty Greenway compares Willie Weaver to Hamlet, who realizes that "'success' is a matter of adjusting our spiritual readiness with the readiness of the events around us" (20), just as Hamlet learns that "the readiness is all" (V.ii.222) and Brutus says, "There is a tide in the affairs of men, / When taken at the flood, leads on to fortune" (IV.iii.218–219). Brutus, Hamlet, and Willie learn they play a part in their own ability to create who they are, what they become, and what they do. They also learn they cannot do everything completely by themselves. Brutus relies on the politicians around him; Hamlet relies on Horatio, his father's ghost, and the gravediggers; and Willie relies on Lisa, Sammy, Andre, and Lacey. Betty Greenway also recommends Gary Soto's "Oranges" and a Gary Snyder haiku as further connections to *Crazy Horse* (21).

All of these activities help students increase use of strategies for reading comprehension; write and speak for a variety of audiences and purposes; increase use of critical thinking skills; and increase recognition and application of literature's connections to life.

Impact of the Material on Readers

Studying about teenagers who experience realistic problems and the issues they raise will help students broaden their thinking and understanding about the connections between these themes and their everyday lives. They will have to confront fears they may be experiencing themselves or those they know their friends have experienced. Students can deepen their understanding of rhetorical devices that create imagery, allusion, symbolism, character, and voice. Ultimately, they can continue to develop their own identities. As a result, students will gain insight into their own self-esteem and identity by applying Willie's situations and solutions to themselves. They can also use the novel as a tool for possible ways to help friends and families deal with similar situations. Ultimately, students will see firsthand how literature reflects life. In addition, they will become better readers by recognizing literary techniques and analyzing the author's purpose behind them. This analysis, too, will demonstrate a connection between literature and life.

Potential Problems with *The Crazy Horse Electric Game* and Ways to Address Them

This book contains many controversial issues, from experimenting with alcohol and drugs to dysfunctional families, runaways, contemplation of suicide, and prostitution. While these topics may offend the sensitivities of parents, students find them genuine and germane issues. Betty Greenway reports that students told her that they "*loved* what they perceived as Crutcher's realism. He was in tune with their real lives, and he wrote about their interests and concerns and about what they knew was going on all around them" (19, emph. in original). A sensitive teacher can help students discuss these issues or know when to ask that they be addressed in small groups or individually in writing.

Drug and alcohol use

Drugs and alcohol are not glorified. Instead, they are shown to be detrimental as Willie becomes violently ill and demonstrates that using drugs or alcohol can cause painful problems. The very fact that this issue is raised in the novel opens a door for teachers to communicate with students about drug and alcohol abuse, allowing students to discuss scenarios and discover truthful information about drugs and alcohol.

Adults portrayed as overly protective and controlling

While Willie's father apparently wants to dictate Willie's life, his character should be perceived as demonstrating the reality that people are not just one-sided. There is no such thing as a perfect family that lives happily ever after. Willie's family illustrates how adults and children must deal with adversity throughout their lives. This topic also invites teachers to help students make connections between literature and life. Teachers can use this opportunity to roleplay a variety of scenarios of family life and hold open discussions of problems and solutions.

Suicide and prostitution

Willie briefly considers suicide, but does not attempt it because he knows it is not a solution to his problems, and Willie has complete disgust for Angel's prostitution and wants her to stop, to realize that she doesn't need to sell herself to define herself. Again, these issues are facts of life, and their presentation in the novel creates a forum for frank discussion.

Students may find these mature themes challenging, but this very challenge can enhance their cognitive skills. They will have to think hard about the issues raised and how they feel about them. They will have to decide how they feel about the decisions Willie makes—what they would do if they were in Willie's shoes and why. Students with personal or family problems similar to those Willie experiences may have difficulty reading and discussing the novel. In cases where students or parents have valid objections, an alternative selection should be offered.

Although many of the themes introduced in this novel may be considered too mature for high school students, their relevance to the everyday lives of children emerging into young adulthood far exceeds any opposition to the teaching of this book. With guidance and an open forum for discussion, students can understand Willie's growth and identity as well as their own.

References

Chris Crutcher was raised in the small lumber town of Cascade, Idaho, and his novels reflect his life and values. Crutcher worked as director of a K-12 alternative school for inner-city kids in Oakland, California, and used this experience as a foundation for *Crazy Horse Electric Game.* He holds a B.A. in sociology and psychology and a teaching credential from Eastern Washington State College. He also worked as a child and family therapist in a mental health center in Spokane, Washington, where he focused on families and child abuse. One of his books was named a *School Library Journal* Best Book of the Year, all of his books for adolescents have been recognized as an ALA (American Library Association) Best Book for Young Adults, and three have been named to a list of best young adult novels of the 1980s by ALAN (Assembly on Literature for Adolescents NCTE) members.

The Crazy Horse Electric Game has received positive reviews:

> Chris Crutcher manages to create truly believable male adolescent characters . . he makes sports and the young boys who play them come

> alive and in the process presents the issues and problems of adolescence . . . [the book] is a testimony to the indomitability of the human spirit. (Silvey 741)

> Crutcher gives us believable glimpses of locker rooms and practice sessions, spiced with irreverent, sometimes coarse, male humor. He shows brief awkward moments of romance in contrast with the honesty, ease, and trust of male friendships. For all [Crutcher's protagonists], winning is not the goal; doing your best, stretching your limits, is the only true measure of success. (McDonnell 332)

> Crutcher writes powerfully and movingly of Willie's attempts to "become whole" again, the need to readjust his expectations of what his body can do and the means of compensating. . . . The characterization in this book is wonderful; the reader can picture each person introduced, whether it be an amazingly bizarre schoolmate known as Telephone Man, or Dr. Hawk, a huge street dude who initially terrified Willie. (Spencer 76)

Alternative Work

The Island by Gary Paulsen (New York: Dell, 1990) could serve as an alternative for students or parents who object to Crutcher's novel. Will Neuton and his family move to northern Wisconsin. His relationship with his family is strained because his parents are fighting. At his new home, though, Will discovers an island where he learns about himself and the wonders of nature.

Related Works

Books about adolescents, growing up, and self-identity

Chang, Pang-Mei Natasha. *Bound Feet & Western Dress.* New York: Doubleday, 1996. This is an autobiographical look at the life of Chang Yu-i, who did not have her feet bound as a child pursuant to Chinese tradition. The change from tradition foreshadows her exceptional life as a student at Oxford, followed by a move to America, where she served in several prestigious positions.

Cormier, Robert. *The Chocolate War.* New York: Dell, 1986. Freshman Jerry Renault refuses to sell chocolate for the school fundraiser, so he becomes a pawn in a game of control in this story of intimidation and power.

Books about adolescents dealing with handicaps

Maugham, W. Somerset. *Of Human Bondage.* New York: Doran, 1915. Philip Carey, a handicapped orphan, is brought up by a clergyman, but he gives up his religious faith and studies art in Paris.

Orr, Wendy. *Peeling the Onion.* New York: Holiday House, 1996. Anna Duncan was a confident, pretty, popular karate champion who was involved in a car accident that left her with a broken neck and shattered dreams. Now, she must overcome debilitating pain, concentrating long enough to complete simple assignments and sit and walk without falling over.

Works Cited

Claggett, Fran. *Drawing Your Own Conclusions.* Portsmouth: Heinemann, 1992.

Greenway, Betty, "Chris Crutcher—Hero or Villain?" *The Alan Review* 22.1 (1994): 19–21.

McDonnell, Christine. "New Voices, New Visions: Chris Crutcher." *The Horn Book Magazine* 64 (1998): 332.

Silvey, Anita. Rev. of *The Crazy Horse Electric Game* by Chris Crutcher. *The Horn Book Magazine* 63 (1987): 741.

Soto, Gary. "Oranges." *New and Selected Poems.* New York: Chronicle Books, 1994.

Spencer, Pam. Rev. of *The Crazy Horse Electric Game*, by Chris Crutcher. *Voice of Youth Advocates* (June 1987): 76.

About Shirl Chumley

Shirl Chumley has been teaching since 1993, holds an M.A. in Secondary Education, Curriculum and Instruction, and is currently a teacher of Freshman English, Advanced Placement Language and Composition, and Yearbook Production at Ponderosa High School in Parker, Colorado.

IRONMAN

by Chris Crutcher

> Mr. Nak sat back on his desk and said, "Ya know, I've heard folks say 'Life's not fair' in this group a lot. I've even said it myself when the occasion seemed to call for it. But that ain't correct. Life is exactly fair. *People* ain't fair, but life sure as hell is. Life has Ironmen an' Stotans an' American Gladiators, an' Charles Mansons an' Jeffrey Dahmers. Life has ever kind of holy man an' devil. If you're ever gonna beat all the anger an' hurt inside you, you're gonna have to learn to offset the awful with the magnificent. But that requires allowin' for both to have their place in the world. An' whether you know it or not, it's there. The truth don't need you to believe it for it to be true. (226–227)

Crutcher, Chris. *Ironman*. New York: Bantam Doubleday Dell, 1995.

Intended Audience

Students in grades 10–12. Although the central characters in this novel are males, teachers should move past gender stereotypes and use the book with females as well. It could be used effectively in language arts classrooms, from AP classes through lower-level ones.

Summary

Through a series of letters to television personality Larry King, seventeen-year-old Bo Brewster chronicles his senior year. Faced with expulsion, Bo agrees to attend a before-school Anger Management Class led by the wise yet enigmatic Mr. Nakatani. Bo's letters and Crutcher's narrative reveal the source of Bo's anger—his volatile relationship with his father. As Bo bonds with his Anger Management classmates, he begins to put his own life into perspective and is able to help others with their own equally serious and hurtful conflicts. "Ironman" refers to the triathlon race Bo is training for; he receives assistance and support from his classmates and opposition, even sabotage, from his father, which gives the race a powerful significance and becomes a turning point for Bo's emotional growth. The book culminates with Bo's ending his dependence upon anger (and Larry King) and becoming a mature individual who is willing and able to forge a new relationship with his father.

Relationship of *Ironman* to the Program

Ironman, depending on how it is taught, can be used to meet a variety of national, state, and district goals regarding the English language arts. These goals are applicable to teaching the novel, as well as being observable *within* the text. One important goal—adjusting language to communicate effectively with a variety of audiences and for various purposes—is strongly evident throughout the novel as characters must learn to communicate with others in both new and more effective ways. Because Bo is angry and hostile in his classes and to his strict teacher, Mr. Redmond, he is sent to Anger Management Class. There, he and his classmates must learn to decipher the spare sentences of Mr. Nak in order to grasp their deeper meanings. As the members of the Anger Management group move from being combative and antagonistic to one another to being supportive, they learn the value of communication. By talking about their problems, they begin to see solutions. Bo must also relearn how to communicate with his teacher, Mr. Serbousek, after learning of this man's homosexuality, and he explores his own burgeoning feelings for fellow classmate Shelly, his first serious relationship with the opposite sex. Perhaps Bo's greatest adjustment is realizing how alike, rather than different, he and his father are; this discovery spurs them into counseling in the hopes of repairing their relationship.

A second important goal, that of using different writing elements and strategies appropriately to communicate with different audiences for different purposes, is emphasized adroitly in the novel. Bo's letters to Larry King are first-person narrative, and then Crutcher switches to third-person for the rest of the story. Thus, we see the novel's story line from different perspectives—Crutcher's statement of the facts, and Bo's personal interpretation of them. This technique presents the reader with a wealth of opportunity for discussion and critique of the story as it unfolds. It must also be noted that Bo is a good writer and presents a positive role model: a boy who enjoys writing and uses it as a tool to deal with the conflicts in his life.

Another goal, using a variety of resources to gather and synthesize information and to create and communicate knowledge, is also demonstrated by Crutcher's characters. Bo comments on Larry King's broadcasts, applying them to his own life. He later uses the library to discover that his teacher, Lionel Serbousek, was once a Stotan; this is a reference to Crutcher's earlier novel *Stotan* (1986), in which Lionel was a main character. (The "Stotans," named for a cross between a stoic and a Spartan, underwent a grueling week of training supervised by a coach resembling Mr. Nak.)

Mr. Nak is the main resource for each character in the novel; his students must synthesize his comments and learn how to implement the advice he gives. Readers (and the characters) learn a great deal about triathlons and American Gladiators, as well as the equipment and training required. Finally, readers see the Anger Management Class members transforming into Stotans as they use their new knowledge to work as a sophisticated team to assist Bo during his triathlon race.

Over time, readers see the goal of developing an understanding of and respect for diversity across cultures, ethnic groups, geographic regions, and social roles. *Ironman* presents a wealth of diversity. Mr. Nak is a Japanese-Texan with a horrific past of drunk driving. Shelly is a female American Gladiator in training who was severely beaten by her father; Italian Joey also faces a combative household. African American Shuja faces the prejudice of others every day, as does homosexual Lionel Serbousek, who witnessed the deaths of his entire family in a terrible boating accident. Elvis's sister mails to their father the bullet used by their mother to commit suicide. Watching his father open the envelope, Elvis realizes his sister is a victim of incest. Hudge witnesses his father murder his beloved dog out of spite. In other novels, these characters could easily become caricatures or stereotypes, but through Crutcher we see them as real, worthwhile individuals desperately struggling to lead the life all good people deserve. Perhaps Mr. Nak describes his Anger Management group best in saying, "They're a little raw, but I'm bettin' they got all the same workin' parts as the fancier models" (45).

Finally, reading, class discussion, writing, and various class assignments would address the broad goals of reading a wide range of literature to understand human experience and applying knowledge of language structure and conventions, figurative language, and genre to create, critique, and discuss texts.

Impact of the Material on Readers

Readers will feel the devastating pain and resentment caused by the conflicts between Bo and his father. Most of the situations faced by members of the Anger Management group are horrifying, as are the pasts of Lionel Serbousek and Mr. Nak. However, the characters are also resilient and resourceful, and we see the strength of the human spirit triumphing over adversity; these people are survivors. Readers will see the power of teamwork and caring; all of the characters become stronger through their interactions with each other and they demonstrate cohesiveness during Bo's Ironman race. Diversity (racial, sexual, and class) is emphasized, yet not stereotyped; tolerance and acceptance are themes that recur without didacticism.

Potential Problems with *Ironman* and Ways to Address Them

This book contains mature themes, events, and language. Students with family problems similar to those presented in the book may find it difficult or impossible to read; in such cases an alternative book could be made available. On the other hand, acknowledgment and discussion of the problems found in the story may encourage previously silent students suffering from these problems to seek help. Students with no experience with such severe family problems and situations may need assistance with perspective regarding the characters and their actions. Class discussion, additional information, and companion reading of novels with similar themes may be beneficial to students.

Some students may object to Lionel Serbousek's homosexuality being presented positively. However, Bo's father voices his objections over the issue, and Bo himself is initially torn over his feelings for Lionel when he discovers the truth. Discussion should center on these responses and emphasize the difficulties of Lionel's everyday life, rather than promoting or denigrating the concept of homosexuality.

Adults are generally not presented in a positive light, and are seen as the cause of much of the difficulties faced by the characters. Anger and hostility are main themes. Those adults actively trying to assist Bo and his peers (his mother, Lionel, Mr. Nak) are flawed and also have painful pasts. Nevertheless, Crutcher has created real people whom students will recognize. Theme maps, webbing, or other organizers can assist students in charting character motivation for a deeper understanding of the novel and its characters.

At first glance, the book has few female characters, but it should be emphasized that the existing ones are important to the story. Bo relies on his mother and Shelly for stability and perspective; his principal, Dr. Gail Stevens, encourages Lionel to work with Bo, eventually leading to his admission into Anger Management Class. Students should discuss the absence of lead female characters as well as the impact of the existing females.

Although there is much in this book that adults could object to, Crutcher reaches—and teaches—students with his characters and their situations. Shielding students from Crutcher's realities will not necessarily protect or benefit them, but open and thoughtful discussion of this novel will help students gain insight and grow together with Bo.

References

Chris Crutcher has written eight novels (seven for adolescents) and is recognized for his ability to combine serious, thought-provoking issues with electric prose; his novels appeal to both contemporary adolescents and adults. He has been a director of a K–12 alternative school for inner-city students and a child and family therapist in a mental health center. His novels have arisen from his personal experiences in these positions.

All of Crutcher's adolescent novels have been named an ALA Best Book for Young Adults as well as receiving numerous state and national nominations and awards. He is also an NCTE/ALAN Award Winner. *Ironman* was additionally named an ALA Quick Pick, a *School Library Journal* Best Book of the Year, and a *Horn Book* Fanfare. *Ironman* has received many positive reviews:

> It is compellingly done—an engaging and important story, brilliantly written (Crutcher at his best, which is, of course, very good), with a memorable protagonist and a distinctive cast of minor characters, and with truly provocative ideas about school, family, and personal relationships. (Hipple 23)

> This may be Crutcher's best book . . . Crutcher's reputation ought to help get it in most young reader's hands. That's a good place to start in taking it one step closer to the reader's mind and heart. (Nilsen and Donelson 134)

> The heart of the story is small and painful, and rings thoroughly true. . . . He's a terrific storyteller with a wonderful handle on what it's like to be an adolescent. (Gorman 13)

Alternative Work

Alden Carter's *Bull Catcher* (New York: Scholastic, 1997) could serve as an alternative for those who object to the issues and language in *Ironman*. In it, Bull and Jeff chronicle their friendship and love of baseball as they travel from ninth grade through high school in their small town.

Related Works

By Chris Crutcher with characters from *Ironman*

Stotan! New York: Dell, 1986. Lionel Serbousek and his three best friends are high school swim team members. Together, they pledge to accept the challenge of Stotan Week—a series of grueling physical and emotional tests of endurance.

Problem novels featuring sports

Cheripko, Jan. *Imitate the Tiger.* Honesdale: Boyds Mills, 1996. Alcoholic high school senior Chris shares his story and problems via flashbacks while receiving treatment in a detox clinic.

Deuker, Carl. *Painting the Black.* Boston: Houghton, 1997. Ryan's life and senior year change dramatically when star athlete Josh moves in across the street.

Klass, David. *Danger Zone.* New York: Scholastic, 1996. Jimmy, a talented high school basketball player from a small town, is selected to play for an American "dream team" in Italy.

Thomas, Rob. *Rats Saw God.* New York: Aladdin, 1996. To graduate, Steve agrees to write a hundred-page essay in lieu of English class. His writing helps him sort out his troubled relationship with his famous astronaut father and shows how he went from good student to troubled teen.

Wallace, Rich. *Wrestling Sturbridge.* New York: Knopf, 1996. Wrestler Ben is stuck in a small town and overlooked by his coach. His best friend is the team's wrestling star, but Ben decides he can't let the season pass without challenging his friend and maybe changing his future.

———. *Shots on Goal.* New York: Knopf, 1997. Fifteen-year-old Bones pursues his goal of winning the league championship in soccer. He must also deal with his attraction to his best friend's girlfriend.

Problem novels with parental/family conflicts

Hautman, Pete. *Mr. Was.* New York: Simon, 1996. After his dying grandfather tries to kill him, Jack discovers a door that allows him to travel fifty years into the past. His travels to the past involve him in events that will influence his future.

Hobbs, Will. *Changes in Latitudes.* New York: Avon, 1988. While vacationing in Mexico, Travis must deal with family problems and, ultimately, tragedy after his younger brother becomes involved in the controversial fight to save endangered sea turtles.

Howe, James. *The Watcher.* New York: Atheneum, 1997. A lonely, troubled girl sits on the beach and watches a vacationing family and lifeguard. She projects herself into their lives—and eventually needs their help to deal with her troubled family.

Mazer, Norma Fox. *When She Was Good.* New York: Scholastic, 1997. The death of her abusive and controlling older sister prompts seventeen-year-old Em to recall their lives together and ultimately allows her to begin a new life of her own.

Naylor, Phyllis Reynolds. *The Year of the Gopher.* New York: Atheneum, 1987. George's parents want him to go to an Ivy League college after high school—but George has other ideas, such as taking the year off to discover himself and what he wants to do.

Short stories about sports

Crutcher, Chris. *Athletic Shorts.* New York: Dell, 1989, 1991. This is a collection of six short stories with athletic themes. "A Brief Moment in the Life of Angus Bethune" first appeared in *Connections,* edited by Donald R. Gallo, published in 1989 by Delacorte Press.

Gallo, Donald R., ed. *Ultimate Sports.* New York: Delacorte, 1995. Sixteen stories feature athletic themes. "Superboy" (51–57) was written by Chris Crutcher.

Short stories about contemporary problems

Bode, Janet, ed. *Trust and Betrayal.* New York: Bantam, 1995. Nineteen real-life stories tell of friends and enemies.

Gallo, Donald R., ed. *No Easy Answers.* New York: Delacorte, 1997. Sixteen short stories feature teens who find themselves in situations that test their strength of character.

Testa, Maria, ed. *Dancing Pink Flamingoes.* New York: Avon, 1995. Teens and the harsh realities of life are the focus of ten short stories.

Works Cited

Gorman, James. *The New York Times Book Review* 2 July 1995, sec. 7: 13.

Hipple, Ted. *The ALAN Review* 22.3 (1995): 23.

Nilsen, Alleen Pace, and Kenneth L. Donelson. "1995 Honor Listing: Can Less Be More?" *English Journal* 85.7 (November 1996): 130–134.

About Lisa A. Spiegel

Lisa A. Spiegel is currently an associate professor of secondary education at the University of South Dakota, where she teaches courses in young adult literature and middle/secondary education. She recently served as chair of WILLA (Women in Literature and Life Assembly of NCTE) and serves on the board of directors for ALAN. Her publications and presentations focus on her special interests—gender issues, rural education, and middle-level students.

THE EAR, THE EYE, AND THE ARM

by Nancy Farmer

He felt gently around the bag and found a Rita-sized lump pressing against the cloth. Tendai still had his Scout knife, so he carefully cut a small opening and looked out. To the right, also bouncing along on Fist's back, was a second bag. Farther away, Knife carried a third one.

So they were all together. Tendai could rip through the cloth and yell for help—except that he didn't see people or buildings through the hole. They were being carried through a vast wasteland. Greasy gray hills rose on either side. The ground squelched under Fist's heavy feet, and his footprints filled with sludge. Everything looked impossibly used and discouraged. (41)

Farmer, Nancy. *The Ear, the Eye, and the Arm.*
New York: Puffin Books, 1995.

Intended Audience

Students in grades 7–9. We advise that this book be used as one of several selections for individual reading or for small-group reading and discussion in a readers' workshop structure. This book could be used effectively in a genre study of science fiction as Farmer's book deals with futuristic technologies and political and social systems. *The Ear, the Eye, and the Arm* could also be one of several texts available for students to read in units that examine the conflict of good versus evil or that explore the theme of coming of age.

Summary

The year is 2194 in Zimbabwe and General Matsika's three children, Tendai, Rita, and Kuda, with the assistance of the Praise Singer, steal away from their fortified home. Tendai, the oldest, wishes to cross the city of Harare in order to earn his Explorers Scout badge. The children delight in their freedom as their father has forbidden them to travel about the city on their own. However, the children are kidnapped and taken to Dead Man's Vlei, where they must work for the She Elephant and mine refuse from toxic-waste dumps. Immediately General Matsika realizes that by overprotecting his children he has inadequately prepared them for living in the real world.

General Matsika's wife is extremely distressed about the disappearance of the children and hires three unusual detectives, the Ear, the Eye, and the Arm, to locate the children. As well as unusual physical features, the detectives possess paranormal powers due to their mothers' exposure to nuclear waste.

Although Tendai, Rita, and Kuda escape from the She Elephant, they find themselves prisoners in two other locations as the story unfolds. Through their adventures, the children mature, learn about the realities of life outside their sheltered home, and learn more about African tribal heritage and mythology. Although persistent in their pursuit, the detectives are always one step behind the children. Finally, the detectives must prove their worth and rescue the children from The Masks, a feared group of people determined to kill the spirit of the land of Zimbabwe.

Relationship of *The Ear, the Eye, and the Arm* to the Program

One of the most important goals that can be achieved through literature is that of personal enjoyment. *The Ear, the Eye, and the Arm* is indeed an entertaining and thought-provoking novel. The following suggestions provide teachers with reasons for using and ways of approaching the book.

Students can understand the diversity of human experience, apply critical thinking skills, and explore historical and current events through an examination of the futuristic political and social systems described in the text. Readers can imagine living in Zimbabwe in 2194 and discuss the strengths and drawbacks of the existing systems. They may generate questions and research issues through an examination of the influence of African mythology on the political and social systems described in the novel. They might explore the interdependence of past and present in the structure and shaping of the systems. Readers could also compare the political and social systems in the novel to current systems in Africa and Canada or the United States. In addition students might explore the human condition by examining those elements that seem universal to societies in 1998 and 2194 (e.g., discrimination, class systems, communities within communities). Readers can imagine their country in 2194 and speculate on future political and social systems, considering their current structures. Further, students could be encouraged to understand cultural contexts by exploring the living conditions of Canadians or Americans from various cultural and socioeconomic groups in the year 2194.

For a comparison activity that requires critical thinking and explores intertextual links, students can read Lois Lowry's *The Giver,* a selection that describes future political and social systems. Students compare the systems in each book, examine the strengths and drawbacks of each, discuss the elements of each system that they prefer, and provide reasons to support their choices.

Farmer's book can also help students gain insight into the role of technology in human society. Readers should speculate on the origins of the future technology in *The Ear, the Eye, and the Arm* and analyze the strengths and shortcomings of such technology. Readers can compare the references to these elements in the Farmer and Lowry books. The futuristic technologies used in specific television programs such as *Star Trek: The Next Generation* or films such as the *Star Trek* movies, *Men in Black*, or the *Star Wars* trilogy could also be discussed in light of the technologies in Farmer's novel.

Readers may see themselves in the literature through an exploration of the coming-of-age theme in *The Ear, the Eye, and the Arm.* Students should be encouraged to explore the changes that occur to Tendai as the story unfolds, including his maturation and discovery of latent abilities. As with many journeys in literature, the journey that Tendai and his siblings experience contributes to Tendai's coming of age. Although Tendai is bored at home, he later realizes that the excitement of adventure is not without its dangers. Readers might explore the significance of the tension between the boredom of "home" and the adventure of "being away." Students could explore their own journey of coming of age in comparison to Tendai's.

The conflict between good and evil is a common element of many excellent works of literature. Students might analyze the role of this conflict in *The Ear, the Eye, and the Arm* or compare its role in other texts, such as Madeleine L'Engle's *A Wrinkle in Time.* Thus, as well as exploring the human condition, readers would be encouraged to examine intertextual links and literary structures in similar or other genres.

Farmer's novel serves as a medium to introduce students to archetypes and the role they play in society, particularly in our films, literatures, and dramas. There are many archetypes, specific symbols and patterns, in Farmer's novel. These serve as a type of intertextuality for readers since they appear and reappear throughout the book. Through the character of Tendai, readers experience the classical male journey, the male hero, and the coming-of-age archetypes. There are several other archetypal figures in the novel, including the innocent child (Kuda), the "village idiot" (Trashman), the misfits of society (the detectives), and an evil force (The Masks). Students should compare these archetypal figures in the context of contemporary society and their use in the African context, both past and present. Through an exploration of archetypal patterns, students may explore what archetypes reveal about how we perceive the life journey as it is expressed in archetypal imagery across time, place, and culture. Several books listed in the Related Works section contain examples of archetypal figures for further comparison and discussion.

The preceding suggestions allow students to express their ideas, explain their opinions and consider the ideas of others, and develop, clarify, and extend their understandings. Students may write diary entries, draw satirical cartoons, engage in class debates, write newspaper editorials or articles, participate in roleplay situations, write response journal entries, create scrapbooks, write and perform readers' theater scripts, create artwork, engage in research, complete Venn diagrams or other graphic organizers, write poetry or song lyrics, create travel brochures, and engage in oral storytelling. In addition, we believe students should be invited and encouraged to generate their own questions and issues to discuss and explore in small- or large-group settings. By responding personally and critically to the literary work through various activities and structural formats, students will have opportunities to explore their thoughts, ideas, feelings, and experiences.

Impact of the Material on Readers

The discussion of topics such as current and future political and social systems and future technologies can encourage students to think about the evolution of these systems and technologies and their influence on people's lives. Students can explore how they can become involved in specific activities that would contribute positively to prospective political and social systems.

Literature is a medium for readers to learn about other cultures. Farmer's novel demonstrates the powerful role of the past in shaping the future, a fundamental aspect of human civilizations. Students may want to research additional information about specific topics and issues related to African heritage and mythology presented in the novel.

Although the novel takes place in the future and on a continent foreign to many readers, students will no doubt detect similarities between themselves and the characters. For example, the story deals with love, hate, human relationships, rites of passage, journeys, family structures, independence, identity, and good versus evil. Understanding the existence of these similarities—regardless of time, race, and gender—can help students better understand what is often referred to as the human condition.

Potential Problems with *The Ear, the Eye, and the Arm* and Ways to Address Them

The Ear, the Eye, and the Arm includes references to witchcraft, spirits, magic powers, sacrifices, and religion. There may be individuals who are uncomfortable with some of these topics and require alternative selections that have connections to the issues and themes in Farmer's novel. We advise providing these students with an alternative work. We also advise that this book be used as one of several selections for individual reading or for small-group reading and discussion in a readers' workshop structure.

A frequent challenge to reading material is that it deals with witchcraft and the occult. However, Farmer's inclusion of witchcraft, spirits, magic, sacrifices, and religion are fundamental to the novel's setting: Zimbabwe, 2194. The inclusion of witchcraft is appropriate to the historical and cultural setting of the novel and should be discussed in that context. A glossary and appendix at the end of the novel explain textual references to African history, culture, and mythology. Farmer explains the significance of the spirit world of Shona, witchcraft, praise singing, the tribes of Zimbabwe, Great Zimbabwe, and Monomatapa. She describes how these elements are representative of African cultures and also outlines the historical significance and meaning of each element. For example, Tendai discovers a *ndoro* in the toxic-waste mines and when others see this artifact, they immediately recognize and respect its significance. The *ndoro* ultimately saves the life of Tendai and the land of Zimbabwe. In the appendix, Farmer explains the historical significance of the *ndoro* and its role in both past and present African cultures. The witchcraft, spirits, and magic are fundamental to the development of the characters and plot and hence the overall impact of the book.

Book challenges can come from people who link Satanism with witchcraft. Teachers need to be clear about the distinctions between the two and to discuss Farmer's factual account of witchcraft in the appendix. To emphasize the importance of understanding cultural, historical, and societal factors when judging behaviors and beliefs, students could examine a variety of current cultural practices, such as the prevalence of television violence, and consider how this practice will be perceived two hundred years from now. As we live in a world filled with media representations of ideas and values, many different from our own, it is important for students to possess the knowledge and strategies that will enable them to think critically about what they read, hear, and view.

References

Subsequent to earning a Bachelor of Arts from Reed College in Oregon in 1963, Farmer worked for two years in the Peace Corps in India. She then studied chemistry at Merritt College in Oakland and the University of California at Berkeley for two years. Farmer then sailed to Africa on a freighter and worked as a freelance scientist in several African countries, including Zimbabwe and Mozambique. Not surprisingly, Farmer identifies African culture and history as two of her interests and explains that her work is shaped by her seventeen years in Africa.

Farmer has written *A Girl Named Disaster*, which became a 1997 Newbery Honor Book; *Lorelei*; *Tapiwa's Uncle*; *Do You Know Me*; and *The Warm Place*. As well as writing novels for children, Nancy Farmer has written books for adults. She has also worked as a lab technician, a chemist, an entomologist, and a freelance writer.

The Ear, the Eye, and the Arm, a 1995 Newbery Honor Book, has received many positive reviews:

> Rich in setting, the story is as complete as a weaver's kente pattern, as symbolic as an eijiri figure, as sophisticated as a Benin bronze. Demanding and intricate, but often convoluted, it will be rewarding to readers willing to travel beyond everyday places and to work to untangle its many strands. (Manning 147–148)

> Farmer's impeccable creation of the futuristic society is a remarkable achievement; the story addresses multiple sociopolitical aspects that parallel or are extensions of modern problems. The fully developed, unique characters struggle with personal issues—courage, identity, the discovery of latent abilities, relationships among family members—that are meaningful to young adults of any era. (Deifendeifer 597–598)

Alternative Work

An alternative to Farmer's novel is *The Story Box* by Monica Hughes (Toronto, Ontario: HarperCollins Canada, 1998). The inhabitants of the island Ariban, mainly fishers and herders, have deliberately isolated themselves from foreign influences and live highly regimented and controlled lives. The Aribans view dreams as lies, expressions of the imagination that present alternatives to the truth as defined by the Ariban community. In Ariban society, dreaming is punishable by banishment or death. After a storm, fifteen-year-old Colin, one of the community members, discovers a young woman, Jennifer, washed up on a beach. Jennifer is clutching a beautfully carved, locked chest and even though strangers are not permitted ashore, Colin takes her to his parents' home. Life becomes very complicated for Colin when the community discovers that Jennifer is a storyteller, a teller of untrue things, that her chest contains stories, and that Colin's younger sister has been dreaming.

Related Works

There are many possibilities for topics when considering related works for Farmer's novel. Some of these possibilities include future political and social systems, the conflict of good versus evil, the theme of coming of age, sibling relationships, the genre of science fiction, cultural mythology, and the archetype of the male journey.

Dickinson, Peter. *Eva.* New York: Dell-Laurel Leaf, 1991. This futuristic novel is about Eva, the daughter of a scientist. Eva is in a terrible car accident and, in order to save her mind, the scientists implant her brain into the body of a female chimpanzee.

Haddix, M. P. *Running Out of Time.* New York: Aladdin-Simon, 1995. Jessie believes herself to be a frontier child living in the nineteenth century. She is shocked when she discovers it is 1996, not 1840, and that she is actually living in a reconstructed village that serves as a tourist site. Jessie must venture outside the fence into the twentieth century in order to seek assistance for a medical emergency. Her quest is impeded by modern innovations and a sinister individual who is determined to keep the village residents locked in the nineteenth century.

Hughes, Monica. *The Tomorrow City.* Toronto, Ontario: Reed, 1994. In this science fiction adventure, Hughes considers the role of technology in future social and political systems. A computer called C-Three is programmed to make the city of Thompsonville an ideal place to live. However, Caro and David discover that the computer's values, including its disrespect for anything that is old, are actually destroying their city.

L'Engle, Madeleine. *A Wrinkle in Time.* New York: Farrar, 1962. Three children, Meg, Calvin, and Charles, with the assistance of three very unusual women, travel to another dimension to confront an evil force in order to save their father and themselves.

Lowry, Lois. *The Giver.* Boston: Houghton, 1993. Twelve-year-old Jonas is a member of a future society where all controversy, pain, and choice have been eliminated, where each childhood year has its privileges and responsibilities, and where family members are selected for compatibility. Jonas is chosen to be the community's next Receiver of Memory, and under the tutelage of an elder known as The Giver, Jonas discovers the disturbing truth about his utopian world and its hypocrisies.

Pullman, Philip. *The Golden Compass.* New York: Ballantine, 1995. While eavesdropping, Lyra becomes privy to information about an extraordinary microscopic particle called Dust. Her father, Lord Asriel, explains how the magical particle, rumored to possess profound properties, is found in the Arctic. Lord Asriel is one of many determined to discover the origin and power of Dust. Lyra becomes involved in the struggle and journeys into unbelievable danger.

———. *The Subtle Knife.* New York: Knopf, 1997. The second book in the series begins as Lyra has slipped through a newly formed astral portal. She meets Will Parry in this other world and together they search for her father (and hence Dust), battle soul-eating Specters, flee enemies (including Lyra's mother), and discover an object of extraordinary and devastating power.

Rubinstein, G. *Galax-arena.* London: Mammoth, 1995. In a novel about the future, three siblings are kidnaped from an Australian train station and forced into a spaceship. They believe they have been taken to the planet Vexa. They are trained to perform as gymnasts for the insectlike inhabitants of Vexa, but one of the children, Joey, is unathletic and becomes a Vexan's pet. However, she is able to discover the truth about their captivity.

Works Cited

Deifendeifer, Anne. Rev. of *The Ear, the Eye, and the Arm,* by Nancy Farmer. *The Horn Book Magazine* 70 (1994): 597–598.

Manning, Patricia. Rev. of *The Ear, the Eye, and the Arm,* by Nancy Farmer. *School Library Journal* 40.6 (1994): 147–148.

About Sylvia Pantaleo and Rebecca Luce-Kapler

Sylvia Pantaleo is an assistant professor in the Faculty of Education at Queen's University in Kingston, Ontario. Her twelve years of elementary and middle school teaching experience inform her university teaching of language arts and children's literature courses. Sylvia's research explores aspects of using children's literature in elementary and middle school classrooms including students' experiences with literature, teaching strategies and resources, and teachers' professional development.

Rebecca Luce-Kapler teaches English curriculum courses at Queen's University, Kingston, Ontario. She has taught English at all grade levels and has been on the board of the Young Alberta Book Society, which promotes reading and authors to students across the province. When not teaching, she writes poetry and fiction.

A LESSON BEFORE DYING

by Ernest J. Gaines

"Do you know what a myth is, Jefferson?" I asked him. "A myth is an old lie that people believe in. White people believe that they're better than anyone else on earth—and that's a myth. The last thing they ever want is to see a black man stand, and think, and show that common humanity that is in us all. It would destroy their myth. They would no longer have justification for having made us slaves and keeping us in the condition we are in. As long as none of us stand, they're safe. They're safe with me. They're safe with Reverend Ambrose. I don't want them to feel safe with you anymore.

"I want you to chip away at that myth by standing. I want you—yes, you—to call them liars. I want you to show them that you are as much a man—more a man than they can ever be. That jury? You call them men? That judge? Is he a man? The governor is no better. They play by the rules their forefathers created hundreds of years ago. Their forefathers said that we're only three-fifths human—and they believe it to this day. Sheriff Guidry does too. He calls me Professor, but he doesn't mean it. He calls Reverend Ambrose Reverend, but he doesn't respect him. When I showed him the notebook and pencil I brought you, he grinned. Do you know why? He believes it was just a waste of time and money. What can a hog do with a pencil and paper?"

We stopped. His head was down. (192)

Gaines, Ernest J. *A Lesson Before Dying*. New York: Vintage Books, 1994.

Intended Audience

Students in grades 11–12. A mature group of students should read this book with close guidance from the teacher. It could be used effectively in a survey of American literature, or in classes focused on contemporary African American authors, Southern writers, or twentieth-century American literature. It would also be effective as supplementary reading in a U.S. history class for its realistic portrayal of the South before civil rights or in a civics class for its critique of our social, political, and religious institutions.

Summary

Set in the fictional community of Bayonne, Louisiana, in the late 1940s, *A Lesson Before Dying* tells the story of Jefferson, a twenty-one-year-old uneducated black field worker who is wrongfully accused and convicted of the robbery and murder of a white man. He is sentenced to death by electrocution. At his trial, Jefferson's court-appointed attorney argues that Jefferson lacks the intelligence to plan a robbery, and that sentencing him to death would be like putting a hog in the electric chair. In spite of this "defense," the all-white jury finds Jefferson guilty. To compound the horror of his situation, Jefferson internalizes the attorney's racist depiction of him as a dumb animal.

Determined that Jefferson will die with dignity, his godmother, Miss Emma, turns to Grant Wiggins, a black teacher at the local plantation school, and asks him to teach Jefferson to be a man. Although convinced that there is nothing he can do, Grant reluctantly agrees to visit Jefferson in jail. Over the next several months, while Jefferson awaits execution, he and Grant forge a bond that enables both men to regain their dignity, reconnect with their community, and learn "the importance of standing."

Relationship of *A Lesson Before Dying* to the Program

There are many good reasons for teaching this novel to high school students.

It illustrates the transformative power of language.

In her 1993 Nobel Lecture, Toni Morrison focused on the power of language to shape and transform reality. Gaines illustrates this powerful concept, beginning with the defense attorney's reference to Jefferson as a "hog," a term that resonates throughout the novel. The incident affirms Morrison's contention that "oppressive language does more than represent violence; it is violence" (Robinson C1). Students not familiar with the legacy of slavery in America might view Jefferson's response to this term as extreme and unrealistic. After all, why would someone who has just been accused of murder be so devastated by a verbal insult? When students analyze the term within the context of slavery and the hostile racial climate of the pre–civil rights South, they begin to understand its devastating impact on Jefferson. They come to realize that, historically, slavery in America was especially brutal and dehumanizing. Instead of being treated like indentured servants or prisoners of war, enslaved Africans were perceived as property and branded like animals.

Both Grant and Jefferson must seek ways to establish their manhood. In Chapter 24, when Grant convinces Jefferson that he is a man worthy of respect and dignity, he destroys the racial myth and transforms the reality of Jefferson's life.

The novel demonstrates the power of myths and stories.

Characters learn valuable lessons through the myths and stories passed down to them. For example, Grant releases Jefferson from psychological bondage not only by exploding the myth of white supremacy, but by replacing the myth with a new story that transforms his reality. Grant uses the example of Mr. Farrell Jarreau's carving the slingshot handle (198) to teach Jefferson a powerful lesson about his own self-worth. Jefferson responds because Grant has taken the time to connect with Jefferson's experience. Consequently, he enables Jefferson to relinquish the destructive racist myth that depicts him as an animal, helping him to embrace a new story that depicts him as a man capable of shaping his own destiny. The power of oral tradition is illustrated in the scenes where the women gather in Tante Lou's kitchen to share stories of their families and the men gather at the Rainbow Club to reminisce about their heroes.

The novel offers insights into black heritage and culture.

Jefferson's diary, which records the last few days of his life, is a first-person historical document. Like Dr. Martin Luther King, Jr.'s "Letter from a Birmingham Jail," the diary not only documents his prison experience but also enables him—for the first time—to speak freely and in his own voice.

Teachers can encourage students to find out more about significant historical events that affected black Americans, such as the Three-Fifths Compromise, the Civil Rights Acts of 1866 and 1964, Black Codes, Jim Crow laws, and the terrorist tactics of the Ku Klux Klan. Students could also research major Supreme Court decisions such as the Dred Scott Decision (1857), *Plessy v. Ferguson* (1896), and *Brown v. the Board of Education of Topeka, Kansas* (1954).

The novel also introduces students to issues concerning interracial as well as intraracial conflicts, such as racism and colorism. Gaines depicts various cultural and ethnic groups, such as Cajuns, Creoles, mulattoes, and Southern whites. He illustrates the strength of the black family and community and the importance of rites and rituals such as 'Termination Sunday and the annual Christmas program. Many of the historical and cultural issues he addresses—the plantation system, religion and the role of the church in the black community, the lack of communication between blacks and whites, the role of sharecroppers in the South, and the men meeting at the local bar while the women congregate in their kitchens—are based on a combination of experience and research.

The novel explores universal concepts.

Truth, freedom, and justice lie at the heart of the novel. For example, at Jefferson's trial, we hear three different versions of the attempted robbery at Alcee Grope's store, each claiming to be "the truth." We also realize that, despite the biblical adage that "The truth shall make you free" (John 8:32), telling the truth is not enough to free Jefferson. The concept becomes even more complex when we listen to the conversation between Grant and Reverend Ambrose, in which the Reverend admits that at times he feels compelled to lie to his parishioners. Gaines also examines the concepts of freedom and justice. Even though Grant is physically free, he is imprisoned by a racist system that devalues his humanity and dismisses his accomplishments. Until his mind is set free through his friendship with Jefferson, Grant perpetuates the system that keeps his people mentally enslaved by accepting the negative stereotypes created by racist whites.

Impact of the Material on Readers

A Lesson Before Dying introduces various concepts unique to African American culture, such as the role of music and the black church, which provided a source of spiritual and psychological sustenance for black people during the era of slavery. It also offers hope for change by exploding the racial myth of white supremacy and smashing racial stereotypes such as the deferential "Uncle Tom" and "Aunt Jemima," the fanatical black preacher, the racist white sheriff, and the violent black youth. The novel provides an alternative view of life in the pre–civil rights South and offers an ideal segue into teaching about the civil rights movement of the 1950s and 1960s and exploring the legacy of slavery that continues to plague black Americans. Through its powerful nature imagery, epitomized by the sugar cane fields and reinforced by the cyclical ritual of "the grinding season"—a motif that forms the backdrop for key events in the novel—the novel also establishes the relationship of black Americans to the land that shaped them.

Potential Problems with *A Lesson Before Dying* and Ways to Address Them

The novel deals with powerful issues such as murder, racism, and capital punishment. Experienced teachers will concur that we cannot shelter students from the harsh realities of life, and that good literature is not always uplifting and positive. However, reading and discussing this novel in a classroom with teacher guidance enables students to explore these issues in a safe, protected environment. Mature students can handle the complexity of these issues.

The novel criticizes many of our social, political, and religious institutions. This criticism provides teachers an opportunity to discuss free speech and First Amendment rights. To generate discussion, they might ask students to respond to James Baldwin's bold assertion: "I love America more than any other country in the world, and, exactly for this reason, I insist on the right to criticize her perpetually" (9).

The novel poses a series of moral and ethical questions and presents a number of philosophical concepts such as fatalism, determinism, and existentialism that some may deem too sophisticated for high school students. Here again, sensitive teachers can seize the opportunity to further explore these issues. Students who are juniors and seniors in high school are interested in such questions as they struggle to determine their own philosophies. When the book is taught to a whole class, students will be able to discuss the diverse perspectives that make up human thought and determine human action.

The language of the novel may offend some readers. Characters sometimes curse and use racial epithets, and there is one sexually explicit love scene. Teachers can help students explore the occurrence of such language to discover when it is used to impart a sense of realism or to portray the devastating impact of racist language. The language used is integral to the love scene, which depicts an intimate encounter between two mature, committed adults. It is not exploited for its sensational or voyeuristic value.

References

Ernest James Gaines was born January 15, 1933, on River Lake Plantation in Oscar, a hamlet in Pointe Coupée Parish, near New Roads, Louisiana.

The oldest of twelve children, he was raised by his great-aunt, Augusteen Jefferson, who provided the inspiration for Miss Jane Pittman in *The Autobiography of Miss Jane Pittman.* His birthplace serves as the model for his fictional world of Bayonne and St. Raphael Parish.

Gaines' works include six novels: *Catherine Carmier, Of Love and Dust, The Autobiography of Miss Jane Pittman, In My Father's House, A Gathering of Old Men,* and *A Lesson Before Dying.* He has also written a children's book, *A Long Day in November,* and a collection of short stories, *Bloodline.*

Gaines is a graduate of San Francisco State College (now University) and pursued graduate studies at Stanford University. He holds several honorary degrees and has received numerous literary awards, including a Guggenheim Fellowship, the Louisiana Library Association Award, the Black Academy of Arts and Letters Award, and the prestigious MacArthur Fellowship. Recently, he was elected as a member of the National Academy of Arts and Letters and a Chevalier in the Order of Arts and Letters, France's highest literary honor.

Critical acclaim for *A Lesson Before Dying* reveals the value of this novel. Charles Larson wrote in the *Chicago Tribune,* "This majestic, moving novel is an instant classic, a book that will be read, discussed, and taught beyond the rest of our lives" (5). Merle Rubin wrote for the *Christian Science Monitor,* "Gaines has a gift for evoking the tenor of life in a bygone era and making it seem as vivid and immediate as something that happened only yesterday" (13). Jonathan Yardley noted that Gaines has much to contribute toward a more knowledgeable society: ". . . he has the breadth and depth of mind to understand that generalizations are always suspect, that one must look at individual humans instead of stereotypes if there is to be any hope of understanding them" (3).

Other reviewers praise Gaines' talents as a writer. Alice Walker noted his ability with characterization: "It is a credit to a writer like Ernest J. Gaines, a black writer who writes mainly about the people he grew up with in rural Louisiana, that he can write about whites and blacks exactly as he sees them and *knows* them, instead of writing of one group as a vast malignant lump and of the other as a conglomerate of perfect virtues" (19, emph. in original).

Early in Gaines' career, Jerry H. Bryant wrote:

> I can think of no other contemporary American novelist whose work has produced in me anything like the sense of depth, the sense of humanity and compassion, and the sense of honesty that I find in Gaines's fiction. It contains the austere dignity and simplicity of ancient epic, a concern

with man's most powerful emotions and actions that arise from those emotions, and an artistic intuition that carefully keeps such passions and behavior under fictive control. Gaines may be one of our most naturally gifted storytellers." (106)

Alternative Works

Books that explore racism are often challenged. It would be difficult to find a true alternative to *A Lesson Before Dying* that might not, itself, be targeted for removal.

Related Works

Many fine books could be paired with this novel to enhance the most important topics.

Books that explore death and dying, the prison experience, transformation, and spiritual redemption

Camus, Albert. *The Stranger.* New York: Vintage, 1989 [1942]. Camus' story of Meursault, an estranged, apathetic young man who commits a murder, explores the spiritual and personal alienation of human beings in the twentieth century. The book chronicles Meursault's transformation from meaninglessness and emotional detachment to a sense of passion and purpose as he awaits his trial.

Kafka, Franz. *The Metamorphosis.* New York: Bantam, 1981 [1915]. Kafka's bizarre tale of Gregor Samsa, who awakens one morning to find himself transformed into a giant insect, explores the integral links between self-concept, human dignity, and personal relationships.

Malcolm X. With Alex Hailey. *The Autobiography of Malcolm X.* New York: Ballantine, 1992 [1964]. This autobiography traces the transformation of Malcolm X (El-Hajj Malik El-Shabazz) from hustler and con man "Detroit Red" to one of the most powerful and articulate speakers for human and civil rights.

Morrison, Toni. *Song of Solomon.* New York: Penguin, 1987 [1977]. Morrison tells the story of Macon (Milkman) Dead, a disillusioned, apathetic young man who, with the help of his eccentric Aunt Pilate and best friend Guitar Baines, embarks on a physical and spiritual quest for his identity and heritage that radically transforms his life.

Books by black writers about the South

Angelou, Maya. *I Know Why the Caged Bird Sings.* New York: Bantam Books, 1980 [1969]. The first volume of her autobiography chronicles her traumatic experiences growing up black and female in the South during the 1930s and 1940s.

Hurston, Zora Neale. *Their Eyes Were Watching God.* New York: Harper, 1990 [1937]. Set in southern Florida during the early 1900s, Hurston's coming-of-age novel tells the story of Janie Crawford, a young black woman who, through the course of her marriages, evolves into a strong, independent woman whose identity is no longer defined by her relationships with men.

Walker, Alice. *The Color Purple.* New York: Washington Square, 1982. Walker's epistolary novel chronicles the life of Celie, a southern black woman who has been physically and emotionally abused by her stepfather and her husband. As she learns to cope with her past and free herself from her abusive environment, Celie achieves strength, dignity, and personal identity through spirituality and friendships with other women.

Books that explore racism in America

Houston, Jeanne Wakatsuki, and James D. *Farewell to Manzanar.* New York: Bantam, 1974 [1973]. Set in the 1940s, during and after World War II, this book tells the true story of Jeanne Wakatsuki and her family who spent three and a half years at Manzanar internment camp in Owens Valley, California. Like *The Diary of Anne Frank, Farewell to Manzanar* is especially powerful because it explores the devastating impact of racism and discrimination from the perspective of a young girl.

Marshall, Paule. *Brown Girl, Brownstones.* New York: The Feminist Press, 1981 [1959]. Set in Brooklyn during the 1930s and 1940s, this novel tells the story of Selina Boyce, the daughter of Barbadian immigrants, who strives to define her identity and values as she struggles to cope with the racism and poverty that surround her.

Works Cited

Baldwin, James. *Notes of a Native Son.* Boston: Beacon, 1983 [1955].

Bryant, Jerry H. "'From Death to Life': The Fiction of Ernest J. Gaines." *The Iowa Review* 3.1 (Winter 1972): 106-20.

Larson, Charles. "End as a Man." *Chicago Tribune* 9 May 1993: 5.

Robinson, Eugene. "Toni Morrison's Measured Words in Her Nobel Lecture, A Meditation on the Power of Language." *The Washington Post* 8 Dec. 1993, final ed., Style sec.: C1.

Rubin, Merle. "Convincing Moral Tale of Southern Injustice." *Christian Science Monitor* 13 April 1993: 13.

Walker, Alice. "The Black Writer and the Southern Experience." *In Search of Our Mothers' Gardens: Womanist Prose.* San Diego: Harcourt, 1983: 15–21.

Yardley, Jonathan. "Nothing But a Man." *Book World Washington Post* 28 March 1993, final ed.: x3.

About Durthy A. Washington

Durthy A. Washington is a writer, a teacher, and an independent scholar focusing on American ethnic literature. An advocate of multicultural education, she is the founder and owner of Springs Seminarz, a Colorado Springs–based company offering culturally responsive seminars for the mind and spirit. Durthy holds masters degrees in English and Education from San Jose State University and the University of Southern California, Los Angeles, respectively. She is the author of more than one hundred articles, essays, and book reviews, and recently accepted a teaching position at the U.S. Air Force Academy.

Lynne Alvine

ANNIE ON MY MIND

by Nancy Garden

> It was like a war inside of me; I couldn't even recognize all of the sides. There was one that said, "No, this is wrong; you know it's wrong and bad and sinful," and there was another that said, "Nothing has ever felt so right and natural and true and good," and another that said it was happening too fast, and another that just wanted to stop thinking altogether and fling my arms around Annie and hold her forever. There were other sides, too, but I couldn't sort them out. (93)

Garden, Nancy. *Annie on My Mind.* New York: Farrar, Straus, and Giroux, 1982.

Intended Audience

Students in grades 10–12 might read this novel in small groups or individually in a thematic unit on difference and tolerance or as part of a study of changes in contemporary American culture. With a very mature group, the novel might be read as a whole-class selection. Since the book focuses on sexual identity, students reading the novel in school are likely to need the support and guidance of an informed teacher. Although there is sexual content, it is handled sensitively and, for the most part, implicitly. In addition to whatever group readings may be set for this novel, it is important that it and other texts about sexual identity also be available to students for individual selection.

Summary

Annie on My Mind is the story of two girls who fall hopelessly, helplessly in love with each other and of the homophobia deeply rooted in the social structures within which they live. The novel opens with Liza's attempt to renew contact with Annie after many months of silence. A "here-and-now" frame surrounds Liza's retrospective on their meeting, on the wonder of their mutual awakening to each other, and on the events that led to their separation. As their feelings intensify, they acknowledge the depth of their love and begin to contemplate acting on the physical attraction they feel for one another. During her private school's spring break, Liza volunteers to cat-sit for one of her teachers who, she later learns, shares her life with another female teacher. Liza and Annie have a wonder-filled week, spending whole days alone together at the teachers' house, until a well-intentioned classmate arouses the suspicion of a meddling neighbor. Liza and the two lesbian teachers soon find themselves sitting in the "court" of a self-righteous headmistress. Liza denies her true feelings; the teachers are fired; and Annie leaves for summer camp and, subsequently, a college three thousand miles away. Torn by the pain of their public exposure, Liza is unable to respond to Annie's letters. Through retelling their story, Liza realizes that her love for Annie cannot be denied. In the end, Liza phones Annie, who is in California, and the two make joyful plans to spend Christmas together.

Relationship of *Annie on My Mind* to the Program

In the past decade, instructional leaders have complemented the reading of classics in schools with various young adult titles—with books many teenagers find more relevant to their lives than those stories set very long ago and far away. In doing so, educators have embraced the writings of many cultures and established a more diverse perspective on life and literature in our nation's secondary English classrooms. By reflecting a society that is increasingly multicultural, the opening of the canon has allowed more children to see themselves in the characters they read about in school. Unfortunately, however, most gay and lesbian high school students still find nothing that matches their reality reflected in the literary mirrors English teachers hold up to them.

Nothing in their society says to young people that it is OK to be gay. Nothing in the books they read offers images of happy, healthy gay teens or adults as role models. Left feeling unwanted and invisible, gay and lesbian teens are killing themselves in disproportionate numbers. According to a report released by the Department of Health and Human Services in 1989, gay and lesbian young people are two to three times more likely to commit suicide than their heterosexual counterparts (Remafedi). Books such as

Annie on My Mind can offer gay and lesbian teens legitimacy for the powerful feelings that other aspects of their culture would have them deny.

In addition to containing a sensitive, loving portrayal of an adolescent lesbian couple, *Annie on My Mind* is quite well-written. Beginning with Liza's attempt to renew contact with Annie, her retelling of the events of their relationship pushes toward the tearful telephone reunion at the end. Though the framed novel is not unfamiliar in young adult literature, it is handled particularly well in *Annie on My Mind.* Thus, the novel could help students extend their understanding of nonlinear plot structure.

Garden's development of the characters of Liza and Annie is superb. With her rich imagination and playfulness, Annie is quite ingenuous and infectious. The reader falls in love with her too. The pain and bewilderment Liza experiences at the hand of her cruel headmistress also has the power to sting the empathetic reader. Even minor characters such as Annie's grandmother, Nan, come to life through Garden's skillful handling of description and dialogue. Though the two teachers are carefully closeted, earlier-generation lesbians, some aspects of their characters are quite interesting and atypical.

If teachers intend to bring into their English classrooms literature that represents diverse perspectives, they should not overlook including books that focus on sexual identity. Because *Annie on My Mind* portrays lesbian love in such a positive light, and because it is a high-quality work of literature, it deserves careful consideration as a classroom selection for older high school students.

Impact of the Material on Readers

Young readers who are experiencing homoerotic feelings can find comfort in the story of these two girls who discover that their feelings may signify more than just friendship. Such a literary mirror may help gay and lesbian teens to regain some of their lost self-esteem and become less invisible to themselves.

Many homosexual youths fear they will be rejected if they do not hide who they really are—and with good reason. According to the Department of Health and Human Services, one in four teens who disclose their gay or lesbian identity to their families are thrown out of their homes.

For gay and lesbian teens who fear that their coming out will mean rejection by those whom they most love, this novel offers a bit of hope. Though her mother and father struggle with their fears that Liza's relationship with

Annie may mean their daughter is lesbian, and though initially her mother sets Liza up to deny that Annie is her lover, both parents eventually offer her the love and support she needs to sort out her true feelings. Liza's brother also rises above his own homophobia and defends his sister against the hateful taunts and behaviors of his more narrow-minded classmates. In many ways, the novel offers a positive message about family reactions to a lesbian teen.

Heterosexual readers come away from this novel with new understandings of how love can also be part of the experience of those whom they have been taught are so different, so unnatural. Before the undergraduate and graduate students in my adolescent literature classes at the university read *Annie on My Mind*, I do not tell them about its characters or story line. When we discuss the novel, students often report that they had to remind themselves as they read that the two main characters are both girls. Many indicate their surprise at the intensity of feelings between Liza and Annie and note that their love seems to be natural—just like a boy-girl romance. When they register surprise that this is a "love story," I ask students if they can articulate why they are surprised. I ask those who register an adverse reaction to the lesbian couple if they can identify the origin of that negative response. The result is usually a very open discussion of how homophobia is sustained in our culture. Because Garden has captured so effectively what it is to be young and so totally lost in another person, the heterosexual reader comes to see the lesbian relationship as completely natural. Readers, then, can come away with new perceptions of what it may mean to be gay—beyond the homophobic stereotypes they have had deeply imprinted in their subconscious.

In addition to its numerous positive images, this novel also presents many of the difficulties of being gay. When they are "caught" alone together, Liza and Annie undergo public exposure and humiliation. In order to protect her mother from knowing she lied to her, Liza denies her true self and her love for Annie. The two lesbian teachers are fired when their lifestyle is revealed. Even so, the novel offers some evidence of a "just world." The person who is the most unyielding in her self-righteous, homophobic intolerance is punished. Near the end, we learn that Mrs. Poindexter, the sanctimonious headmistress who conducted Liza's "trial" and who had the lesbian teachers fired, has been released from her job by the school's Board of Trustees for "frequent demonstrations of poor judgment and overreaction to trivial incidents" (219). Readers who have been intolerant of non-heterosexual lifestyles in the past may find themselves empathizing with the girls and cheering when Mrs. Poindexter's villainy catches up with her.

Potential Problems with *Annie on My Mind* and Ways to Address Them

It is estimated that one in ten individuals is gay; thus, it is likely that each classroom will have one or more young people who are dealing with an emerging awareness of their own homosexuality. It is imperative, then, that any teacher planning to work with *Annie on My Mind* in the classroom broach the subject of sexual orientation with a great deal of sensitivity. Preliminary discussions of tolerance for difference and clear messages that homophobic jokes, snickering, and gestures will not be tolerated are important to set the classroom climate for the reading of this novel. Some teachers may want to discuss ways of responding sensitively with the students before the class or the small groups tackle this book.

The best way to head off parental complaints about selection of reading materials in the classroom is to approach them openly and positively. Teachers who are working with texts that explore differences are advised to keep parents fully informed by sending home in advance a rationale for discussing such topics in the English classroom. Parents of students who are to read *Annie on My Mind* as part of their course work should be asked to give permission for their child to read the novel.

Teachers who are themselves gay or lesbian may be unable to overcome their own homophobia sufficiently to bring literature with gay and lesbian characters and homosexual themes into the curriculum. In many contexts they may still have good reason to fear punishment or even loss of employment for doing so. Thus, it is imperative that heterosexual teachers come forward as allies to gay and lesbian teens and teachers if curricular reform in this area is to go forward.

References

In addition to *Annie on My Mind*, which has been both "widely acclaimed and widely condemned" (Estes 34), Nancy Garden has written four other young adult novels, including *The Lovers*; *Peace, O River*; *Lark in the Morning*; and *Good Moon Rising*; and one nonfiction young adult title, *Berlin: City Split in Two*. Throughout her twenty-five-year career, she has also written many books for middle graders and young readers as well as a children's mystery series.

Mary K. Chelton, a reviewer for *Voice of Youth Advocates,* celebrated the arrival of *Annie on My Mind,* saying ". . . the body of adolescent literature has waited for this book a long time, and it is superior to all its predecessors." She also noted, "The writing is clear, consistent, at times lyrical, but best of all gut-level believable" (30).

Even though *Annie on My Mind* has enjoyed critical acclaim, it has also drawn the venom of anti-gay censors. In Kansas City, the book was banned by the city school board. Although the board's decision was eventually ruled unconstitutional, and they were ordered to put it back on the shelves, the novel was publicly burned in that city.

Though only a small percentage of her work addresses gay themes, Garden returns to the genre of young adult lesbian novel in her latest work, *Good Moon Rising.* In it, two female high school dramatists discover their love for each other while working on a production of *The Crucible.* In using Arthur Miller's play about the Salem witch hunts, Garden offers an ironic nod toward the social pressures and censorship she experienced with her first lesbian novel, *Annie on My Mind.*

Alternative Works

No other novel will achieve the objectives of teaching *Annie On My Mind* without it, in turn, being challenged.

Related Works

Numerous related books could supplement a study of this novel.

Sexual identity—fiction

Bauer, Marion Dane, editor. *Am I Blue? Coming Out from the Silence.* New York: HarperCollins, 1994. The sixteen stories in this collection focus on characters dealing with the pain and loneliness of growing up gay or lesbian and their family members' and friends' struggles to understand. Written by Jane Yolen, Bruce Coville, William Sleator, M. E. Kerr, and other well-known young adult authors, these stories include a grandmother who understands better than the parents and seniors who use a class video project to "come out."

Durant, Penny Raife. *When Heroes Die.* New York: Macmillan, 1992. Gary's Uncle Rob is his surrogate father and best friend. When Rob, who is gay, becomes very sick with AIDS, Gary worries that he himself may be gay because he has trouble relating to girls. Uncle Rob reassures Gary and helps him find answers to his questions.

Kerr, M. E. *Deliver Us from Evie.* New York: HarperCollins, 1994. Evie Burrman, who loves farm work and disdains the dresses her mother wishes she would wear, falls in love with the very feminine Patsy, a banker's daughter. In his confusion, Evie's brother Parr takes an action that results in the lesbian couple's being "outed" in the community, and both families must come to terms with their feelings about the girls' sexuality and with their running away to New York.

Salat, Christina. *Living in Secret.* New York: Bantam/Skylark, 1993. Despite her pleas to live with her lesbian mother, Amelia has been forced to live with her father since her parents' divorce. Then, Amelia, her mother, and her mother's partner move to San Francisco, where they assume new identities and must deal with many new challenges.

Scoppettone, Sandra. *Happy Endings Are All Alike.* Boston: Alyson, 1991. Janet's mother knows about Peggy and Janet's lesbian relationship and accepts them. Peggy's sister, however, does not. A brutal attack against Janet forces the two girls, their families, and their community to deal with their relationship and different perspectives on sexuality.

Sexual identity—nonfiction

Cohen, Susan, and Daniel Cohen. *When Someone You Know Is Gay.* New York: M. Evans, 1989. Teenage homosexuality is discussed in a straightforward manner and with sensitivity. The authors offer historical and scientific information, including information about AIDS. Interviews with gay and lesbian teens are included.

Kuklin, Susan. *Teenagers Take on Race, Sex, and Identity.* New York: Putnam, 1993. Kuklin asked students to talk among themselves about prejudice, race, sexuality, and being different. The discussions resulted in increased awareness and indications that the youths had made gains in self-esteem and respect for others.

Rench, Janice E. *Understanding Sexual Identity: A Book for Gay Teens and Their Friends.* Minneapolis: Lerner, 1990. The author pushes against violence, ignorance, and hatred. Her goal is to dispel myths and help all readers become more comfortable with homosexuality, regardless of their sexual orientation. Chapter titles include "Facts about Homosexuality," "Friends," "Families," "Religion," "Coming Out," and "Healthy Sexuality."

Sexual identity—resources for teachers

Harbeck, K. M. *Coming Out of the Classroom Closet: Gay and Lesbian Students and Curricula.* New York: Harrington, 1992.

National Education Association. *NEA Human and Civil Rights Action Sheet: Teaching and Counseling Gay and Lesbian Students.* Washington, DC: NEA, 1993.

Stover, D. "The At-Risk Students Schools Continue to Ignore." *Education Digest* 57.9 (1992): 36–40.

Zera, D. "Coming of Age in a Heterosexist World: The Development of Gay and Lesbian Adolescents." *Adolescence* 27.108 (1992): 849–854.

Works Cited

Chelton. M. K. Rev. of *Annie on My Mind,* by Nancy Garden. *Voice of Youth Advocates* 5.3 (1982): 30.

Department of Health and Human Services. *Sixty Minutes.* CBS. WCBS, New York. 1 Mar. 1998.

Estes, Sally. Rev. of *Good Moon Rising,* by Nancy Garden. *Booklist* 1 Oct. 1996: 340.

Remafedi, G. *Death by Denial.* Boston: Alyson, 1994.

About Lynne Alvine

Lynne Alvine taught middle school and high school English for seventeen years in Iowa and Virginia before becoming an English teacher educator. She is currently Professor of English at Indiana University of Pennsylvania, where she directs the Southcentral Pennsylvania Writing Project and coordinates the Master of Arts in Teaching English degree program. In her graduate and undergraduate courses she encourages preservice and inservice teachers to find ways to create a positive climate for gay and lesbian students in their classrooms.

OUT OF THE DUST

by Karen Hesse

Rules of Dining

Ma has rules for setting the table.
I place plates upside down,
glasses bottom side up,
napkins folded over forks, knives, and spoons.

When dinner is ready,
we sit down together
and Ma says,
"Now."

We shake out our napkins,
spread them on our laps,
and flip over our glasses and plates,
exposing neat circles,
round comments
on what life would be without dust.

Daddy says,
"The potatoes are peppered plenty tonight, Polly,"
and
"Chocolate milk for dinner, aren't we in clover!"
when really all our pepper and chocolate,
it's nothing but dust. (21)

Hesse, Karen. *Out of the Dust: A Novel.*
New York: Scholastic Press, 1997.

Intended Audience

This book appeals to readers ranging from thirteen to eighty. Although the Newbery Medal is reserved for books for children, this 1998 winner will work best for readers at the upper end of childhood—and beyond. Because this novel presents grim life and death issues, younger readers may find it difficult or unpleasant, suggesting the book is a better choice for more mature adolescents. Those interested in historical fiction and readers with rural connections—particularly in western Oklahoma, Texas, and Kansas—will be especially attracted to this work. Because this novel is a connected series of narrative poems in diary form, some readers may find the genre more challenging than traditional prose narratives even though the free-verse poetry is easily accessible. Parents and teachers will probably appreciate reading this novel as they decide on its appropriateness for their young readers.

Summary

Billie Jo, the fourteen-year-old daughter of an Oklahoma Dust Bowl farmer, narrates the individually dated, journal-like poems that comprise this novel. From January 1934 through December 1935, the two years near the close of the long drought, the high points of her meager existence are her love of family and piano playing. These positives are followed closely by the more numerous low points in the unrelenting dust, her perceptions of guilt about the accidental fire leading to the deaths of her mother and infant brother, her own burned and disabled hands, her father's skin cancer, and his distance from Billie Jo after his wife's death.

The tragic fire changes Billie Jo's life dramatically. She suffers with her own severely burned hands while ineffectively nursing her mother, who barely clings to life long enough to give birth to an ill-fated boy. Fire and dust result in physical and emotional pain for Billie Jo and her devastated father in their struggle to forgive and understand each other in the midst of desperate times. Her painful hands render piano playing impossible; her father continues to battle the dust and the grief; and her own feelings of loss overwhelm her. Overcome by despair, Billie Jo escapes to the West in a brief attempt to change her life, only to realize that she misses home—however problem ridden. When she returns, her father welcomes her back, and they begin to rebuild their lives. Louise, the night school instructor who cautiously enters their lives, brings hope with her. The end of the novel suggests that these gritty souls will survive.

Relationship of *Out of the Dust* to the Program

This historical, poetic novel offers many opportunities to learn. If we agree that literature functions as a record of human existence, this novel is an excellent choice to help young readers recognize that concept. Reading it will provide students the opportunity to empathize with the real hardships of the Great Depression as experienced by the fictional adolescent narrator. This novel will dramatize for readers the events of this dark period as few other texts will, presenting a long-awaited companion piece to Steinbeck's *Grapes of Wrath*.

Short, sparse poems recount how to set the table in a dust storm to minimize the ingestion of dirt, what must be done with starving cattle, the devastation of dust pneumonia, and the tentative hope that springs from a brief sprinkling rain. The reader peers through omnipresent dust to the novel's events, rooted in the history of the Depression. The poetic vignettes capture historically accurate episodes such as neighbors' migration west in defeat, rabbit slaughter to save vegetation, and grasshopper infestation.

Out of the Dust is an unexpected coming-of-age story set in an unusual time and place. This is indeed a love story but not a typical one. This is about love of family, home, and self, with only a nod to emerging interest in boys (and that dominated by the boy's musical connection). Other themes worth exploring include forgiving, grieving, struggling against seemingly insurmountable odds, dealing with guilt, and surviving in the face of daunting prospects. More positive themes are those of indomitable spirit, strength, and courage. This novel will work easily into thematic units focused on any of these issues.

The interdisciplinary possibilities are obvious ones as students study American history, economics, ecology, and biology. Interviews with Depression survivors can be a part of social studies and English course work, offering opportunities to research, write, and speak with purpose. Conservation study can emphasize the connections between the farmers' early techniques and current attitudes about natural resources.

Because this novel is comprised of journal entries, reading it can help students understand that form as an unusual one for developing narrative. Students may explore their own abilities as diarists by modeling journal entries on the ones in this book.

The unconventional format of the novel offers opportunities to teach about narrative poetry and free verse, as well as about language choices matched to the austerity of the subject. The study can spur discussions about Hesse's choice of poetry to tell this story.

Helping students understand how symbols and metaphor work is often an important part of literature study, and this novel offers an accessible opportunity to explore the symbolism of grit. In the real and symbolic senses of the word, Billie Jo has both kinds. The literal dirt buries everything in sight; the figurative grit this young woman exhibits enables her to cope with real tragedies as well as troublesome adolescent anger at her father. Despite the two years of unrelenting hard times, this novel is about learning to forgive—others and oneself—and about healing and hope. Billie Jo's hands heal, as does her heart, her relationship with her father, her life, and the land. The most significant aspect of this novel is the message of survival, love, and hope. Grit permeates this novel just as the dust seeps in around their lives.

Impact of the Material on Readers

In spite of their distance in time and precise conditions, middle and high school students will identify with the internal struggles of the protagonist, especially her efforts to understand and be understood by a parent. Wrestling with wishing things were different and wanting to run away to a dream of a better life are common issues for today's young readers, as is the need to deal with guilt and grief. Getting past the grim specifics of Billie Jo's life to the hopefulness will be a lesson in itself. Students will no doubt marvel at her courage and tenacity in the face of devastating circumstances.

Readers from rural settings will identify more thoroughly with the agrarian aspects of the novel, but even those from urban environments will recognize the messages of suffering and loss and the determination of the human spirit. Whether they read this on their own or study it with a group, students will gain insights into this era of American history.

Many young readers may be surprised that they are drawn to the poetry; others will forget entirely that it is poetry as the story progresses. The simple, descriptive language and its images will stay with readers.

Potential Problems with *Out of the Dust* and Ways to Address Them

Detractors find this novel too harsh for young readers. However, if students are to understand the real issues of this historical era, those readers must deal with the rough truth. Although the unrelenting difficulties of the Dust Bowl cannot be softened, they deserve exploration just as other unpleasantness does. Young readers can handle harsh realities and often find that the vicarious experiences in literature allow them to reach new understandings about human nature. Teachers and parents can guide students to this book when readers are ready to wrestle with the difficulties of death, guilt, and growth, knowing that *Out of the Dust* tempers those harsh elements with hope, forgiveness, and love.

Language and disturbing situations may give rise to objections. Some people will be likely to object to the first poem as inappropriate for young readers. The book's first few lines recount the story of Billie Jo's birth, a story she has heard often enough to tell of its harshness herself. As she introduces herself, Billie Jo says that her mother "crouched, / barefoot, bare bottomed / over the swept boards" of the kitchen for the delivery. While strongly dramatic, these few words capture the scene without further detail and help set the atmosphere as one of little comfort. The language is clear but not objectionable. Again, to soften the language is to reduce the reality of the content.

Similarly, when Billie Jo notices her mother, too long parched, standing nude in the long-awaited drizzle to catch as much moisture as possible, the poem alerts the reader to the false promise of this paltry sprinkle. Censors may worry about a teenager watching her nude, pregnant mother, but the episode is not lewd or titillating. There is no explicit description of body to mar the moment and its message. The clear picture of this woman who "aches for rain" adds to the historical accuracy of the long, devastating drought by personalizing the dryness. Discussion of this scene, if it arises at all, can center on the desperate need for moisture.

"The Accident" and its companion, "A Tent of Pain," draw details in specific language to depict the horror of the mother's accident, both her and Billie Jo's pain, and the groaning, faceless figure that her mother becomes. Some objectors will cite this episode, and perhaps the description of the doctor tending Billie Jo's wounds, as too graphic for young readers. Because this is the personal disaster in the novel, its strong presentation is essential. Surrounded by the general grimness of the austere Dust Bowl life, this monumental event cannot be couched in kinder terms or downplayed into less emphasis. The lives of Billie Jo and her father are forever altered by this event and by the accompanying guilt each carries; strong images in strong language are appropriate here. Discussions of sparse word choices to convey tone as well as message will help readers see the importance of the language Hesse has chosen.

This book is for readers who are ready for a tougher kind of historic fiction than most books for this age group offer. *Out of the Dust* asks readers to tackle painful subjects and emotions but does not require that they enter the mean streets of gangs, sex, violence, drugs, and foul language to do so. Neither does it gloss over the realities of this dark period's demands on those who lived and died in the Dust Bowl.

References

Karen Hesse has authored ten books for children of various ages. Until *Out of the Dust* won the Newbery Medal in 1998, her most notable title was *The Music of Dolphins*, named a Best Book of 1996 by *Publishers Weekly* and *School Library Journal*. Her other titles include *A Time of Angels*, *Phoenix Rising*, *Letters from Rifka*, and *Wish on a Unicorn*. For younger readers she has written *Lavender*, *Sable*, *Poppy's Chair*, and *Lester's Dog*. She makes her home in Williamsville, Vermont, with her husband and two daughters.

Though some reviewers suggest that *Out of the Dust* is inappropriate for the young readers who normally trust Newbery Medal titles to appeal to them, most reviewers have been very positive.

In *The Horn Book Magazine,* Peter Sieruta remarked on the format and language: "Filled with memorable images . . . the sparse verses showcase the poetry of everyday language; the pauses between line breaks speak eloquently, if sometimes melodramatically. . . . Yet her voice, nearly every word informed by longing, provides an immediacy that expressively depicts both a grim historical era and one family's healing" (74).

Indicating that the book is appropriate for ages eleven to thirteen, the review in *Publishers Weekly* notes, "This intimate novel, written in stanza form, poetically conveys the heat, dust and wind of Oklahoma along with the discontent of a narrator Billy [sic] Jo, a talented pianist growing up during the Depression" (72).

Kirkus Reviews recognizes that "In Billie Jo, the only character who comes to life, Hesse presents a hale and determined heroine who confronts unrelenting misery and begins to transcend it. The poem/novel ends with only a trace of hope; there are no pat endings, but a glimpse of beauty wrought from brutal reality."

I have given this book to teenagers and to older adults with Depression and Dust Bowl experiences. While the young readers appreciated the story, the adult readers wept from their memories of dust storms and ruined dreams.

Alternative Work

This unique work should be read and studied. To offer alternatives seems to defeat the purposes reading this book would fulfill. However, if an alternative is absolutely necessary, a possible basis for selection lies in format or genre rather than in content. Karen Cushman's historical novel *Catherine,*

Called Birdy (New York: Clarion, 1994) is written in diary format and has a female protagonist, qualifying as an alternate on those aspects.

Related Works

Companion pieces, not alternative ones, can enrich the learning, and two books that might work well with *Out of the Dust* are John Steinbeck's *Grapes of Wrath* (New York: Viking, 1939) and Irene Hunt's *No Promises in the Wind* (New York: Berkley, 1970), serving a range of reading abilities. Jerry Stanley's informational *Children of the Dust Bowl: The True Story of the School at Weedpatch Camp* (New York: Crown, 1992) depicts the poverty of the Dust Bowl, drawing from sources including interviews and photographs. Because it, too, is a poetry collection and deals with a historically grim era, *I Never Saw Another Butterfly: Children's Drawings and Poems from Terez Concentration Camp, 1942–44*, edited by Hana Volavková (expanded 2nd ed., New York: Schocken, 1993), would be an interesting companion for *Out of the Dust.*

Works Cited

Kirkus Reviews 15 Sept. 1997. *Amazon.com.* Online. 30 June 1998.

Rev. of *Out of the Dust,* by Karen Hesse. *Publishers Weekly* 25 August 1997: 72.

Sieruta, Peter D. Rev. of *Out of the Dust,* by Karen Hesse. *The Horn Book Magazine* 74 (1998): 73–74.

About Jackie E. Swensson

Jackie E. Swensson is an associate professor who teaches English and English Education courses at Metropolitan State College of Denver, where she also directs the MSCD Writing Center. Before the move to higher education, she taught middle and high school English for twenty years. As a high school English teacher, department chair, and administrator, she was involved in challenges to both books and films in classroom settings.

JACK

by A. M. Homes

> My father was banned from the grounds. That's what my mother's lawyer called the lawn in the front and back of the house, "the grounds." It was illegal for him even to step on the grass without calling and getting permission from my mother. At first, he called every night. My mother would yell and scream at him for a half hour and then hang up before I even got a chance to say hello. Eventually, she laid down the law. No explanations offered. She said I wasn't going to see my father for a while and that he would only be allowed to call the house once a week. Even though I probably should have hated her for cutting him out, I was relieved. At least with my dad not sneaking in to water plants and my mother not crying all night every night, I could pretend things were normal. (11–12)

Homes, A. M. *Jack*. New York: Vintage Contemporaries, 1989.

Intended Audience

Students in grades 7–12. This book should be used by a teacher who is comfortable leading discussions on provocative issues. The book does contain strong language at times but in a realistic and nongratuitous fashion. *Jack* could be taught in a contemporary American fiction class; a psychology or sociology class; any humanities class emphasizing coming of age, family, gender, and sexuality; or as part of a unit on understanding difference and diversity.

Summary

Like many middle-class American twelve-year-olds, Jack is faced with figuring out how to deal with his parents' messy divorce. By the time he turns fifteen, things have settled down into a routine. He lives with his mother and her retro-1960s boyfriend and is regularly taken out by his father for dinner and a movie. Jack is an average basketball player, has a best friend, Max, and wonders if he will ever be popular enough to find a real girlfriend. But Jack's typical life is turned upside down when his father rows him out into the middle of a lake and explains that he is gay. Most of the book follows Jack through a series of complicated emotional stages and significant interactions with parental figures, friends, teachers, administrators, and a love interest, Maggie, as he denies, questions, and finally understands what it means to accept his father for who he really is.

Relationship of *Jack* to the Program

Jack is an important young adult novel to include in curricula with an emphasis on teaching for diversity and social justice. The increasing visibility of gay people on television, in the movies, and in advertising has created a need for teachers to find texts like *Jack* that help create a framework for conversations about different lifestyles. Teaching *Jack* gives teachers an opportunity to help students understand the ways homophobia maintains strict and narrow definitions of gender roles. Recent studies reveal school-aged adolescent males as being the typical perpetrators of gay hate crimes. *Jack* helps readers develop an understanding of the impact of homophobia on individuals both gay and straight.

Discussing *Jack* over several weeks will invite students from heterogeneous and homogeneous backgrounds to challenge each other's perspectives as each reader rejects or sympathizes with the main character's strategies for dealing with the changes in his life. Because the issues in *Jack* are provocative, students will come to terms with, tolerate, and defend various characters in the novel to differing degrees, depending on their relative comfort and understanding of each issue as it gets presented and developed. Discussing the events in *Jack* will provide students with the opportunity to listen and learn from different opinions that will in turn help them practice sharing and negotiating across conflicting social and moral values.

My own experience reading and discussing *Jack* with a group of adolescents emphasized several issues related to working with young adults and young adult literature. Adolescents are ready to challenge and be challenged by their peers and adults. *Jack*, like many young adult novels, presents youth who are challenged by adult role models. Addressing this challenge requires teachers to question student assumptions, responses, and opinions, while creating opportunities for students to question both the teacher and each other. Because adolescents are moving through a time of continual change, both physically and emotionally, they are in a critical position to process what it means to change. Stories like *Jack* that emphasize change provide a great place to begin some of these conversations.

It is important to give students the opportunity to write their thoughts and feelings regarding the development of Jack's actions as they relate to his perspective on divorce and homosexuality. Personal response journals are an important starting place for defining ideas and questions raised when reading *Jack*. By using a double-entry journal, students can trace how their own perspectives on divorce and sexuality change over time in relation to the comfort level of a major or minor character. In a double-entry journal the student uses the left side of a page to record important events in the novel through self-selected summaries and quotes. On the right side of the page the student responds to summaries and quotes with personal connections, thoughts, and feelings.

The responses my students wrote about Jack and his family helped them identify what they were each most interested in or concerned about. My written responses back to each student created an important layer of communication where I could push students to develop issues they were raising, often in the form of questions. For example, when one student suggested in writing that Jack and his father had a lot to work out, I asked her what she thought could help make this happen. My questions were invitations that often helped students develop reasoning skills around important issues like adult and adolescent relationships.

While reading *Jack*, students can develop written reports on the historical and social changes that have in some ways made it easier for gays and lesbians and their friends and family to be public about who they are and with whom they live and love. Students can define through research and writing the policies, practices, and beliefs that continue to make life difficult for gays and lesbians.

Impact of the Material on Readers

Jack presents himself as a Holden Caulfield–type persona, who continually describes, analyzes, revises, and re-presents his perspective on the people he needs and loves. Much of Jack's coming to terms with his father's sexuality involves a kind of self-examination and reexamination of the qualities and behaviors that provide a person's gender identity. Reading and discussing *Jack* will:

1. encourage students to ask questions about lifestyles different from their own
2. provide many moments to examine and reflect upon the complicated and complex relationship between an adolescent and his or her parent
3. create a window of opportunity for teachers who believe in the importance of challenging the stereotypes most students hold about homosexuals and heterosexuals.

These three outcomes will certainly give teachers the frameworks they need to help students become better and more thoughtful communicators.

Potential Problems with *Jack* and Ways to Address Them

Students may have trouble understanding each other's level of acceptance of provocative issues. It is important to validate each student's opinions regarding divorce, homosexuality, and domestic violence while creating opportunities for students to share, examine, and reexamine the information presented to substantiate an opinion. For example, one student might reject Jack's father's sexual preference based on religious teachings or the opinions of an adult in his or her home. A confident teacher will be able to help students translate student opinions into an explanation of a personal value rather than a direct attack on an individual in or outside the group. Learning information that contradicts stereotypes about people who are divorced, gay, or victims of domestic violence often helps students who silently identify with these categories feel empowered and accepted. Bringing in videotapes of other adolescents discussing homosexuality, and *Jack* in particular (see reference to *It's Elementary* in Related Works), will allow students to become more objective when processing their own group conversations.

Students may have trouble understanding why homosexuals are feared by specific individuals and groups in American society. Materials such as those included in the "Facing History and Ourselves" curriculum (also referenced in the Related Works section of this chapter) will give students a historical overview of the dangers of indifference and the values of civility and will connect other civil rights movements in the United States to the current gay rights movement. It is important for students to explore indifference on a personal, local, and national level through the use of primary and secondary resources. Students need to understand how their opinions and decisions fit into a historical, social, and economic context.

Students who have family problems similar to those presented in the story might find *Jack* difficult to read. It is always recommended that before reading *Jack* students need to be made aware of the issues that will be touched upon and discussed. Teachers should provide students with a private opportunity to opt out of reading and/or discussing issues that they are uncomfortable with. It is also important to suggest that reading and discussing *Jack* may also provide an opportunity to clarify or understand an issue that may be confusing or unfamiliar. It is always a good idea to give students the opportunity to pass when others are sharing written responses and to assure students that what they write is confidential unless the teacher feels a student's safety may be threatened.

Parents may have problems with the use of curses and/or the nature of the conversations Jack has with his parents and friends. Parents may need to be reminded that in order to create realistic and believable dialogue, Homes has refrained from censoring the language of her characters as well as the topics Jack, his family, and his friends are brave enough to acknowledge.

References

A. M. Homes is a graduate of Sarah Lawrence College and the University of Iowa Writers Workshop. In addition to *Jack*, Homes is also the author of several other novels, including *In a Country of Mothers*; the short story collection *The Safety of Objects*; *Appendix A*, an artists' book; and *The End of Alice*. Homes is a contributing editor to *Vanity Fair*, *Bomb*, *Blind Spot*, *Story*, and *Mirabella*. She has been awarded a James Michener Fellowship, a New York Foundation for the Arts Fellowship, and NEA and Guggenheim Fellowships. Homes currently resides in New York City and teaches in the writing programs at Columbia University and The New School for Social Research.

Jack was voted one of the Best Books for Young Adults in 1989 by the Young Adult Library Services Association of the American Library Association and won the *New York Times* Notable Book Award in 1990. *Jack* has been published in eight languages and in 1993 received the highest literary award in Germany, the Deutscher Jugendliteratur Preiz.

Jack has been widely praised for its literary merit. Kathryn Harris in *School Library Journal* wrote, "The adults in the story are . . . fully developed and sympathetically portrayed. The bewilderment, fear, and shame that accompany a revelation of . . . [homosexuality] are well represented, but the gradual acceptance and sensitivity that come with understanding and maturity are also depicted. An excellent, credible novel that strongly describes the maturation of a young man into a person with an identity all his own" (126).

Crescent Dragonwagon wrote in *The New York Times Book Review*, "Ms. Homes handles the big subjects and adolescent passions subtly, deftly and with an appealing lack of melodrama, growing overwrought only when Jack himself naturally would. Even the minor characters have dimension and draw our sympathy, as does Jack himself, who is likable from the first paragraph. If *Jack* is at times imitative, it still has much to recommend it. Without pat answers, A. M. Homes has given us a good youngster who in the end convincingly grows larger than his circumstances—as all of us, good and otherwise, must do on that arduous journey to adulthood" (24).

Jack also garnered praise from Nancy Vasilakis in *The Horn Book Magazine*, who said, "The excellent characterizations of Jack and his friends, and of both his parents, make up for the lack of action in this story whose tone and theme are reminiscent of Ron Koertge's *The Arizona Kid* (Joy Street) . . . [w]hile the first-person narrative occasionally lapses into idiomatic excess, this first novel read, for the most part, naturally and without self-consciousness, and it keeps strictly within the bounds of realism as it discloses yet another new wrinkle in the fabric of family relations" (206).

Alternative Works

No other book would achieve the objectives of teaching *Jack* without its also being challenged.

Related Works

Fiction

Bauer, Marion Dane, ed. *Am I Blue? Coming Out from the Silence.* New York: HarperTrophy, 1995. This is a powerful and engaging collection of sixteen short stories emphasizing gay awareness and positive, credible gay role models, and showcasing the work of authors such as Bruce Coville, Lois Lowry, Jane Yolen, and Nancy Garden.

Garden, Nancy. *Annie on My Mind.* New York: Farrar, 1982. Two high school girls in New York City fall in love and weather the storm of a critical community with the help of their teachers, who are two caring role models.

Kerr, M. E. *Deliver Us from Evie.* New York: HarperCollins Children's Books, 1994. The story of eighteen-year-old Evie Burrman is told through the eyes of her younger brother, Parr, who tries to understand and make sense of his sister's lesbian identity. Set in rural Missouri, the book describes how Evie pursues and falls in love with Patty, the daughter of the local banker. She is also interested in animals and farm machinery and resists her family's attempts to make her more "feminine."

———. *"Hello," I Lied: A Novel.* New York: HarperCollins Juvenile Books, 1997. Lang Hugh, a happily adjusted gay teenager, spends a summer in the Hamptons working part-time for a retired rock star. Lang's boss asks Lang to entertain the daughter of a long-deceased band member and to his surprise, Lang finds himself attracted to her. In the end, Kerr's novel becomes a thoughtfully narrated story about the sometimes complicated nature of friendship when the lines between intellectual and sexual attraction become blurred and confusing.

Walker, Kate. *Peter.* London: Omnibus, 1991; Boston: Houghton Mifflin, 1993. In this novel set in Australia, fifteen-year-old Peter hangs out with a group of dirt-bikers and develops a trusting relationship with his older brother's gay friend, who helps Peter answer questions about sexuality and male identity.

Books and articles for teachers

Adams, Maurianne, Lee Anne E. Bell, and Pat Griffin, eds. *Teaching for Diversity and Social Justice: A Sourcebook.* New York: Routledge, 1997.

Facing History and Ourselves: Holocaust and Human Behavior. Brookline: Facing History and Ourselves National Foundation, Inc. 1994.

Hamilton, G. "Reading Jack." *English Education* 30.1 (1998): 24–40.

Harris, Simon. *Lesbian and Gay Issues in the English Classroom: The Importance of Being Honest.* Philadelphia: Open UP, 1990.

Heron, A., ed. *Two Teenagers in Twenty.* Boston: Alyson, 1994.

Film

It's Elementary: Talking About Gay Issues in Schools. New Day Films, 22D Hollywood Avenue, Ho-ho-kus, NJ 07423. 800-343-5540. Parents, teachers, administrators, and students explore what happens when schools (K–12) openly discuss homosexuality.

Works Cited

Dragonwagon, Crescent. Rev. of *Jack,* by A. M. Homes. *The New York Times Book Review* 15 July 1990, sec. 7: 24.

Harris, Kathryn. Rev. of *Jack,* by A. M. Homes. *School Library Journal* 35.15 (1989): 126.

Vasilakis, Nancy. Rev. of *Jack,* by A. M. Homes. *The Horn Book Magazine* 66 (1990): 206–207.

About Greg Hamilton

Greg Hamilton is an assistant professor of English in the Department of Arts and Humanities at Teachers College, Columbia University. Greg has taught language arts, social studies, and mathematics for twelve years at The Center School, a public middle school in New York City. His writing and research interests include the preparation of secondary school English teachers, young adult literature, adolescent literacy development, and the teaching to, for, and about issues of race, gender, and sexual orientation. Greg studied abroad in Mysore, India and is currently working on a novel for young adults related to his experiences in India.

THEIR EYES WERE WATCHING GOD

by Zora Neale Hurston

In a little wind-lull, Tea Cake touched Janie and said, "Ah reckon you wish now you had of stayed in yo' big house 'way from such as dis, don't yuh?"

"Naw."

"Naw?"

"Yeah, naw. People don't die till dey time come nohow, don't keer where you at. Ah'm wid mah husband in uh storm, dat's all."

"Thanky, Ma'am. But 'sposing you wuz tuh die, now. You wouldn't git mad at me for draggin' yuh heah?"

"Naw. We been tuhgether round two years. If you kin see de light at daybreak, you don't keer if you die at dusk. It's so many people never seen de light at all. Ah wuz fumblin' round and God opened de door."

He dropped to the floor and put his head in her lap. "Well then, Janie, you meant whut you didn't say, 'cause Ah never knowed you wuz so satisfied wid me lak dat. Ah kinda thought—"

The wind came back with triple fury, and put out the light for the last time. They sat in company with the others in other shanties, their eyes straining against crude walls and their souls asking if He meant to measure their puny might against His. They seemed to be staring at the dark, but their eyes were watching God. (151)

Hurston, Zora Neale. *Their Eyes Were Watching God*. New York: HarperPerennial, 1990. (Note: This book was originally published by J. B. Lippincott, 1937.)

Intended Audience

Students in grades 10–12. Read by mature readers with a teacher's guidance, this novel would supplement the curriculum in classes focusing on African American literature, women writers, authors of ethnic diversity, African American and Southern history, or the Harlem Renaissance.

Summary

African American Janie Crawford tells her life story to her friend Pheoby. Raped by a school teacher, Janie's mother abandoned Janie at birth. Her grandmother, who displaces her hopes and fears onto Janie, subsequently raises Janie. At seventeen, Janie marries an older man, Logan Killicks, at her grandmother's urging so that Janie will be provided for in the event of her grandmother's death. Although Janie obeyed her grandmother when she married for convenience, she disobeyed her own heart that told her to marry for love. When a young man, Joe Starks, passes through and captures Janie's fancy, Janie runs off to marry him. This second marriage spans two decades of financial prosperity and rising social status but results in Janie's emotional decay. After Starks' death, Janie meets a man twelve years her junior, Vergible "Tea Cake" Woods, an itinerant laborer. Despite the town's gossip and warnings about Tea Cake's gambling and Janie's sinking social status, Janie follows her heart and finally discovers the love she had yearned for so long. Tea Cake takes Janie into the Florida Everglades, where they labor side by side in the muck. When a hurricane hits, Tea Cake is bitten by a rabid dog while attempting to save Janie from drowning. He subsequently goes mad and attempts to shoot Janie during his delirium. Janie is forced to kill him in order to save herself. Quickly acquitted of Tea Cake's murder, Janie returns to the African American town she and Joe Starks helped found. The story ends there, with Janie recovering from Tea Cake's loss by gathering her memories of love and life around her as a shawl, feeling the fulfillment of having followed her heart and of living on her own terms.

Relationship of *Their Eyes Were Watching God* to the Program

Teaching *Their Eyes Were Watching God* would meet several common district, state, and national goals for students.

Read and understand a variety of materials and rhetorical styles.

A study of Janie's rhetorical styles can help students understand the relationship of audience and purpose to style. Students can examine the different contexts for Janie's speeches and detail how her language changes while addressing a group of townspeople, other characters individually, and, indirectly, the reader.

Much of the novel consists of dialogue in a dialect that may be unfamiliar to many readers. To ensure comprehension, the teacher could read aloud passages featuring the dialogue or play recordings of the novel in class to give students an accurate portrayal of the southern, rural African American intonations and pronunciations. Double-entry journals that contain a quote on one-half of the page and a rewriting of the passage in standard written English on the other half would confirm students' understanding of the dialogue and of the conventions of language. Additional activities could include students' written responses to the chapters, dialogue journals among students about their understanding of key passages, double-entry journals in which students copy a quote on one-third of the paper and respond to it on the remainder of the paper, and story log activities in which students paste newspaper headlines, pictures, and/or articles into a pamphlet format in order to represent their comprehension of key events in the plot.

Use critical analysis to explore narrative techniques in students' writing.

Analyzing the novel from the perspectives of both reader and writer will enrich students' understanding of the book and enhance their writing skills if they apply to their own writing several of the narrative techniques that Hurston employs. The novel begins and ends at the same moment, with forty years of Janie's life placed in between. Students could explore various narrative devices to manipulate time. Activities could include writing a short story completely as a flashback, starting a story in the middle of the plot (in medias res), returning to the past to fill in key plot elements, and ending the story in the future. Writing a series of letters or diary entries would also encourage students to explore and manipulate elements of form, voice, verb tense, and narrative stance.

Because Hurston employs both first- and third-person narration in the novel, students would benefit from an extended study of point of view. Exploring the effects, perspectives, and flexibility of first- and third-person narratives by reading other literary works in addition to *Their Eyes Were*

Watching God and by writing their own blended-narrator pieces will help students better comprehend the novel. Students could rewrite passages, most notably the trial scene, in an alternate point of view and critique the impact of the shift on the reader, the plot, the character of Janie, and the social statements and feminist themes of the novel.

Hurston's use of metaphor, simile, point of view, personification, dialogue, and symbolism provide an excellent opportunity for the teacher to assign writing and discussion projects in which students employ these devices in journals, critiques, essays, or other projects. Teachers could share excerpts of other literary works or pair shorter works such as poems with the study of this novel so that students could better comprehend a range of devices.

Read and recognize literature as a record of human experience.

By reading and discussing *Their Eyes Were Watching God*, students can find connections between their lives and numerous themes that recur in literature across genres, times, and cultures. Class discussion and assignments such as those already suggested can help students make important connections. Issues such as arranged marriages, ethical treatment of all people, self-discovery and fulfillment, social status, and the role of work in one's life are socially, historically, and culturally relevant themes for study.

Furthermore, this novel provides insights to the astute reader about a specific historical time and place. Hurston details the impact of racism, living as an itinerant laborer, and the devastation that occurs in the wake of natural disasters. By helping students study and compare Hurston's life and times to Janie's, the teacher can assist students in discovering further historical, cultural, and literary insights. Hurston and *Their Eyes Were Watching God* also represent the Harlem Renaissance and challenge the conventions of that era. Reviled by contemporaries such as Richard Wright for not being aggressive enough in rejecting stereotypes of African Americans in her writings and for giving readers a repeated view of African Americans as carefree and shiftless, Hurston's writings lay dormant for decades, unread and unrevered.

In *Their Eyes Were Watching God* Hurston presents both an independent female protagonist and women who had been repressed yet managed to live fulfilling lives. She chronicles the avenues and adventures that one may experience when following one's dreams and one's heart. She allows her characters to make life choices and her readers to experience the results—both happy and sad—of those choices. There is no doubt that *Their Eyes Were Watching God* represents a chronicle of human experience through the rich language, numerous literary devices, and subtle commentary on being an African American female.

Impact of the Material on Readers

The potential benefits of studying this novel are as varied as the themes this book presents. Learning about the lives of African American women in the South, discussing issues associated with slavery's impact on the repression and unethical treatment of generations of African Americans, and discussing the numerous themes of this novel will help students expand their thinking about race relations, human interactions, the importance of love in one's life, and a number of other relevant issues. Consideration of gender perspectives and interactions will make for lively discussion topics. Students will gain an increased appreciation for various uses of language, dialect, and dialogue. By working closely with students to overcome any difficulty they have with the vernacular used in this book, teachers enable readers to approach more skillfully other texts that use dialect. The wealth of historical information regarding ethnic diversity, cultural backgrounds, and social strata will broaden students' minds and knowledge bases. Opportunities abound for considering the time, setting, and values of the characters and comparing them with students' own situations. Finally, appreciation of the story's numerous literary devices will enhance students' own literary skills.

Perhaps the most powerful impact of the novel is simply the appreciation for Janie's strength and self-acceptance and the facility with language that Hurston imparts in this novel. It is an inspiring read.

Potential Problems with *Their Eyes Were Watching God* and Ways to Address Them

This novel could face criticism for its use of dialect, portrayals of marriage and abuse, and use of a racial epithet. Although controversial issues raise valid concerns for young adults as they confront these concepts, each issue is an integral component of this book that contributes to the themes, pathos of the characters, and historical and cultural premises of the novel.

Dialect

The strong Southern black dialect used in this novel is critical for conveying the linguistic history of African Americans. For students to gain full knowledge of the particular slice of African American history that is represented in this novel, they need to examine a full range of historical and cultural concepts, including the political, social, religious, economic, and language use issues of the era. An understanding of the fact that most African Americans in the South during this time spoke in ways similar to this vernacular will impress upon students the power of this dialect to express the human condition of the people using it, to convey African Americans' social limitations as compared to those of their privileged white counterparts, and to connote social and class differences that existed in this culture during this time. Beyond race and privilege, however, the dialect of the characters in this novel conveys their sense of poetry, their understandings of life, and their very personal perceptions of events often beyond their control. In many ways, it is the dialect that distinguishes this novel and that conveys the human pathos so evident in it. Nonetheless, the students' difficulties with the dialect may be circumvented if the teacher initially discusses the history, stereotypes, and social implications surrounding the dialect, and carefully instructs students in how to read the phonetically written words. Daily question-and-answer sessions and other activities suggested previously could further aid students' understanding of the language used in the novel.

Challenges to conventional ideas of marriage

Not only did Hurston break with literary tradition by using black vernacular in this novel, but she also challenged the conventional American perception of marriage. Although arranged marriages have occurred throughout United States history, a fact that may surprise some students who think that such practices occur only in other countries, these marriages were not the prevalent custom. It is important for students to be aware of the social, political, and economic influences that provided the backdrop and impetus for arranged marriages. In order to understand Janie fully, the reader must comprehend such influences and their impact on Janie's life and subsequent development. It is precisely Janie's first marriage that prepares her for a marriage characterized by mutual respect and love. It is also Janie's relationships, including those with her husbands, that pave the way for her full development as a self-fulfilled woman. By investigating Janie's marriages and relationships, students may compare the treatment of these issues in *Their Eyes Were Watching God* to their treatment in other literary works and in the customs of other cultures. Many cultures approve of and utilize arranged marriages for a variety of reasons, and having students understand these contexts would enhance their understanding of Janie's particular situation as represented in the novel. By comparing and/or contrasting contemporary instances in which diverse cultures have retained the practice of arranged marriages to the situation in the novel and to students' own family histories and anticipated marriage arrangements, students broaden their cultural understandings. Individual journals, class discussions, and writing could help students clarify these issues.

Another instance of Hurston's feminist approach to breaking many of the confining Western social norms is evident in the "May/December" romance between Tea Cake and Janie. Tea Cake is twelve years Janie's junior, a fact that causes some consternation to many in Janie's community, even though the romance ultimately leads to marriage. Janie's determination to be true to herself and to find her own happiness is underscored by her defiance of her own community's social norms. Janie possesses the courage and strength to assert herself and to stand up for what she deems to be right for her personal fulfillment. If Janie had bowed to custom and to peer pressure, she would have lost herself and in the process become antithetical to Hurston's portrayal of strength, endurance, and individuality. Thus, one of the novel's primary themes would not have been developed. As with the issue of arranged marriages, students have the opportunity to investigate, discuss, and learn from other cultures about this issue. Students may also link this issue to other instances of a change in or a challenge to social norms. Historical events in the United States such as the women's movement, suffrage, desegregation, the abolitionist movement, and women entering the work force and the political arena might all be discussion topics that relate to the larger issues associated with this novel.

Instances of abuse

The physical and emotional abuse that are presented may pose difficult reading for students who have histories of abuse in their lives or families. These possible personal connections serve to underscore the novel's value and importance in addressing a range of relevant issues. Unfortunately, instances of abuse and maltreatment occur in every era and in every culture to both child and adult victims. The masterful way in which Hurston crafts the instances of abuse in this novel illustrate the humanity of the victim, leading readers to sympathize with the sufferer, decry the abuse, and realize that abuse is neither acceptable nor unique. The realization that one who has been abused is not alone in this experience may help students who have suffered abuse to seek the appropriate avenues of healthful support and assistance. However, if the student is uncomfortable with the novel on these grounds, the teacher can offer an alternative reading selection.

Use of a racial epithet

The use of a particular racial epithet, "nigger," is prevalent in this novel. Primarily, the African American characters use the term in reference to each other. Janie's grandmother uses the term to refer to her race in general, an indication of the ways in which she has been referenced, deprecated, and maltreated by her white owners while a slave. It is further an indication of the ways in which oppression has become institutionalized within African American and mainstream cultures.

The one character who uses the term as a racial slur is Mrs. Turner, a woman who has both white and African American ancestors and who reviles the dark, Negroid features of her peers. She judges her own appearance against Janie's lighter skin and more Anglicized features, including Janie's long, flowing hair, and finds herself lacking. Mrs. Turner's attitudes puzzle and disturb Janie, and thus disturb the reader.

In any context, the use of this or any racial epithet is offensive. However, Hurston presents the term as part of a particular mindset during a specific era. Readers recognize the self-deprecation and racism that engender the term's use, bringing focus on an alternative viewpoint and again reinforcing several of the novel's themes about surviving against all odds, self-fulfillment and acceptance, and the power of love in one's life. Far from encouraging such language and racism, the use of the term within the context of this novel causes readers to disavow it and to empathize with characters caught in challenging circumstances.

When adequately preceded by relevant socio-historical and cultural information, students should have little trouble understanding the context and themes of this novel. *Their Eyes Were Watching God* will enhance students' language understanding, human empathy, and literary knowledge. Further, it will open their minds to a writer just recently taking her deserved place in literary annals as one of the most important voices of African American women.

References

Zora Neale Hurston was an iconoclastic yet private woman who rose to brief literary recognition during the Harlem Renaissance, faded from prominence, and died poor and forgotten. Hurston was buried in an unmarked pauper's grave until her rediscovery by noteworthy African American writer Alice Walker, who journeyed to Florida in search of Hurston's grave to mark it, literally and symbolically. Walker's journey is chronicled in her tribute article "In Search of Zora Neale Hurston." Walker thus began the literary dialogues that would return Hurston to literary respect and prominence. Hurston's exact birth date is unknown. Some mark it as 1891, others as 1901. She died alone and in poverty in 1960. According to Alice Walker, local townspeople believe that Hurston died of complications following a stroke and of malnutrition. On the tombstone that Walker ordered for Hurston's gravesite, Walker had the following inscription engraved: "Zora Neale Hurston, 'A genius of the South,' Novelist, Folklorist, Anthropologist, 1901–1960."

Hurston wrote a play with Langston Hughes, several novels, numerous journal articles, several shorter works, two anthropological works, and an autobiography. She was the recipient of two Guggenheim Fellowships to study West Indian practices and folklore, and she attended Barnard College, working with Franz Boas, a noted anthropologist. Hurston received Howard University's Distinguished Alumni Award and an honorary Doctorate of Letters degree from Morgan State College, and she worked on the faculty of several colleges in the South. Numerous conferences are now held in her honor.

Hurston is perhaps most noted for her weaving of African American traditions and folklore into her fiction. Such artistry is clearly evident in this novel.

Praise for Hurston and for *Their Eyes Were Watching God* includes the following:

> What I loved immediately about this novel besides its high poetry and its female hero was its investment in black folk traditions. Here, finally, was a woman on a quest for her own identity, and, unlike so many other questing figures in black literature, her journey would take her not away from, but deeper and deeper into blackness, the descent into the Everglades with its rich black soil, wild cane, and communal life representing immersion into black tradition. (Washington x–xi)

> Hurston's evocations of the lifestyles of rural blacks have not been equaled; but to stress the ruralness of Hurston's settings or to characterize her diction solely in terms of exotic "dialect" spellings is to miss her deftness with language. In the speech of her characters, black voices—whether rural or urban, northern or southern—come alive. Her fidelity to diction, metaphor, and syntax—whether in direct quotations or in paraphrases of characters' thoughts—rings, even across forty years, with an aching familiarity that is a testament to Hurston's skill and to the durability of black speech. (Williams ix)

> Her best novel, *Their Eyes Were Watching God* (1937), is regarded as one of the most poetic works of fiction by a black writer in the first half of the twentieth century and one of the most revealing treatments in modern literature of a woman's quest for a satisfying life. (Hemenway 6)

Alternative Work

No other novel can replace the imagery, language, period-awareness, and character revelations that occur in *Their Eyes Were Watching God.* That is why the novel has become a classic that is widely read, studied, and critically acclaimed. If objections to the novel arise, however, an alternate selection could be *Jubilee Journey.*

Meyer, Carolyn. *Jubilee Journey.* San Diego: Harcourt, 1997. Thirteen-year-old Emily Rose Chartier thinks of herself as being a "double," not a "bi-" or "half" anything. Her mother's roots are southern and black, and her father's heritage is French. Living in Connecticut and helping her mother run their French restaurant, Café au Lait, does nothing to prepare Emily for a visit to Dillon, Texas, to celebrate the Juneteenth Diamond Jubilee with the great-grandmother she has never met. In Dillon, Emily discovers her southern black heritage, the story of the blacks in Dillon, her family history, and a new culture and perspective on life that she has never before experienced. Emily must come to grips with the fact that, in the South, she is black, not a double of anything. Emily, with the help of her sometimes-enemy, sometimes-friend Brandy Woodrow, discovers that, indeed, being black is something she wants to explore and understand better. Through all of their discoveries and encounters with the past and with this deep-rooted African American culture, Emily's mother, grandmother, brothers, and newfound friends support her so that Emily begins to understand herself and her roots more fully.

Related Works

Baldwin, James. *Go Tell It on the Mountain.* New York: New American Library, 1963 [c. 1953]. Long noted as the book Baldwin said he had to write even if he never wrote anything else, this novel expanded America's use of language and changed America's social and cultural perceptions. The stepson of a Pentecostal minister, a fourteen-year-old boy comes to terms with his moral and spiritual identity in 1935 in Harlem. This classic novel deals with issues of race, self-understanding, and the powers driving a hierarchical society.

Dove, Rita. *Through the Ivory Gate.* New York: Pantheon, 1992. Artistic Virginia King returns to her hometown of Akron, Ohio, to deal with her own career, racism, love, and, ultimately, family truths. The story is set in America during the aftermath of the Vietnam War. The social and political turmoil of the time and of the war is mirrored in the protagonist's own life as she encounters racism, failing relationships, and her own past.

Hurston, Zora Neale. *Dust Tracks on a Road.* New York: Arno, 1969 [c. 1942]. Hurston's autobiography details her impoverished childhood and subsequent placement among the leading artists of the Harlem Renaissance. She also recounts her personal struggles as a feminist African American standing against racism and a patriarchal society.

Thurman, Wallace. *The Blacker the Berry.* New York: Arno, 1969. Emma Lou Brown, a young African American woman living in the 1920s, battles discrimination within her own family in Boise, Idaho. She travels to Harlem in an attempt not only to find her own identity, but also to explore her cultural heritage.

Walker, Alice. *The Color Purple.* New York: Washington Square, 1982. In this Pulitzer Prize–winning novel, Celie, an abused and uneducated African American woman, overcomes her own fears to find her own identity and sense of personal empowerment. Central to her self-awakening are the insights of her female friends, especially those of Shug. This novel also uses the black vernacular to reveal insights about the characters.

Fictional works by Zora Neale Hurston

Jonah's Gourd Vine. New York: HarperPerennial, 1990 (new edition).

Moses, Man of the Mountain. New York: HarperPerennial, 1991 (new edition).

Mule Bone (a play written with Langston Hughes). New York: HarperPerennial, 1991 (new edition).

Seraph on the Swanee. New York: Scribner's, 1948.

Nonfiction anthropological works by Zora Neale Hurston

Mules and Men. New York: HarperPerennial, 1990 (new edition).

Tell My Horse. New York: HarperPerennial, 1990 (new edition).

Works Cited

Hemenway, Robert E. *Zora Neale Hurston: A Literary Biography*. Urbana: U of Illinois P, 1977.

Walker, Alice. "In Search of Zora Neale Hurston." *Ms*. Mar. 1975: 74–79.

Washington, Mary Helen. Foreword. *Their Eyes Were Watching God*. By Zora Neale Hurston. New York: Harper, 1990: ix–xvii.

Williams, Sherely Anne. Foreword. *Their Eyes Were Watching God*. By Zora Neale Hurston. Urbana: U of Illinois P, 1978: v–xv.

About Dawn Latta Kirby and Angela Dykstra

A veteran high school English teacher, Dawn Latta Kirby is now an associate professor in the Department of English at The Metropolitan State College of Denver, where she teaches young adult literature courses. She pairs *Their Eyes Were Watching God* with *To Kill a Mockingbird* by Harper Lee for critical reading and pedagogical discussion in a senior capstone course for English education majors. Angela Dykstra is an undergraduate English major, avid reader, skilled writer, and research wizard who is specializing in Creative Writing and who plans one day to teach.

THE BEAN TREES

by Barbara Kingsolver

I jumped when she pecked on the windshield. It was the round woman in the blanket.

"No thanks," I said. I thought she wanted to wash the windshield, but instead she went around to the other side and opened the door. "You need a lift someplace?" I asked her.

Her body, her face, and her eyes were all round. She was someone you could have drawn a picture of by tracing around dimes and quarters and jar tops. She opened up the blanket and took out something alive. It was a child. She wrapped her blanket around and around it until it became a round bundle with a head. Then she set this bundle down on the seat of my car.

"Take this baby," she said.

It wasn't a baby, exactly. It was probably old enough to walk, though not so big that it couldn't be easily carried. Somewhere between a baby and a person.

"Where do you want me to take it?"

She looked back at the bar, and then looked at me. "Just take it." (17)

Kingsolver, Barbara. *The Bean Trees*. New York: HarperCollins, 1988.

Intended Audience

Students in high school, grades 10–12. This book would be most successful read in small groups, using a readers' workshop format that would encourage a great deal of discussion and writing. Working in this way offers students the opportunity to explore the dynamics of group relationships within their own collective as a corollary to the themes of the book. The book has the flavor of South American literature and borders on magic realism. Thus it would be an excellent introductory novel for this style of writing. The themes of relationships, family, and cooperation can be explored in conjunction with this novel, as can Native American and refugee issues.

Summary

The story is told from the perspective of Taylor Greer, a young woman who leaves Kentucky to avoid the fate of early pregnancy and a life of poverty. She heads west across the country in a dilapidated Volkswagen toward an undetermined destination. Along the way, she meets a Cherokee woman who hands her a three-year-old girl, asks her to care for her dead sister's child, and disappears. Not knowing any details about the child except that she was born in a Plymouth, Taylor names her "Turtle." When the two arrive in Tucson, Arizona, Taylor stops at "Jesus Is Lord Used Tires" to get her flat tires fixed. She decides that this city is where she will stop her journey, and she sets out to find work.

Early in the book, we are given a parallel story of Lou Ann Ruiz, a pregnant young woman also living in Tucson. When the baby arrives, her husband leaves her and Lou Ann advertises for a roommate to help share expenses. Taylor and Turtle offer to move in, and from that point the two women's stories come together. Taylor begins to work at the "Jesus Is Lord" tire store, where the owner, Mattie, houses political refugees as part of the sanctuary movement.

The story then centers on this small community of people: Taylor and Turtle; Lou Ann and her baby; two Central American refugees, Estevan and Esperanza; two elderly ladies next door; and Mattie. The relationships among these unique characters tell a story of caring, friendship, and interdependence.

Relationship of *The Bean Trees* to the Program

In working with literature, we hope that students will have their interpretations of the world challenged and broadened. Reading novels about characters who live in various circumstances and come from different cultures or regions, or who are not living in conventional contexts, offers the opportunity for students to explore different thoughts, feelings, ideas, and experiences. If students explore a variety of texts and genres outside their personal preferences and understandings, they can analyze, explain, and synthesize connections between these diverse experiences, their prior knowledge, and many different texts. *The Bean Trees* offers such an opportunity for many students.

Because this novel does not rely on a fast-paced plot but rather depends on a story unfolding from the development of characters' lives, students have the opportunity to discuss the values of the choices of characters in their reader-response groups. The teacher can develop a number of questions or compile questions from students about the story to which students can prepare journal responses followed by debate and discussion. In a fast-paced world where students are offered a plethora of choices, *The Bean Trees* offers the possibility of learning how to make considered and ethical decisions in their lives.

One of the book's thematic threads is about the creation of community and the challenges and benefits of collaboration. Since students work in small response groups, the study is a good opportunity to further develop their cooperative learning skills. The discussions about the story can result in collaborative assignments that help students explore their interpretations of the text. For instance, one of the issues in the novel deals with refugees and the sanctuary movement. Students can debate if and how their country should accept people fleeing difficult political situations. This discussion could be connected to exploration of actual national policies for refugees, statistical information about recent refugees, and investigations of the political situations from which they have fled. In this way, *The Bean Trees* offers students the possibility of understanding issues facing their country from a new perspective and relates the reading of literature directly to their daily lives.

The topic of families could also be explored in similar groups. *The Bean Trees* offers a context for students to consider the meaning of "family" and compare a variety of descriptions, relating these to their own experiences and the composition of families they see in their community and in the media. For many students who do not come from traditional family structures, reading *The Bean Trees* can be an affirming experience. From a broader perspective, questions that are relevant to young people in the rapidly changing social structures of modern society can be explored and addressed to develop their understanding of the issues of diversity.

Opportunities for writing in response to their reading of the novel can help students experience the interdependence of plot, character, setting, and mood in enhancing meaning in this story. Such activities reveal how the context of where we live and the culture from which we come influence our actions, an important theme in the novel. One activity begins with students writing a short description of a location with which they are very familiar. Then the teacher presents a list of four or five characters, such as a young woman who has just escaped from a frightening situation. Students are asked to bring one of the characters into the location they've written about. They are not to mention the circumstances of the character's life; instead they are to depend on sensory details to leave the reader with a particular mood. Writing within such constraints, the students perceive how character, setting, and events interact in a particular context. Through such realizations, students can make connections to their own lives and begin to understand how they can work to make change within such contexts.

The atmosphere of the novel is reminiscent of magic realism stories, such as those from Central or South America. This book could be a good lead into readings of that genre by such authors as Marquez, Allende, Alvarez, and Esquivel. Students often enjoy trying to create their own short magic realism texts afterwards as a further exploration of that form of writing. Understanding this genre helps students experience perspectives of different cultures.

Impact of the Material on Readers

Readers have the opportunity to discover and consider a variety of characters and situations in *The Bean Trees* that would not be considered mainstream. Students may need some assistance and encouragement to make some of the connections between characters and events.

Students can see a broader perspective of what defines family as they read about the different family groups in the novel. They can develop a greater empathy and understanding for the varieties of family in their society and can feel a sense of affirmation about their own family circumstances.

Students can consider issues relevant to political refugees. For instance, how can refugees "prove" they are fleeing difficulty when they often can bring no proof with them? What kind of information should be accepted as evidence? What are the immigration policies? Students will become more attuned to the political climate in their country and be more informed in their future decision making in the political system.

Issues relating to Native Americans can be explored through this novel, including conditions of life on reservations and adoption of Native

American children by white parents. (The latter issue is explored further in *Pigs in Heaven*, a sequel.) Students can develop deeper awareness of issues concerning Native Americans.

Students can develop an awareness of differences among different regions of the United States. Taylor leaves to escape a particular lifestyle in Kentucky and sees other possibilities in her travels and in Tucson. They can also explore the themes of interconnectedness and communities of support. This understanding can help students find sources of support when they need them. Kingsolver's novel also offers the possibility of discussion of feminist issues such as single parenthood, abuse, male and female relationships, "women's work," and so on.

Taylor's story is a female journey story. She does not come back full circle as in the traditional hero story, but she does come back home in other ways. Students can compare the two archetypes of male and female journeys and perhaps discover structures that more closely resemble their own life stories.

Potential Problems with *The Bean Trees* and Ways to Address Them

Kingsolver's characters use straightforward language and "tell it like it is." Therefore, words such as "pecker" and "homosexual" appear in the story. But for the characters to speak otherwise would not be realistic in that context. Kingsolver has not overused such language to create shock effect but rather has carefully chosen just a few words to give the flavor of such characters' daily talk. This novel also offers an opportunity to talk about the difference between gratuitous sexual detail and everyday talk. Teachers can discuss differences between colloquial and standard language as well as the importance of considering the contexts for such language, relating to the world in which the students live. For instance, what language is appropriate for school hallways, for classrooms, or for social occasions with peers?

Another potential challenge is that Kingsolver's novel does not exemplify what some call "traditional family values." Comparing the family structures in the novel to those in the community clearly show that Kingsolver's perspective is very much a part of the fabric of modern society. Teachers could certainly defend the novel on this basis by using a simple statistical profile of the students in the school in terms of the variety of family structures.

Objectors might raise questions about the illegal activities around the refugees' story. However, this thread of the story gives teachers an opportunity to explore the differences between moral and legal questions, and the importance of students' learning such distinctions could well justify the use of this novel. Students could learn about Kohlberg's Scale of Moral Development through this discussion, although it should be noted that this scale has been criticized for being too white, Anglo-Saxon, and most specific to North American males. These questions, too, could become part of the discussion, and using Carol Gilligan's work, *In a Different Voice*, would broaden students' perspectives.

Some might object to the name of Mattie's tire store in Tucson, "Jesus Is Lord Used Tires," as being sacrilegious; however, because there is a range of opinions regarding religion, discussions could center on what points Kingsolver is trying to make about religion. Understanding the American perspective of freedom of speech and beliefs could also be part of this exploration.

References

The Bean Trees, Barbara Kingsolver's first book, was published to critical acclaim in 1988. She has since published three other novels, collections of poetry, short stories, and essays, as well as a nonfiction book. Kingsolver grew up in rural Kentucky, received a B.A. at DePauw University, and studied biology at the University of Arizona, graduating with a Masters of Science degree in 1981. Afterwards, she worked first as a technical writer and then moved into journalism and fiction writing. Kingsolver has long been interested in issues concerning family, relationships, and community, particularly as they relate to poor women. She has had contact with the sanctuary movement for refugees and is concerned about environmental dilemmas.

Kingsolver has won a number of awards, including the American Library Association award for *The Bean Trees*, a PEN fiction prize, and an Edward Abbey Ecofiction Award. She has also received a citation of accomplishment from the United Nations National Council of Women.

The Bean Trees generated a great deal of critical interest. Diane Manuel praised the novel: "[This book] gives readers something that's increasingly hard to find today—a character to believe in and laugh with and admire. . . . Kingsolver delivers enough original dialogue and wry one-liners to put this novel on a shelf of its own. . . . That's not to say this is merely laugh-a-minute fluff, however" (20). Karen FitzGerald, writing in *Ms.* magazine, said, "Given [its] ostensible contrivances of plot and character, *The Bean Trees* would seem to be on a collision course with its own political correctness. But Barbara Kingsolver has resisted turning her characters into mouthpieces for the party line. Instead, she has written a vivid and engaging novel that is connected more with love and friendship than with the perils of single motherhood and the politics of the sanctuary movement" (28). And Jack Butler further praised the talents of the writer: "Barbara Kingsolver can write. On any page of this accomplished first novel, you can find a striking image or fine dialogue or a telling bit of drama. . . . It is one thing to create a vivid and realistic scene and it is quite another to handle the harmonics of many such scenes, to cause all the images and implications to work together. And it is extremely rare to find the two gifts in one writer" (15).

Alternative Work

One book that could be used as an alternative because of its themes of relationship and Native American spirituality is Martha Brooks' *Bone Dance* (New York: Orchard Books, 1997). In this story, seventeen-year-old Alexandra Sinclair leaves Winnipeg, Canada, after the death of her grandfather and her father to visit the land that has been left to her. She meets Lonny, a young man whose family originally owned that land for generations, and discovers that she and Lonny must work through the spirits of the past to move onward into the future.

Related Works

While there are many possibilities for books that deal with the topics of community, interdependence, adoption, and single parenthood, we have chosen to suggest books that have mood and atmosphere (as well as some topics) comparable to *The Bean Trees*.

Alvarez, Julia. *How the Garcia Girls Lost Their Accents.* Chapel Hill: Algonquin Books of Chapel Hill, 1991. This novel tells about the lives of the four Garcia sisters and their parents, blending family history and expectations with the realities of being immigrants from the Dominican Republic to the United States.

Creech, Sharon. *Walk Two Moons.* New York: HarperTrophy, 1994. Thirteen-year-old Salamanca Tree Hiddle searches for her mother, who has disappeared, by retracing her steps on a car trip from Ohio to Idaho with her grandparents. Her Native American ancestry gives her the strength to face the truth about her mother.

Erdrich, Louise. *Bingo Palace*. New York: HarperCollins, 1994. This novel about contemporary Native American life features the character of Lipsha Morrisey, his return to the reservation, and his romance with Shawnee Ray.

Kingsolver, Barbara. *Pigs in Heaven*. New York: HarperCollins, 1993. Kingsolver continues writing about similar themes to *The Bean Trees* in this novel. She explores Native American issues, including adoption of Native American children by whites; families who do not represent the traditional structures such as single-parent families; the difficulties and challenges of poverty; and community relationships.

Works Cited

Butler, Jack. "She Hung the Moon and Plugged in All the Stars." *The New York Times Book Review* 10 April 1988, sec. 7:15.

FitzGerald, Karen. "A Major New Talent." *Ms.* Apr. 1988: 28.

Gilligan, Carol. *In a Different Voice: Psychological Theory and Women's Development*. Cambridge: Harvard UP, 1982.

Manuel, Diane. "A Roundup of First Novels About Coming of Age." *Christian Science Monitor* 22 Apr. 1988: 20.

About Rebecca Luce-Kapler and Sylvia Pantaleo

Rebecca Luce-Kapler teaches English curriculum courses at Queen's University, Kingston, Ontario. She has taught English at all grade levels and has been on the board of the Young Alberta Book Society, which promotes reading and authors to students across the province. When not teaching, she writes poetry and fiction.

Sylvia Pantaleo is an assistant professor in the Faculty of Education at Queen's University in Kingston, Ontario. Her twelve years of elementary and middle school teaching experience inform her university teaching of language arts and children's literature courses. Sylvia's research explores several aspects associated with using children's literature in elementary and middle school classrooms, including students' experiences with literature, teaching strategies and resources, and teachers' professional development.

SPITE FENCES

by Trudy Krisher

"Let's take you, for instance. Why don't you tell me, Maggie, something that you're afraid of?"

I thought for a long time. "Lots of things, George Hardy," I said. "I'm afraid of lots of things."

"Like what?" He was circling things on math papers while we talked.

"Well, my mama, for one," I said, tightening a stitch.

. . .

"Well, it's the meanness in her, the meanness in her that's not her fault. It's the meanness and the spite that I'm afraid of. I don't know where she got it from." I cut a strand of thread with my teeth.

I could tell he was listening closely. His pencil had stopped moving. "And what about the spite, Maggie? What is it about the spite that scares you?"

George Hardy asked the hardest questions. It was what I liked about him the most. I was quiet a long time. "I think it scares me, George Hardy, because I'm afraid I might catch it too." (159)

Krisher, Trudy. *Spite Fences*. New York: Bantam Doubleday Dell, 1994.

Intended Audience

Students in grades 8–12. Although this book reads easily, the subject matter is more appropriate for discussion with slightly older students. *Spite Fences* would be used appropriately in American literature survey courses, American history and literature courses taught in tandem, or in units focused on the early civil rights movement, moral decisions, family conflicts, and strong female characters.

Summary

Set in Kinship, Georgia, in the 1960s, this book presents Maggie Pugh, who is a poor white girl who lives on the other side of the tracks but has not been "ruined" by her circumstance. In *Spite Fences,* there are many examples of abuse. Maggie's mother is physically and psychologically abusive to her. Maggie's hateful neighbor, Virgil, stalks Maggie and her sister. The blacks in the town face discrimination from the whites, and the poor whites are discriminated against by the rich whites and don't mix with the "coloreds." The history of the civil rights movement is quietly woven in throughout the story. And it is told from the point of view of a young white girl who sees the reality of what is happening around her and realizes it will be up to her to expose the truth.

Maggie selects her friends by their kindness, not their skin color. Her two greatest teachers are black men in the community. Zeke, a black man who sells secondhand goods to everyone in town, has decided it is time to stand up for his rights. After Zeke is beaten and arrested for using the whites-only toilet at the diner, Maggie offers to teach him how to read, thinking he could not read the signs over the doors. Though he cannot read, Zeke admits he understood the signs but used the whites-only toilet on purpose in an attempt to force the whites to see the truth. Knowing Maggie's family's financial troubles, Zeke helps Maggie get a job house cleaning for a Mr. George Hardy. At first Maggie only communicates through notes she leaves for her employer. One day when he returns early, she realizes that she is working for a black man. Slowly a friendship develops. Through their conversations, George teaches Maggie that she ". . . could understand people by figuring out the things they were afraid of" (257). With the strong and courageous role modeling of these two men, Maggie comes to terms with the conditions of her life and chooses to take a moral stand against the injustices surrounding her.

Maggie is unusual and has a special ability to see the world through camera-like snapshots. She sees things happening and uses her mind's camera to take pictures. To thank her for teaching him to read, Zeke gives Maggie a secondhand camera. With this camera, Maggie courageously exposes the racial realities of Kinship, Georgia.

Relationship of *Spite Fences* to the Program

Spite Fences is a great book for teens for several reasons. It is adaptable to any of the standard assignments used in reading, processing, and writing about literature, but it is much more. I am always looking for bridges into the lives of my students. Maggie Pugh is not only a bridge, she is a kid faced with moral decisions that life puts in front of her, just like the young people who sit in my classes every day. She can't help the family she comes from. She can't help that her little sister is picture perfect, the apple of her mother's eye. She is a victim of many circumstances, but she makes all the right choices. Maggie sifts through the realities around her and finds the strength to be courageous. Using reader-response journals, students can explore their realities and sift through them. Will they be brave enough to make the right moral decisions? Will Maggie's insights into her life help them find insights into their lives?

It is my job as a teacher to create the opportunities through discussions and writings for my students to "soul search." The topics for these opportunities abound. We look at family issues and physical abuse, but we also look at Maggie's acceptance of her mother the way she is. Maggie realizes she cannot change her mother, and instead of feeling bitterness and hatred for her, Maggie feels pity and sadness. That acceptance is such a demanding lesson. We discuss economic and social limitations. Maggie is poor, but that does not stop her. Maggie does not interact with the "socially privileged," but she lives her life with honor and integrity.

And, of course, with this book one must discuss racial intolerance. The history of the early 1960s is woven in so subtly and delicately that the lessons are learned without resistance. Maggie is present when beatings occur at the lunch counter, and she is holding her camera. The injustice of the situation rips through Maggie, and she is determined to use her camera to tell the world no matter what the consequences. And she does. We troop to the library and form teams for research. Each team takes a different issue or year and we create a timeline around Maggie's photographs. I ask my students how many of them would have Maggie's courage to fight not only the white pressures in the town but also her mother, father, and nearly every white adult she knows.

In high school, we read many books with strong male characters. We need more books with strong female characters. This book fills that need, and Maggie's story should be read. Maggie is a survivor who carries many others with her. Some of these are students in my classes.

Impact of the Material on Readers

It is necessary that we learn from our history, even the parts we are not proud of. Students will have studied the early civil rights events, but usually as outsiders. In this book, Krisher shows us a town where bigotry exists on several levels. It was not just the cross burners who were racist, and it was not just the northerners who fought to uncover the truth. All readers will have faced moral decisions in their lives; this book asks them if they have been able to step forward in the same way as Maggie did. It gives them the opportunity to plan for future decisions.

Potential Problems with *Spite Fences* and Ways to Address Them

At 283 pages, this book is longer than I usually select for my classes. I move the students through the first part quickly and slow down once we get into the depth of the book. Students may complain when they see the length and size of the print, but they will quickly get involved with life in this small Georgia town.

The abuse that Maggie faces from her mother and the sexual assault by Virgil that comes close to rape may open wounds of some students in class. As always, the teacher needs to be alert to signs of distress some students will display and seek the appropriate referrals or counseling channels for these hurting kids. Virgil is selective in those he abuses; he targets those that society has labeled as weaker or less. He is a bully who has no respect for women or African Americans. Maggie and the reader learn it is Virgil who is the weaker, the lesser. Students need to see that bullies are not heroes.

The word "nigger" used throughout the book certainly is an offensive term. In the context of the novel it is used to show the racism in this town and many towns just like it. The word is never used casually; it is always used by a bigot in a hateful scene. Words have power, and our students need to see the damage words can cause. We spend considerable time discussing this power with many derogatory words. Often, black students explain that they use this word as a way to diffuse its power and to reclaim the word. Each of my students has an opinion, which leads to an enlightening discussion.

References

Trudy Krisher presently lives in Dayton, Ohio, where she teaches writing at the University of Dayton. Krisher grew up in the South; she was born in Macon, Georgia, and later lived in southern Florida. She published her second novel, *Kinship*, in 1997. Set in the same small town, it centers on Pert Wilson, Maggie Pugh's good friend in *Spite Fences*.

Spite Fences is an International Reading Association Award Winner, an ALA Best Book for Young Adults, and a Parents' Choice Honor Book. It has also received many positive reviews, including the following:

> Through Krisher's stunning narrative and achingly real characters, Maggie's pain and redemption are brought to vivid life. (*Kirkus Reviews* 1567)

> The courage and vision of the 1960s South, as well as its ugliness, are posted on *Spite Fences* for all to see. It is a masterful, sobering display. (Bradburn 666)

> The suspenseful story of the civil-rights era provides a believable, courageous heroine. (Anderson 89)

Related Works

Strong female protagonist

Grant, Cynthia D. *Mary Wolf.* New York: Atheneum, 1995. Sixteen-year-old Mary has to hold her family together after her father's business fails.

Krisher, Trudy. *Kinship.* New York: Delacorte, 1997. Pert Wilson, Maggie Pugh's best friend, tries to understand her life and keep her community together in Kinship, Georgia. In the process she learns the meaning of family.

Mason, Bobbie Ann. *In Country.* New York: Harper, 1985. Sam travels to the Vietnam War Memorial to understand the father she did not know.

Wolff, Virginia Euwer. *Make Lemonade.* New York: Henry Holt, 1993. Fourteen-year-old LaVaughn learns the importance of "taking hold" in life as she tries to help seventeen-year-old Jolly and her two small children.

Civil rights history

Free At Last : A History of the Civil Rights Movement and Those Who Died in the Struggle. Montgomery: The Southern Poverty Law Center, n.d.

Haskins, Jim. *Separate But Not Equal: The Dream and The Struggle.* New York: Scholastic, 1998.

King, Casey, and Linda Barrett Osborne. *Oh, Freedom! Kids Talk About the Civil Rights Movement with the People Who Made It Happen.* New York: Knopf, 1997.

Levine, Ellen. *Freedom's Children: Young Civil Rights Activists Tell Their Own Stories.* New York: Avon Flare, 1994.

Powledge, Fred. *We Shall Overcome: Heroes of the Civil Rights Movement.* New York: Scribner's, 1993.

Works Cited

Anderson, Lois F. Rev. of *Spite Fences,* by Trudy Krisher. *The Horn Book Guide* 6.1 (1994): 89.

Bradburn, Frances. Rev. of *Spite Fences,* by Trudy Krisher. *Booklist* 1 Dec. 1994: 666.

Rev. of *Spite Fences* by Trudy Krisher. *Kirkus Reviews* 15 Dec. 1994: 1567.

About C. J. Bott

C. J. Bott is an English teacher at Shaker Heights High School in Shaker Heights, Ohio. She has taught for twenty-six years, the last fourteen at Shaker Heights. She is also cofounder and cosponsor of WHEN (Women Helping Educate Women) and the Gay/Straight Alliance at her school, as well as president of the Cleveland branch of the American Association of University Women and a weekend poet.

MEMOIRS OF A BOOKBAT

by Kathryn Lasky

"Well, look at the facts—Goldilocks gets off scot-free, and this is after she has trespassed, stolen the porridge, and committed vandalism. Remember?" Nettie raised a finger and began shaking it at me. "She broke Baby Bear's chair! Now you don't go around stealing and trespassing and vandalizing, do you, Harper?" She turned to Mom. "Don't we teach our children not to trespass? And not to touch other people's things?"

. . .

"So," Nettie continued, "Goldilocks trespasses and does she get punished? No. Inappropriate punishment as it is shown in these children's books is a real evil today. We cannot have stories in which naughty children get away with misbehaving. You watch it, Beth." Now she was shaking her finger at my mother. "Children start reading this trash and they get real stubborn, a lot of back talk."

"Well." My mom smiled. "Harper does like to read, but she is a very obedient child. I declare, I don't think I've ever heard Harper talk back in her life."

Nettie turned her eyes toward me. "Bookworm, are you?"

The way she said that word absolutely made my skin crawl. She made me sound like I was some spineless, mindless creature living on mold underground. I do love books, but there is nothing wormy about it. I would much prefer to be called a bat than a worm any day of the week. (30–31)

Lasky, Kathryn. *Memoirs of a Bookbat.* San Diego: Harcourt Brace & Company, 1994.

Intended Audience

Because the main character is fourteen, middle school (grades 6–8) is the ideal place for this 215-page, easily read novel. But because the issues of book censorship, hypocrisy, creationism, and parental control are such complex issues, older students will be able to rise above the age of the main character to discuss the thought-provoking topics that this novel examines.

Summary

In the middle of a cross-country bus ride to her grandmother's home in Georgia, fourteen-year-old Harper Jessup reflects on the events that prompted her to run away from her parents and brought her to this point. Moving so often from town to town with her family during the previous four years has, as she says, "pretty much wrecked my life." More specifically, it's the reason for their moving that has caused the problem: Harper's parents say they are "migrants for God." Living out of a trailer, they travel the country representing Family Action for Christian Education (F.A.C.E.), opposing textbooks that describe evolution, attacking novels they find offensive, and marching in an anti-abortion demonstration. The trouble is that books are the most important thing in Harper's life. Always have been. Having no time to make friends, she has let books become her most important companions. And when her parents and their closest allies attack everything from "Goldilocks and the Three Bears" to fantasy novels and "JEWdy" Blume, Harper can no longer stand to be a part of that life. So, with the help of her level-headed boyfriend Gray, she runs away to live with her open-minded, supportive grandmother.

Relationship of *Memoirs of a Bookbat* to the Program

Although this novel will fit comfortably in a unit on parent-child relationships, decision making, or critical thinking in general, its most obvious use is in a unit on intellectual freedom, more specifically on book censorship. Censorship of books in schools and libraries from various quarters, especially from the extreme religious right, presents perhaps the greatest threat to intellectual freedom this country has ever seen. Educators—especially English teachers—need to address the problem aggressively. Unless teenagers understand the complex issues involved in preserving intellectual freedom, our rights to read and discuss controversy may well be lost in the next generation. All of the literary works in this volume have been challenged, but this novel—better than any other one available—examines some of the reasons and the psyche behind much of the censorship in America today.

Memoirs of a Bookbat contains many issues worthy of discussion, starting with one that many teenagers normally can identify with: getting along with parents. What teenagers haven't disagreed with their parents about their choice of friends, clothing, TV programs, or after-school activities? As students consider how conflicts between parents' beliefs and students' beliefs are handled, they can examine the relationship between Harper and her parents and how, specifically, the characters hold different views about evolution, humanism, other religions, Halloween, and homosexuals.

Once students discuss the disparate attitudes about various aspects of their own lives, they can look at their different perspectives of books. Teachers can then broaden the scope of that issue by talking about what specific books, and what types of books, have been attacked in recent years, what kinds of people seem to be doing the most censoring, in what type(s) of communities most censoring occurs, and the manner in which disgruntled people go about getting books removed from schools and libraries. Students researching recent censorship cases might be able to figure out the various reasons that some people want to remove certain books from schoolrooms. Discussing *Memoirs of a Bookbat* can help students better understand the real cases they read about. Although the book is fiction, the books and authors mentioned in the novel are real books and real authors that have been attacked in recent years, and the actions and beliefs of the religious fundamentalists in this novel are based on the actions of real people.

Somewhere along the way, of course, the class should debate the pros and cons of book censorship (and the censoring of movies, music, art, and performances): What, if anything, should be censored? Who should do the censoring? What are the likely results of censorship? Is it better to know or not know about hurtful or controversial things? Finally, students might propose procedures for what to do if someone attacks a novel, a textbook, a teaching method, a film, and so on used in their school system. Obviously, all of these explorations should help develop students' critical thinking skills and enable them to see the dangers that can result from the kinds of censoring that Harper's parents and their friends engage in.

Students can also discuss the rights and responsibilities of parents. As they focus their attention so much on "saving" others, are Harper's parents guilty of neglecting her and her younger sister? Hypocrisy is another important topic, especially when it's coupled with the value of religion in a person's life. Students could consider ways that the behaviors and attitudes of Harper's parents and other members of F.A.C.E. might not be considered very Christian or the question of whether or not a person can be religious and not impose his or her values on others in the negative ways that the members of F.A.C.E. did. Finally, a class discussion on the value of fairy tales could be useful. What lessons do students remember that fairy tales taught them? What was believable and what was not in the tales they grew up with? How difficult was it to tell the difference?

If there is time and interest, students can discuss some of the other issues that Harper describes: the celebration of Halloween, differences between Catholics and Protestants, anti-Semitism, homophobia, humanism, and evolution versus creationism.

Teachers might also choose to develop a short unit on logic. Students can then apply the principles of logic they have learned to the reasoning used by various characters in the novel.

The reading skills of prediction and cause-effect can be applied throughout this novel. For prediction, teachers can ask students to stop reading at certain points in the novel and write down what they think might happen next. Similarly, given a list of statements or events from the novel, students can be asked to explain what resulted from those. In some cases, students' predictions of what will happen next and what does happen will be identical.

Among the literary devices that deserve attention is point of view. Of what value is it to have Harper tell us the story in her own words? How might the story have been different if it had been told by Harper's mother, Gray, or an omniscient author? Another is the use of flashback. How might this novel have been different if Harper had narrated it as it happened instead of when she was on her way to the safety of her grandmother's home?

This novel can inspire several writing and speaking activities. Teachers can ask students to recall books that were important to them when they were younger and describe them to the class. Response journals can reveal students' personal connections with the books mentioned in the novel and with the kinds of activities Harper's parents engage in. Students can write a series of diary entries that Harper's mother or father could have written about their experiences in different towns. Some students can use newspapers and the Internet to investigate a recent case of book censorship, write to Judy Blume to express their feelings about one of her books, or contact Kathryn Lasky to ask what kind of research she did for this book and where this novel itself has been censored. Small groups of students can prepare and engage in a debate about whether book censorship is generally good or bad for students. If there is an organized group of self-identified Christian fundamentalists in town or nearby, certain students might interview one or more of them about their views on some of the topics brought up in this novel and report findings to the class.

And, of course, interested students might want to read one or more of the books mentioned in *Memoirs of a Bookbat*, examine another book that has been censored somewhere and consider the reasons for the controversy, investigate one or more articles about book censorship published in professional journals, or read another novel written by Kathryn Lasky (see Related Works).

Impact of the Material on Readers

Any students who love to read, especially those whose favorite books might be ones mentioned by Harper, will likely share Harper's perspective and be shocked to learn the reasoning behind attacks on those books. Even less enthusiastic readers will have heard of some of the books mentioned—certainly everyone knows "Goldilocks"—and be equally as shocked that anyone would want to prevent kids from reading them. Not wanting to read a book is one thing; being *prevented* from reading it is something else.

Some teachers reading this novel for the first time will be equally surprised by the perspectives of some censors. In my college classroom, most of the experienced teachers find this novel extremely enlightening; in fact, this novel has been the most effective book I have ever used to show how one group—possibly the largest and currently the most influential group—of censors thinks and acts.

Students who come from homes where their parents share the beliefs of the Jessups may see nothing wrong with their actions and might be offended by this book. Some teachers, too, will find the portrayal of religious extremists offensive if they share those same beliefs. Teachers who wish to use this book will need to be conscious of this potential impact and remember that discussions of all sides of controversial topics require students to develop their critical thinking skills and form the foundation of a democratic society.

Potential Problems with *Memoirs of a Bookbat* and Ways to Address Them

Without question, any book that deals with the topic of book censorship is itself going to be attacked. Ray Bradbury's *Fahrenheit 451* is one of the most censored books in America today, and *Memoirs of a Bookbat* is controversial because it, too, deals with the power of books and reading and the desire of some people to limit or completely eradicate all books. All the more reason for teaching it.

If individual students are likely to feel uncomfortable dealing with the religious aspects of *Memoirs of a Bookbat*, they certainly need to be given the opportunity to read something else, as has been suggested with other books examined in this resource. See "Alternative Works" for suggestions.

Some readers may find the novel too didactic, as *Booklist* reviewer Hazel Rochman did. "Thinly disguised as a novel, this is an essay about the dangers of the religious Right," she boldly stated. The religious "fundamentalists are all caricatures of fools and villains," she asserts (1526). No other reviewers shared Rochman's opinion. Elizabeth Poe, for example, writing in *The ALAN Review*, calls the novel "Poignant and provocative" and concludes with "This is an important book" (27). And, having grown up on the fringe of the kind of culture Lasky describes, I find the characters all too real.

Negative remarks are made in this book toward blacks, Catholics, Jews, and gays. Immature or weak readers may take these remarks at face value. However, mature readers and those who have teacher assistance through class discussion will understand their role in the book immediately. Teachers can help students analyze who makes the remarks, for what reasons, and in what contexts. This kind of analysis will reveal that neither the protagonist nor, presumably, the author supports such attitudes.

References

Books were a major part of Kathryn Lasky's life growing up in Indianapolis. She started writing stories for children when, as an elementary teacher, she discovered how dull the reading workbooks were. Since then she has published nearly fifty books, both fiction and nonfiction, including picture books for children and novels for young adults in various genres: mysteries, historical fiction, nonfiction, and contemporary realistic fiction.

Her *Sugaring Time* was a Newbery Honor Book; *Monarchs* received the Parents' Choice Silver Medal; and *The Weaver's Gift* received the *Boston Globe-Horn Book* Award—all three of those books were illustrated with photographs by her husband, Christopher Knight. *The Night Journey* , a true story about her grandmother's escape from Czarist Russia, won the National Jewish Book Award for Children. *Beyond the Divide, Prank, Pageant,* and *Beyond the Burning Time* were all selected as Best Books for Young Adults by the American Library Association.

Alternative Works

Students who may object to the portrayals of Harper's parents and friends can still read about and discuss some of the issues associated with censorship.

Hentoff, Nat. *The Day They Came to Arrest the Book.* New York: Dell, 1982. This is an excellent examination of both sides of the issue of censoring *The Adventures of Huckleberry Finn* in a fictional high school.

Neufeld, John. *A Small Civil War.* New York: Atheneum, 1996. Neufeld's novel concerns the censoring of *The Grapes of Wrath* in a fictional town. There is a 1982 version and a newer revised 1996 version; try the newer one.

Related Works

Additional books by Kathryn Lasky

Beyond the Burning Time. New York: Scholastic, 1994. Fourteen-year-old Mary Chase gives us an inside view of the panic surrounding the Salem witch trials in 1692.

A Journey to the New World: The Diary of Remember Patience Whipple. New York: Scholastic, 1996. In diary form, the narrator describes her experiences on the Mayflower in 1620.

True North. New York: Scholastic, 1996. The lives of a fourteen-year-old Boston society girl and an escaped slave girl named Afrika meet dramatically on the Underground Railroad

Young adult novels that deal with the influence of religion on the lives of teenagers

Brooks, Bruce. *Asylum for Nightface.* New York: HarperCollins, 1996. Although he is a very spiritual person, fourteen-year-old Zimmerman feels compelled to do something radical after his parents become fanatical born-again Christians.

Greene, Bette. *The Drowning of Stephan Jones.* New York: Bantam, 1991. Using their fundamentalist religious beliefs as a shield, Andy Harris and his friends become responsible for the death of a local gay man, and Andy's girlfriend Carla has to decide whose side she's on.

Howe, Norma. *God, the Universe, and Hot Fudge Sundaes.* Boston: Houghton, 1984. When her sister dies and her parents separate, Alfie has to face what she believes about life, death, and religion.

Kerr, M. E. *Is that You, Miss Blue?* New York: Harper, 1975. In a girls' boarding school, Flanders Brown and her classmates discover that their faculty guide, Miss Blue, keeps a picture of Jesus on the bathroom wall.

———. *What I Really Think of You.* New York: Harper, 1982. Opal Ringer's father is a poor, Pentecostal preacher; Jesse Pegler's father is a wealthy television evangelist. This novel is about what happens when they get involved with one another.

Newton, Suzanne. *I Will Call It Georgie's Blues.* New York: Viking, 1983. At home Reverend Sloan is quite different from how he behaves in public. Aileen rebels against her strict father, and Neal copes through his music, but little Georgie doesn't have the resources to cope.

Nolan, Han. *Send Me Down a Miracle.* New York: Harcourt, 1996. In a small town with outlandish characters, the preacher's daughter Charity falls under the influence of a local artist who says she has seen Jesus sitting in one of her chairs.

Ruby, Lois. *Miriam's Well.* New York: Scholastic, 1993. When Miriam gets seriously ill from cancer and her family refuses medical help because it is against their religious beliefs, her friend Adam feels he needs to take extreme measures to save her life.

Novels dealing with censorship

Malmgren, Dallin. *The Ninth Issue.* New York: Delacorte, 1989. Malmgren explores newspaper censorship in a fictional high school.

Miles, Betty. *Maudie and Me and the Dirty Book.* New York: Knopf, 1980. Two sixth-grade girls read a book about dogs to first graders and react to the kids' questions about puppies and birth, thus getting into trouble for discussing sex with younger kids.

Peck, Richard. *The Last Safe Place on Earth.* New York: Dell, 1995. Peck provides a look at a variety of types of censorship in a small town (books, sex education, Halloween) by religious extremists.

Nonfiction works about book censorship

Edwards, June. *Opposing Censorship in the Public Schools: Religion, Morality, and Literature.* Mahwah: Lawrence Erlbaum, 1998.

Monks, Merri M., and Donna Reidy Pistolis. *Hit List: Frequently Challenged Books for Young Adults.* Chicago: ALA, 1996.

Simmons, John R., ed. *Censorship: A Threat to Reading, Learning, Thinking.* Newark: IRA, 1994.

Works Cited

Poe Elizabeth. Rev. of *Memoirs of a Bookbat,* by Kathryn Lasky. *The ALAN Review* 22.3 (1995): 27.

Rochman, Hazel. Rev. of *Memoirs of a Bookbat,* by Kathryn Lasky. *Booklist* 15 Apr. 1994: 1526.

About Donald R. Gallo

Donald R. Gallo is a specialist in young adult literature. A former professor at Central Connecticut State University, he is now writing full time. He is the editor of several award-winning collections of short stories for young adults, including *Sixteen* and *No Easy Answers.* With Sarah K. Herz, he coauthored *From Hinton to Hamlet.* He is also the author of "Censorship of Young Adult Literature" in *Censorship: A Threat to Reading, Learning, Thinking,* edited by John S. Simmons.

IN COUNTRY

by Bobbie Ann Mason

Cawood's Pond was famous for snakes, but it also had migrating birds—herons, and sometimes even egrets, Emmett claimed. She saw the egret so often in her mind she almost thought she had really seen it. It was white, like a stork. Maybe her father had seen egrets in Vietnam and thought they were storks. The stork bringing her. Emmett went over there soon after, as though he were looking for that stork, something that brought life. Emmett didn't look hard enough for that bird. He stayed at home and watched TV. He hid. He lived in his little fantasy world, she thought. But Sam meant to face facts. This was as close to the jungle as she could get, with only a VW.

A blue jay fussed overhead. A fish splashed. She leaned over the railing of the boardwalk and watched the Jesus bugs. The place was quiet, but gradually the vacancy of the air was filled with a complex fabric of sounds—insects and frogs, and occasional whirring wings and loud honks of large birds.

The insects were multiplying, as though they were screwing and reproducing right in the air around her. A gnat flew into her eye. She went back to the car and put on her jeans and boots. She hadn't brought any Bug-Off. With the space blanket and her backpack and the picnic cooler, she followed a path through the jungle. The cypress knees, little humps of the roots sticking up, studded the swamp, and some of them even jutted up on the path. She had to walk carefully. She was walking point. The cypress knees were like land mines. There would be an invisible thread stretched across the path to trigger the mine. She waded through elephant grass, and in the distance there was a rice paddy. (211)

Mason, Bobbie Ann. *In Country*. New York: Perennial Library, 1986.

Intended Audience

Students in grades 10–12. This novel will be most successfully read by students with at least some experience dealing with contemporary literature. Frequent references to popular culture and controversial themes will be best dealt with in conjunction with teacher guidance prior to starting the reading. Frequent class discussion will help students understand the material at several levels. This book can be used in courses specializing in American literature, twentieth-century literature, and female authors, as well as general grade-level courses.

Summary

Having just graduated from high school in the small Kentucky town of Hopewell, Samantha Hughes is feeling restless. Her father, Dwayne, was killed in Vietnam before she was born, and Samantha finds it increasingly difficult to look toward the future before coming to terms with the past. Learning about her father becomes an obsession filled with dead ends. The veterans in town, including her uncle Emmett Smith with whom she lives, offer little information about their experiences in Vietnam ("in country"), and indeed all seem to have trouble taking charge of their own lives. Her mother has remarried and moved to Lexington and, having been married to Dwayne for just a short time, has little to share with Sam. Adding to Sam's unsettled life are the feeling that she is rapidly outgrowing her relationship with boyfriend Lonnie; the pregnancy of her unwed best friend, Dawn; the fear that Emmett is suffering the effects of Agent Orange; and the attempt at a relationship with a much older veteran named Tom, who carries the scars of war in his own way. In spite of everything Samantha remains strong, and both she and Emmett come to terms with the past through a series of events that culminate in a visit to the Vietnam Veterans Memorial in Washington, D.C.

Relationship of *In Country* to the Program

In Country can be used in a variety of ways to meet numerous educational goals. Themes of the novel should be discussed in small-group settings, with each student expressing personal thoughts and perspectives as well as responding to those of others. Throughout the study of the novel, teachers should encourage students to use a variety of media to express their ideas. They can use letter writing, audio- and videotapes, and Internet connections with other schools to address the concerns that emerge from discussions.

Reading and writing for understanding

The subject matter of *In Country* lends itself to any number of suggested assignments. Thesis/support papers on cross-disciplinary topics can address the potential effects of chemicals such as Agent Orange, historical and geographic aspects of the southeast Asia region, and the conflict and its social implications. Students are thirsty for information about the Vietnam conflict. They have parents and other relatives who experienced it firsthand but refuse to talk about it. This book sheds some light on the reasons for the silence.

Incorporating expert information to support a thesis should lead students to interviews with veterans in the community as well as exploration of related Internet websites where connections can be made. Students will need to find both electronic and print data to be analyzed and evaluated for inclusion in their work.

Literary structure

Reading *In Country* will help students understand the structure of a contemporary novel by a writer who incorporates both contemporary and traditional techniques. Mason's prose abounds with references to popular culture. Students can catalogue these and analyze the picture they offer of the time period. The journey of Sam, Emmett, and Sam's grandmother to the Veterans Memorial serves as a frame for the story, with the rest presented in flashback. Teachers can discuss the tradition of framed stories in literary history with examples from *The Decameron, The Canterbury Tales,* and the various versions of the *Arabian Nights.* The novel also provides information in the form of letters Dwayne sent to Sam's mother while he was "in country" and in a diary he kept while at war. Students can use these to study various forms of narration.

War and its effects on those directly and indirectly involved is a theme that dates back at least as far as Homer and extends through all time periods and literary genres. Students can select a work with a similar theme and identify common concepts and literary techniques. This book is particularly relevant because Mason takes a classic theme and develops it with contemporary times and characters. This makes the book more accessible and interesting to today's readers.

Evaluating divergent viewpoints and perspectives

Students can prepare speeches and debates using both formal evidence and personal opinion/analysis. Entire courses could be taught on the debate over the United States' involvement in Vietnam. Students can discuss whether Emmett, Sam's mother, and other characters owe Sam information about her father and the past. Do people have to come to terms with the past in order to successfully move on to the future? Students can first discuss this in the context of the novel and then, if they are comfortable doing so, prepare oral presentations incorporating personal experience. Students can also play the role of a character in the novel and describe the growth that character has experienced.

Impact of the Material on Readers

Students will probably have preconceived notions of the Vietnam War and its aftermath. These notions will most likely have been shaped by Hollywood accounts of action heroes jumping out of helicopters with machine guns and bringing long-lost P.O.W.s safely home. If so, students will come away from *In Country* with a new perspective of the situation. Vietnam was a conflict that affected an entire generation, one person at a time, changing the lives of those who served but not by making them heroes. Through *In Country*, students can see that the conflict also affected those whose loved ones served. From Samantha's viewpoint, students will see how the war affected even those Americans who were not yet born when their ancestors were "in country." Above all they should come away with the understanding that this was not a glamorous time but one that changed the lives of a nation, not just for one generation but for many.

Potential Problems with *In Country* and Ways to Address Them

Students' view of war as an adventure-filled romance will be challenged. They may have difficulty understanding that the small, personal impacts of war can be far more significant than the conflicts on the battlefield. Teachers should encourage students to think about how major events in their lives—such as death, serious illness, the breakup of a family, or losing a boyfriend or girlfriend—affect all aspects of their lives, often in small ways that do not become evident for a long time. Students should come to realize that all of a person's experiences have the potential to influence every subsequent event in that person's life.

While not an overriding theme, sexuality is a significant topic in driving the plot. Although high school students might seem to be obsessed with sexuality, they are not, for the most part, experienced in dealing with it on an academic level in the classroom. That Sam and boyfriend Lonnie are sexually active is alluded to in a matter-of-fact way. Dawn's pregnancy is used largely as a metaphor for getting stuck in the small-town cycle. The situation dealing with sex that is most significant and that should be addressed is Sam's evening with Tom. She goes home with him following a dance in honor of the Vietnam veterans. They attempt to have sex but ultimately Tom is unable. Tom is another casualty of war, his impotence a result of the fact that his mind "takes me where I don't want to go." This can be discussed in a clinical manner and as an example of the unseen implications of the war.

Sam's and Emmett's recreational use of marijuana may be focused on by students. It is, however, presented almost as an afterthought in the context of the novel. It is significant in that it bridges the generations, with both characters lost in a world of meaninglessness and dead ends. It is simply another example of Emmett's dulling his senses and of Sam's going through the motions of a life she desperately wants to understand.

The novel contains much language that some may find offensive. While there is little language that high school students have not heard and likely used, teachers should point out that the vocabulary of a novel must be consistent with the language of the time period, characters, and setting of the novel.

References

Her native Kentucky is frequently the setting for the novels and short stories of Bobbie Ann Mason, who was born in 1940 and educated at the University of Kentucky in Lexington. Her work began appearing frequently in *The New Yorker* in 1980. A short story collection, *Shiloh and Other Stories,* won the Hemingway Award in 1983. Along with such authors as Alice Hoffman, Anne Tyler, and Anna Quindlen, Bobbie Ann Mason is part of a generation of contemporary female authors who individually and collectively provide a powerful body of work of interest to adolescents and adults. A well-received first novel, *In Country* was praised upon its release along with its author:

> Miss Mason has not only mastered the way teenagers talk—their speech filled with allusions to television and rock-and-roll, non sequiturs and

> sarcastic comebacks—but she has also understood and captured the ambivalence of youth: a young woman's craving for both knowledge and pristine innocence, her need to be both idealistic and cool. In doing so, Miss Mason has written a novel that, like a flashbulb, burns an afterimage in our minds. (Kakutani C20)

Wendy Smith praised Mason's characterization:

> While *In Country* provides a rich character study in a style accessible and relevant to a wide audience, it does so using subject matter that is controversial and of high interest: Mason's sensitive, profound understanding of character and place, her clear-sighted yet compassionate examination of the most divisive issue in recent American history, seem to strike a deeply sympathetic chord in almost everyone. (425)

Alternative Work

Palmer, Laura. *Shrapnel in the Heart: Letters and Remembrances from the Vietnam Veterans Memorial.* New York: Random House, 1987. This is a collection of letters and poems left at the Veterans Memorial by loved ones of those who died in Vietnam.

Related Works

Mason, Bobbie Ann. *Shiloh and Other Stories.* Lexington: UP of Kentucky, 1995. The first collection of stories by the author of *In Country.*

Books about Vietnam

Greene, Bob. *Homecoming: When the Soldiers Returned from Vietnam.* New York: Putnam, 1989. The syndicated columnist presents a collection of actual letters from veterans describing their treatment upon returning home from Vietnam.

Karnow, Stanley. *Vietnam: A History.* New York: Viking, 1983. Written to accompany the PBS series, this is a comprehensive account of the conflict.

Kovic, Ron. *Born on the Fourth of July.* New York: McGraw-Hill, 1976. This is a powerful autobiography of a paralyzed veteran.

O'Brien, Tim. *The Things They Carried.* Boston: Houghton, 1990. A collection of interconnected stories that mesh to read as both a novel and a work of nonfiction about a platoon of soldiers in Vietnam.

Contemporary novels with strong female characters

Berg, Elizabeth. *Durable Goods,* New York: Random House, 1993; and *Joy School,* New York: Random House, 1997. These novels chronicle the turbulent adolescence of "army brat" Katie struggling to cope with the death of her mother and first love.

McMurtry, Larry. *Some Can Whistle.* New York: Simon, 1989. Writer Danny Deck has his life changed by T. R., the daughter he has never known.

Works Cited

Kakutani, Michiko. "Books of the Times." *The New York Times* 4 September 1985: C20.

Smith, Wendy. "PW Interviews." *Publishers Weekly* 30 August 1985: 425.

About Lou Orfanella

Lou Orfanella teaches English at Valhalla Middle School, writing and poetry at Western Connecticut State University, and communications at Dutchess Community College. His work has appeared in numerous magazines, journals, and newspapers, including *The New York Daily News, Teacher Magazine, English Journal, New York Teacher, The Humanist, Statement, College Bound, Wordwrights!, Discoveries, Remember, Inland, Baby Boomer,* and *World Hunger Year Magazine.*

OUT OF CONTROL

by Norma Fox Mazer

At home, she tacks Kara's letter on her bulletin board to remind her that nothing in life is simple. She puts it up next to the operative words from Janice's horoscope, which are pinned above a scrap of paper on which she has written in black Magic Marker, REFUSE TO BE ERASED. Slogans, admonitions, but they're helpful: they remind her of things, they tell her what she needs to remember.

"You know," Helen Moore says to Valerie the next day at lunch, "I've been thinking. You were really brave to tell as many people as you did what happened to you. I didn't want anyone to know."

Valerie laughs. "I was not brave. I was mad!" Then her nose feels hot and her forehead burns, and she realizes that since it happened, since the first moments of anguish and anger, she has not allowed herself to be that mad again. She has hated and feared and shuddered and shivered, but she has not been plain out-and-out burning mad. Mad that this could happen to her. Mad that the boys went after her as if she were game in a field and they were hunting dogs. Mad that everybody knows and nobody raised a fuss. Mad that Mr. Ferranto wants her out of the school. *Mad, mad, mad.* Mad enough to do something.

That weekend she writes a letter. She isn't sure who's going to receive it. Maybe the newspaper. Maybe the local TV station. She means to write the letter without undue emotion, to simply make clear what happened to her that day, and what has and has not happened since then. (211–212)

Mazer, Norma Fox. *Out of Control.* New York: Avon Books, 1993.

Intended Audience

Students in grades 10–12. This novel would be an excellent introductory text for the issue of gender. It could be the springboard from which the teacher of English language arts, psychology, social studies, or social issues could begin discussion regarding gender issues (similarities and differences) of the older adolescent in and out of school. Although the text addresses harassment, there are other significant issues raised within the text regarding ramifications of the act(s) of harassment and how the characters deal with the issues.

Summary

Three boys, Brig, Candy, and Rollo (friends since grade school), taunt and terrorize a shy, artistic young woman in high school. During a class assembly, the boys stalk and physically attack Valerie on the nearly deserted third floor. Valerie doesn't quite know how to handle this situation. She reports the incident to the administration, but the administration prefers to "soften" the issue to avoid ugly media attention. The boys are suspended for two weeks until things cool down. Valerie no longer feels safe anywhere. She is, literally, out of control. Rollo went along with his friends (because that's what he does) but feels badly about his participation. Things just got out of control. He approaches Valerie and talks to her about it. He can't understand why she feels the way she does. He doesn't have a clue. There is, however, talk around school about "third-floor things." Other girls approach Valerie during lunch and talk about similar events happening to them. A touch, a feel, a sexual innuendo are accepted practices around school and in social situations. The girls feel disenfranchised and powerless. This problem has never been openly addressed by anyone. Valerie decides to write a letter to the editor of the local newspaper, hoping that this issue will be addressed by the school personnel and the community. This letter might bring the issue of sexual harassment to the forefront to make the school and community a safer place for all individuals. She tells Rollo what she is going to do because she feels that he is different, and she wants him to know that his life is going to change. The school and community will know what has happened and become involved and aware.

Relationship of *Out of Control* to the Program

At the secondary level, gender issues need to be discussed in a mixed class where young women and young men can voice their thoughts and concerns about how the "opposite sex" feels and thinks. *Out of Control* offers an opening for such discussion and exchange of attitudes, ideas, concerns, and feelings.

Granted, Peggy Orenstein in *Schoolgirls: Young Women, Self-Esteem, and the Confidence Gap* identifies stereotypes of maleness and femaleness being evident as early as the sixth grade, but students at this age are not experienced enough to diagnose reasons and events of gender differences. Therefore, having texts available to readers of all ages with strong, independent, caring male and female protagonists is important. Frank discussion of *Out of Control* and the issues the novel raises would be appropriate for students who are approximately the same age as the characters. Developmental psychologists suggest that students at this age seek literature that lets them explore the sociological and psychological struggles of characters in situations that may soon be theirs as emerging adults. If approached seriously and genuinely, students can and will become involved at a personal level and begin to listen openly to members of each gender. Dialogue just might begin to lead to more understanding and less miscommunication between genders.

A variety of articles, nonfiction texts, and guest speakers could be introduced before students read the text. After students complete the novel, students could choose individual selections from a list of related texts as an extended focus on the topic for purposes of discussion, role-playing, I-Search papers, creative writing, and/or artistic interpretations.

Because of the relevance of, and inherent interest in, the topic of relationships in general and gender issues in particular, this novel offers a plethora of opportunities to enhance critical thinking through discussion, debate, and listening. It also will enhance problem-solving and decision-making strategies. Most important, it will help develop an open, genuine, and sincere understanding and acceptance of gender differences and similarities.

Impact of the Material on Readers

Young people are often confused by what they see going on around them and what they believe to be just or unjust. Sometimes in order to be accepted into a particular group, students forsake (and then rationalize) what they know to be right and wrong. Students at the secondary level are observant, and they mimic the adult world. They observe the interactions of males and females as rendered through the media, but they rarely have the opportunity to scrutinize how the opposite sex feels or thinks about these modeled interactions. Reading *Out of Control* enables students to address gender issues because the text is offered from both Valerie's and Rollo's point of view. Mazer's characters wrestle with issues relevant to today's teens. She does not sensationalize or graphically describe the actual attack. Valerie is not raped, but her personal space is invaded, unwanted touching occurs, and attempts to cover up the situation make the victim feel insecure, vulnerable, and somehow responsible. Yet no one seems to care. The implicit message is this: If it isn't discussed, perhaps it will go away. Actions, reactions, and consequences are presented realistically by the author through Valerie, Rollo, and the people with whom they associate daily. Mazer's *Out of Control* also affords the opportunity for young people to examine mythic conceptions concerning gender-specific needs, thoughts, and feelings.

Orenstein describes an activity that a teacher uses in a middle school class to introduce what she calls the "gender journey." Students are asked to close their eyes and go back in age and grades as far as they can. Once students have envisioned their childhood, the teacher asks the students to begin the same journey back to the present as a member of the opposite sex. Students are then asked to list everything that would be different as a member of the opposite sex. Lists are shared and written on the board. Of this activity, Orenstein states, "Almost all of the boys' observations about gender swapping involve disparaging 'have to's, whereas the girls seem wistful with longing. It is clear that both boys and girls have learned to equate maleness with opportunity and femininity with constraint" (xvi). *Out of Control* portrays this situation dramatically. For example, Valerie asks Rollo what he would do if he was in her place:

> "What if guys attacked you?"
>
> "What?" He almost wants to laugh. What does this mean? Attacked him, like it happened to her? It wouldn't. It couldn't. "I'd fight them off."
>
> "What if there were too many of them?"
>
> "I don't know. . . . I'd get out of it."
>
> "How? What if they were doing stuff to you and there was nothing you could do about it?"
>
> "I'm too big. They don't mess with me."
>
> What does she want him to say? (179)

Valerie questions him further, making it more difficult for Rollo to get out of the situation:

> He doesn't want to answer. He doesn't want to think about being helpless, but she's forcing him to think about it. Forcing him to think about

> how humiliated he'd be, how his cheeks would burn and his heart pound a mile a minute. (180)

Rollo says he would beat them up—he would kill them. He becomes totally defensive and frustrated with this "what-if" scenario. He doesn't have a clue.

Potential Problems with *Out of Control* and Ways to Address Them

The major problem is with the term *sexual harassment.* Discussing the issue in school may be frowned upon by the community or parents. Parents and caregivers must be notified of this project, informed of the focus content, and invited to read the text(s) with their children. Parents, if informed, are usually supportive when teachers deal with controversial issues that will ultimately help adolescents confront their social world. If they trust the teacher to teach realistic novels in a mature fashion, there should be no major problem. For this reason, the text should not be introduced below the tenth grade. It is at this age when students begin to establish personal and societal values. Although there may be initial concern about how the harassment is portrayed, the attack is not graphically described. In fact, the readers will need to use their imaginations concerning the actual abuse. It's not the attack that's the major focus; rather, the focus is on the actions and reactions of the male and female characters, the school community, and the community at large. Mazer just tells the story—she leaves the readers to make decisions. This is not a problem if the text is used with the appropriate age.

References

In her novels, Norma Fox Mazer, author of the Newbery Honor Book *After the Rain*, offers the older adolescent reader a variety of topics for consideration. Her novels are consistently recognized as outstanding literature by the ALA, *Kirkus Reviews*, and *VOYA*. Her texts deal with issues important to young adults: family unity, divorce, family illness, relationships, sibling and parental abuse. She does not sensationalize controversial issues. As an author, she does not become involved. She involves her characters in situations—none of which are isolated. The readers become decision makers and problem solvers. In her texts, all actions of her characters cause reactions, and all character actions affect other people. None of her stories take place in a vacuum. Not all of her stories end "happily ever after" but rather end realistically—usually with hope for the protagonists' future beyond the scope of time in the novel.

Reviewers of *Out of Control* say:

> Mazer deals directly and realistically with the complexities of sexual harassment. That two of the boys feel no remorse and that the boys are punished so lightly for a sexually motivated physical attack on a girl doesn't seem far-fetched given today's headlines. Valerie comes through the ordeal courageously, and Rollo finds the strength to reach for redemption and turn his back on the "friends" he accompanied to the third floor. (DelNegro 1804)

> The third-person narration alternates between Rollo's and Valerie's point of view as Rollo attempts to understand the situation and Valerie tries to come to terms with her post-assault fear and anger. The characterizations and plot are full of interesting ambiguities, with school honor, romantic disillusionment, class hatred, and family dynamics all playing strong parts in the story. (Stevenson 259)

The *Kirkus* reviewer praises Mazer's handling of the topic:

> Accessible, but far from simplistic, Mazer's balanced depiction of both sides is a powerful demonstration of the evils of harassment and how its victims can assert themselves; it may even help harassers see the other side. (376)

Alternative Work

Pitts, Paul. *For a Good Time, Don't Call Claudia.* New York: Avon, 1986. Claudia Baker has been receiving prank calls. She is sure that they are coming from girls at school. She ultimately discovers that her name has been printed on the boys' bathroom wall—*for a good time, call . . .* This was meant to be a practical joke, but the harassing telephone calls proved otherwise. The young man responsible for "this harmless prank" didn't know Claudia when he did it. His explanation was that "no one pays attention to that stuff." This text is age-appropriate for grades 10–12. There are many gender-related issues embedded throughout the novel.

Although many of the issues are similar to those in *Out of Control*, Pitts' book avoids the explicit sexual implications that Mazer includes. There is no physical contact. In addition, people who would object to Mazer's portrayals of adult authority figures would find little to question regarding the adults in Pitts' novel.

Related Works

Fiction related to gender issues

Cole, Brock. *The Goats.* New York: Farrar, 1987. Two young people are stranded on Goat's Island overnight. Both are stripped nude and left to tend for themselves. Howie is left by the boy's camp pranksters, and Laura is stranded by her girl's camp pranksters. Howie is small for his age and Laura just doesn't fit in to camp society. Although these characters are both thirteen, secondary readers will garner insight through retrospect. Howie and Laura were harassed because they didn't fit the summer camp stereotype.

Crutcher, Chris. *Ironman.* New York: William Morrow, 1995. Bo Brewster is placed in an Anger Management Class instead of being expelled from school because he stood up to the English teacher/football coach when verbally harassed in class. The group is composed of students from various "groups" in school. Students in this class listen to each other and come to understand that each is a human being with specific needs to belong, be appreciated, and be accepted on their own terms. This is a subplot of the novel, but serious adolescent concerns are discussed in an open forum. This novel also addresses the pressures (imagined and real) placed on males by society.

Lynch, Chris. *Blue-Eyed Son #1,* New York: HarperCollins, 1996; *Blood Relations: Blue-Eyed Son #2,* New York: HarperCollins, 1996; *Dog Eat Dog: Blue-Eyed Son #3,* New York: HarperCollins, 1996. This trilogy presents a once ethnically tight New England community and shows how population changes cause Mick's brothers and friends to physically abuse and harass those not like them. Mick doesn't understand why everyone is so angry and hateful because people of other cultures are living among them. This trilogy contains graphic and often violent scenes depicting the extent of harassment and physical abuse that "hatemongers" will resort to. Lynch accentuates his thematic focus appropriately and realistically.

Turk, Ruth. *15 is the Pits.* New York: New Win, 1993. Jennifer is being "pressured" to become sexually involved in order to be accepted by her chosen peer group. She has to sort out just what is and is not important.

Voigt, Cynthia. *When She Hollers.* New York: Scholastic, 1994. This novel covers a day in the life of Tish, who has been verbally harassed and sexually abused by her stepfather since early puberty. This is the day she's not going to take it anymore. She would rather die. She is befriended by a friend's father who is a lawyer. He is the first adult who listened to her and helped her. Voigt's novel is controversial and powerful. Like *Out of Control*, it addresses the issues of the lack of control and power that females often experience.

Nonfiction related to gender issues

Gay, Kathlyn. *Rights and Respect: What You Need to Know About Gender Bias and Sexual Harassment.* Brooklyn: Millbrook, 1995.

Marrewa, Al. *The Feminine Warrior: A Women's Guide to Verbal, Psychological, and Physical Empowerment.* New York: Kensington, 1998.

Shoop, Robert J., and Debra L. Edwards. *How to Stop Sexual Harassment in Our Schools: A Handbook and Curriculum Guide for Administrators and Teachers.* New York: Allyn, 1994.

Strauss, Susan, and Pamela Espelund. *Sexual Harassment and Teens: A Program for Positive Change.* Minneapolis: Free Spirit, 1992.

Annotated bibliography

Stitt, Beverly A. *Gender Equity in Education: An Annotated Bibliography.* Carbondale and Edwardsville: Southern Illinois UP, 1994. This annotated bibliography contains reviews of articles, curriculum guides, books, workshop guides, videos, and classroom activities. Pertinent annotations span a period of twenty-five years, which might promote some historical considerations. The object of the text is to provide specific resources for administrators, teachers, and counselors in their attempts to address and begin to overcome gender role stereotyping and sex bias in schools.

Works Cited

DelNegro, Janice. Rev. of *Out of Control,* by Norma Fox Mazer. *Booklist* June 1993: 1804.

Orenstein, Peggy. *Schoolgirls: Young Women, Self-Esteem, and the Confidence Gap.* New York: Doubleday, 1994.

Rev. of *Out of Control,* by Norma Fox Mazer. *Kirkus Reviews* 15 Mar. 1993: 376.

Stevenson, Deborah. Rev. of *Out of Control,* by Norma Fox Mazer. *The Bulletin of the Center for Children's Books* 46.8 (1993): 259.

About Linda Broughton

Linda Broughton recently received a Ph.D. from Florida State University. For twenty-five years she taught English language arts in grades 8–12. She is presently an assistant professor at the University of South Alabama in Mobile in Curriculum and Instruction/English Education. She teaches graduate and undergraduate courses in young adult literature; methods for language subjects at the secondary level; and critical reading and writing practices, methods and strategies. She began to read young adult literature twelve years ago and doesn't plan to stop anytime soon.

SHIZUKO'S DAUGHTER

by Kyoko Mori

She signed the note and took out another sheet of paper. She knew what she wanted to tell Yuki. *In spite of this,* she wrote, *please believe that I love you. People will tell you that I've done this because I did not love you. Don't listen to them. When you grow up to be a strong woman, you will know that this was for the best. My only concern now is that you will be the first to find me. I'm sorry. Call your father at work and let him take care of everything.* Shizuko stopped to read over what she had written. This is the best I can do for her, she thought, to leave her and save her from my unhappiness, from growing up to be like me. Yuki had so much to look forward to. At twelve, she was easily the brightest in her class; all her teachers said so. The art teacher had been particularly impressed by her watercolors. They reflected, he said, her bold intelligence and imagination as well as her skills. *You are a strong person,* Shizuko continued. *You will no doubt get over this and be a brilliant woman. Don't let me stop or delay you. I love you.* As she signed the note, Shizuko pictured Yuki running to her in her new skirt, the white cotton and the maroon trimmings fluttering in the spring breeze like the sail of a new ship. Only, I won't be there to catch you, she thought, but you will do fine by yourself. You will be all right. (6)

Mori, Kyoko. *Shizuko's Daughter.* New York:
Henry Holt and Company, 1993.

Intended Audience

Students in grades 8–12. This work of fiction is appropriate for mature students in grade 8 and all high school students. It fits a variety of thematic units frequently taught in English language arts classes, especially courses focusing on women authors. It could be used as part of a study of genres of literature, in survey classes of twentieth-century American literature, or in world literature classes.

Summary

This fictional work, Kyoko Mori's first novel, is set in modern Japan, primarily in Kobe. The story, based on Mori's life, focuses on Yuki's struggle to deal with the loss of her beloved mother, with her father's emotional distance, and with a rigid and uncaring stepmother. When Yuki is twelve years old, her mother, who feels she cannot live any longer with her husband's unfaithfulness, commits suicide. Yuki feels like an outsider in her home; at school she is separated from peers by her family situation, her intelligence, her athletic skill and academic ability, and her independence. Her grandparents love her, but her father will not permit her to live with them. She is, however, strengthened by her visits with them and by her memories of times when she and her mother enjoyed the beauty of nature and art. Six years after her mother's death, Yuki leaves home to attend college in Nagasaki. As she turns her beautiful memories into art and comes to terms with her mother's death, she becomes the strong woman her mother knew she could be.

Relationship of *Shizuko's Daughter* to the Program

Whether *Shizuko's Daughter* is used for whole-class reading, in literature study groups, or as an individual reading choice, it meets a variety of curricular objectives. In national and state guidelines addressing what students should know and be able to do, multiple standards point to the need for students to read often; to read a variety of texts, including contemporary literature; and to use appropriate strategies for comprehending and evaluating the works they read. It is important that students read for a variety of purposes, including to learn about themselves, their own cultures, and the lives of others. Numerous curricular guides and standards documents also point to the need for students to engage in a variety of activities in which they must use the critical thinking skills necessary to recognize an author's point of view, purpose, and cultural context and to appreciate the artistry of a writer's choices in selecting the particular details and word arrangements that tell the story or convey an idea. While all of these guidelines can be addressed with this unique and powerful coming-of-age story, the primary focus of this rationale is that students who read *Shizuko's Daughter* have the opportunity to see themselves in literature and gain new insights into the lives of others set in a specific cultural context.

The uniqueness and artistry of Mori's contemporary work, a story set in Japan and told in beautiful language from a young person's point of view, is reflected in the words of Michael Cart. He said that reading *Shizuko's Daughter* allowed him to empathetically and intellectually comprehend the lives of the characters and gain an understanding about adolescent life in Japan in a more powerful way than would be possible from reading nonfiction works (133). Young people grow in knowledge of themselves and others when they read about those whose lives are different, yet who experience the same feelings and concerns. This "opportunity and ability to see how others experience life is especially important for young adults who are in the process of becoming independent participants in a world much larger than their own school and community" (Zitlow and Stover 8).

Mori's work is written with such careful word choice that readers feel Yuki's pain and understand how her loneliness makes her feel like an outsider. Kyoko Mori has said she thinks being an outsider is a universal theme of young adult life and literature, yet her literary works are intensely personal accounts of her own experiences. *Shizuko's Daughter* shows how literature written with such artistry can tell one person's story and yet also represent and illuminate the experiences of many others.

Shizuko's Daughter is a well-told story filled with the images and colors of Japan. This exemplary work of fiction helps readers understand a particular cultural context by showing the circumstances of an individual's life and aspects about the country of her birth. In an interview published in the Summer 1998 *Ohio Journal of the English Language Arts*, Mori talked about how she carefully chose the specific words for chapter titles "to reflect the overall images" in each chapter. Because specific colors are right for certain circumstances and times of life in Japan, she included the details about color, something that is very symbolic in Japan (Zitlow and Sanders 41).

Although the book is informative, Kyoko Mori has said it was not written to be representative of all Japanese or Japanese Americans or all Asian Americans; nor was it written with a predefined purpose to teach a specific lesson or recommend a certain moral truth. Yet readers do learn, becoming a part of Yuki's search for answers to the universal questions asked by youth: "Who am I?" or "What is the meaning of life?" and "Where is my place in the world?" Readers learn about the similarities of the questions and concerns of another youth and the unique role played by one particular cultural heritage. As readers imaginatively enter Yuki's world, one that may be very different from their own yet surprisingly similar, they can compare and contrast her experiences, feelings, and reactions with their own and those of their peers. In addition, when they write about and discuss their interpretations with others, they have the opportunity to expand their initial response and increase their knowledge of other people, of other places, and of themselves. They can explore a number of possible themes: identity, independence, dealing with death, relationships with parents, loneliness, and cultural expectations. In addition, the work shows the power of art and is a fine example of a story about a strong female protagonist, a contemporary teen in a diverse setting.

Teachers can suggest prompts to guide students' written responses in literature logs and pose questions to encourage meaningful discussion in small-group formats. Students can also record the key passages that strike them as they read, putting the quote and page number on one side of an index card and the significance of the passage on the other side. It will help readers to understand Yuki if they note the many ways she feels like an outsider and the examples of the strength she derives from remembering what her mother had taught her.

Another book about an independent, determined youth, the autobiographical novel *The Ink-Keeper's Apprentice* written by Allen Say, would work well paired with *Shizuko's Daughter.* Say's book is set in Tokyo, where Say learned to draw while serving as an apprentice to a great teacher and famous cartoonist. Although the events of the stories are very different, readers might compare the protagonists' relationships with their parents, the role of art in their lives, and the reactions to cultural expectations of the two authors, both of whom lived in Japan until they came to the United States as young adults.

Impact of the Material on Readers

The impact of the beautiful images evoked by Kyoko Mori's careful choice of words leaves a strong impression on readers, who can picture the colorful flowers Yuki and her mother had enjoyed and also the beautiful shapes of pottery where no two pieces are exactly the same. The vivid colors associated with her mother contrast sharply with the drab, stark life Yuki experiences with her cold father and rigid stepmother. Readers note how even the chapter titles are an integral part of the story as they reflect Yuki's sense of loss and the intensity of her struggle with the difficult process of accepting change.

When readers become aware of Yuki's ability to see eloquence and beauty in her daily life in spite of the difficult situations she faces, they have a way to deal with disturbing scenes and events in the story. They see how her awareness of beauty and her ability to express her feelings through her art lead to her healing and growth as a strong individual.

Potential Problems with *Shizuko's Daughter* and Ways to Address Them

The problems that students might have with this novel are related to problems that potential challengers would have, namely a death caused by suicide and a youth questioning a parent's decisions. Some readers will need to be prepared for disturbing scenes in the story. It is painful to realize that Yuki is the one who found her mother. Teachers need to help students understand Yuki's reactions to her grief, such as hiding in the closet during the funeral and using an outspoken manner with her loving aunt and grandmother.

Readers must also consider what Yuki has experienced when she decides to leave for college without saying goodbye to her father. Her way of leaving is not out of lack of respect but a result of how isolated her life had been. It is also an example of her courage and developing autonomy. Although it is very disturbing that, after she leaves, her father burns the content of the boxes with her mother's things, readers know that Yuki has found, through her art, other ways to remember who her mother was and what she hoped Yuki would become.

The occurrence of death, particularly suicide, can be problematic for some readers or their parents who do not understand how important it is for young people to have the opportunity to think about the experiences others have with life's realities and the potential and resilience of the human spirit. Guidance from the teacher might be needed to clarify misunderstandings about Shizuko's belief that her beloved daughter would have a better life without her. Class discussion should include exploration of cultural expectations, the similarities and differences of Japanese customs to those in other cultures, and also consideration of changing traditions.

For readers or parents who think the portrayal of the father is too negative, it should be noted that there are other loving male characters in the book, such as the grandfather and Yuki's male friend. Again, it is important to point out that this book is one person's story, not written as a description of all teens in Japan, nor of all stepmothers or fathers. Portions or all of Mori's nonfictional work, *Dream of Water: A Memoir*, can be read by either the teacher or interested students who would like to compare

Mori's memories of specific events in her life to her fictional account. *Dream of Water* and her collection of essays, *Polite Lies*, can be used to supplement discussion about the role of each person's unique experiences and issues of various cultural expectations.

Teachers must be sensitive to the potential difficulty of reading this book for students who have recently lost a parent or who live in an especially oppressive situation. Yet with support, these readers might find it is helpful to read about the strength and resilience of another youth in a difficult situation. Poems chosen from her collection *Fallout*, particularly "To My Ancestral Spirits" and "Messages For My Mother," work well with the novel because they show how Mori makes use of her legacy in her literary works of art.

Shizuko's Daughter, with its snapshots of specific details that become universal, is a literary work of great merit, a book full of haunting, moving images and colors. Its merit was noted by the American Library Association that named it, and also Mori's work *One Bird*, among the ALA Best Books for Young Adults. The beauty in Mori's fictional works, in both their writing and their thematic possibilities, must not be overshadowed by the difficulties various characters experience.

References

Kyoko Mori, who came to the United States in 1977 to study, grew up in a highly Westernized Japanese family. She has returned to Japan for visits but now lives in the United States, where she is an associate professor of English and Creative Writing at Saint Norbert College in DePere, Wisconsin. Her interest in the theme of feeling like an outsider is influenced by her experiences in both cultures. In her work she expresses her desire to claim the unfamiliar landscape of the American Midwest by making internal connections:

> Though I am an outsider in both the landscape in the Midwest and the remembered landscape of Japan, I want to bring them together to create an emotional landscape that is mine. The balance between belonging and not belonging is what I need to write with. I hope there is a metaphor for what I see as the essence of being an outsider as a teenager and as an expatriate. (qtd. in Cart, 134)

She is interested in writing about something she knows but does not completely understand, and the choices she makes as a writer are influenced by aesthetics and by the legacy of her mother, who taught her to appreciate and express a love of beauty and, through her art, to find a home.

Shizuko's Daughter began as a short fictional work, which was published in the literary magazine *The Kenyon Review*. In writing about the book, Michael Cart says Mori's work is one of the best titles in a series of new works by strong writers with something original to say:

> If Mori's theme in her first novel is universal, her treatment of her material is intensely personal and helps the reader to empathetically comprehend the emotional lives of the modern Japanese. Of perhaps greater importance to me as a reader is the fact that Mori made it possible for me to intellectually comprehend the lives of her characters; she took me not only into their hearts but into their minds as well, making it possible for me to understand how different the mind-sets and thought process of nonwestern people can be from our familiar American ones. Mori's wonderfully thought-provoking book gave me, thus, a much more powerful and memorable experience than the reading of half a dozen nonfiction books about adolescent life in Japan could have given. (133–134)

Alternative Work

Mori's fictional work *One Bird* is a book that can be used as an alternative to *Shizuko's Daughter*. In it, the mother of fifteen-year-old Megumi feels she must leave, but she does not die. In *One Bird*, as in *Shizuko's Daughter*, Mori explores the mother-daughter relationship, the desire of a female protagonist to be different and yet still belong, her difficulty in accepting cultural restraints and expectations, and her search for life's meaning. This book, filled with beautiful imagery, is another gripping, poetic, well-told coming-of-age story set in Japan.

Related Works

According to the themes chosen for further exploration by readers or teachers, a variety of young adult works can be paired with, or read in place of, Mori's work. Many young adult works include multiple thematic connections to *Shizuko's Daughter*. For example, Bruce Brooks' *Midnight Hour Encores* (New York: Harper, 1986) and Brock Cole's *Celine* (New York: Farrar, 1989) include strong female protagonists whose art is an important part of their lives and who grow up missing a parent who chooses to live elsewhere. In Trudy Krisher's *Spite Fences* (New York: Delacorte, 1994), Maggie Pugh questions the racist beliefs of her abusive mother and, with the help of her camera, develops her own perspective of her Southern community. A noteworthy example of another story about a strong female protagonist who has difficulty accepting cultural expectations is Suzanne Fisher Staples' work set in contemporary Pakistan, *Shabanu: Daughter of the Wind* (New York: Knopf, 1989). Two works of historical fiction in which young women must deal with the death of a parent are Katherine Paterson's *Lyddie* (New York: Lodestar, 1991), set in nineteenth-century New England, and Katherine Lasky's *Beyond the Divide* (New York: Macmillan, 1983), in which Meribah must survive the death of her Amish father as they travel west. In addition there are collections of short stories, such as *An Island Like You* (New York: Orchard, 1995) by Judith Ortiz Cofer, that would enhance discussion about young people growing up in diverse settings.

Works Cited

Cart, Michael. *From Romance to Realism: 50 Years of Growth and Change in Young Adult Literature.* New York: HarperCollins, 1996.

Zitlow, Connie S., and Tobie Sanders. "Balance, Beauty, and Being an Outsider: An Interview with Kyoko Mori." *Ohio Journal of the English Language Arts* (Summer 1998): 38–42.

Zitlow, Connie S., and Lois Stover. "Japanese and Japanese American Youth in Literature." *The ALAN Review* 26.3 (1998): 7–17.

About Connie S. Zitlow

Connie S. Zitlow is an associate professor at Ohio Wesleyan University, where she teaches reading and methods courses and directs the secondary education program. Young adult literature is an important part of her teaching, presentations, and publications, which include pieces in the *Adolescent Literature as a Complement to the Classics* series and in *The ALAN Review.* She is the coeditor of the *Ohio Journal of the English Language Arts*; has served on the Board of the Assembly on Literature for Adolescents, National Council of Teachers of English (ALAN); and is the 1999–2000 President of ALAN.

FALLEN ANGELS

by Walter Dean Myers

It took me three tries to get the letter even close to something worth saying, and then it was nothing special. In a way I felt real bad just being alive to write it. I could think of her wondering why I didn't do something, why I didn't save him.

Dear Mrs. Carroll,

My name is Richard Perry, and I had the good fortune to serve under your husband. Last night, we ran into heavy fighting in an area we've been trying to protect for some time. Lieutenant Carroll was in the process of getting us out of there safely despite the fact that we had run into more of the enemy than we had expected to, when he was wounded. The medevac choppers got him down to Chu Lai, to the medical unit there, and they tried their best to save him, but could not.

Mrs. Carroll, I know that it is not much comfort to you that your husband died bravely, or honorably, but he did. All of the guys in the squad who served under him are grateful for his leadership and for having known him.

I am sorry to have to write to you under these circumstances.

Yours,

Richard Perry

I read the letter to Peewee and Walowick and they said it was okay. Then I gave it to Sergeant Simpson to take to HQ.

I thought about Mama getting a letter about me. What would she do with it? Would she put it in the drawer she kept Daddy's papers in? Would she sit on her bed in the middle of the night and take it from the drawer to read like she did his stuff? I wondered how Kenny would feel? (130–131)

Myers, Walter Dean. *Fallen Angels.* New York: Scholastic, 1988.

Intended Audience

Fallen Angels is written on a sixth- or seventh-grade reading level; however, the content is appropriate for high school students. The novel can fulfill core reading requirements in an American literature course, a course that focuses on black American authors, or an American history course.

Summary

This coming-of-age novel is about two young soldiers, Richard Perry and Peewee Gates, fighting on the front lines of the Vietnam War. Perry and Peewee, two eighteen-year-old boys from Chicago and New York City, face profound fear and distrust as they carry out their call to duty—to protect and obey their country.

Richard Perry chronicles their war experiences, complete with the inequity of discrimination between the black and white soldiers; the power struggle of the enlisted men versus the officers; and the unanswered questions of the United States' involvement in the war. This historical novel shows the horrific killing of Vietnamese women and children, the brutal massacre of young men killed by the unknown enemy, and the sad reality of "friendly fire" (the accidental killing of our own men). In order to survive, Perry and Peewee learn to live in constant suspicion of what they see and hear.

Relationship of *Fallen Angels* to the Program

Fallen Angels shows students the true horrors of war and brings them to the front lines of battle, not of flag raising and honor, but of death and destruction. Students are intrigued about a part of their history that *Fallen Angels* explores, and they appreciate Myers' frank portrayal of the characters' language and thought. They recognize fear and explore their own history, gaining insight into racism at home and in Vietnam, through a close relationship with Richard Perry, the main character. The novel, through its language and action, encourages students to question what is reported and demands that students think critically.

We teach *Fallen Angels* to high school students to meet four objectives:

1. to help students transact with the authentic story and language of the time period
2. to encourage students to interact with the text by composing pieces of their own
3. to satisfy our cross-curricular goals of having students read about historical events
4. to connect students' own lives and their parents' experiences with the literature

Students are often hungry for information about the Vietnam War, the war of their parents, but often know few facts about American involvement and ultimate decimation. By examining multiple perspectives on the subject of Vietnam, students learn to be critical readers and careful consumers of information throughout their lives. Firsthand experiences and third-person accounts about Vietnam through print, film, music, and guest speakers are essential for students to understand the Vietnam Era. When the students read the final lines of the novel, they reflect on this question: Why were we in Vietnam?

Fallen Angels is the one novel that students of all levels read and remember because it does what teachers hope good literature will do: it bridges all of our lives with the text. The connections that the story builds, however, are just the tip of the iceberg. Drawing on the interest the novel creates in high school classrooms, literature circles that use Vietnam-related books are a natural follow-up activity. Sarah Owens writes that using literature circles "promotes a love for literature and positive attitudes toward reading and invites natural discussions that lead to student inquiry and critical thinking" (3). Students' curiosity about the Vietnam Era often sends them to their parents for book titles for their literature circles and information about the war. This leads to a natural discussion about that time period, the war of the students' parents and other relatives.

Fallen Angels may serve as a powerful prompt for a myriad of writings. In particular, students can write a sympathy letter to the loved one of a dead soldier, which places them in Perry's boots. The creator of this compassionate letter must visualize what it would be like for his or her own parents to read this news. Students cannot leave themselves out of this assignment; they must connect the text to their own lives.

Students say that they have never experienced the same level of fear that Richard Perry feels because of his circumstances: war. But they can empathize with him; they too have fears, dreams, hopes, and doubts. They realize that they are not so different from this eighteen-year-old, even though he lived thirty years before them. First-person narration brings them into his thoughts and out onto the battlefield without a moment's notice; the reader and the soldier are serving in wartime together. Myers creates an intimate friendship between Perry and Peewee that students believe because his characters speak as soldiers, profanity and all. "War is hell," Vietnam veterans tell the students; they don't revise their language to pacify pristine ears.

Impact of the Material on Readers

Studying a novel like *Fallen Angels* allows students to view war, its inhumanity, and its effects on their country. Since the novel unfolds intimately, through a soldier's eighteen-year-old eyes, students will think about their own relationships with their mothers, younger siblings, and friends; their individual opportunity to grow up relatively safe and spontaneous; and their world. As the war forces Richard Perry to grow up, he shares his fears, responsibilities, and private moments with students who may have never before contemplated their own life process past adolescence.

Students in our classes have developed an appreciation for their likeness with another culture, and have come to realize that the enemy wasn't much different than they. This is an important realization for students who face hundreds of images daily that casually glorify violence, including war. *Fallen Angels* demystifies the kind of war that World War II veterans eulogize; presents Vietnam as a hot, muggy jungle, instead of an exotic paradise; and contends that differences are just that: differences.

As the soldiers grapple with their own involvement "in country," students will learn to question everything in their own lives. They will read about "incorrect" body counts, boasting American victories, and nonexistent peace talks in the army paper, *Stars and Stripes.* As a result of analyzing the misinformation fed by the United States Government, as portrayed by Myers, students can become careful consumers of information.

Perhaps the most significant impact of *Fallen Angels* is the communication that it generates between children and their families, particularly their fathers. As a follow-up activity, local Vietnam veterans make excellent guest speakers who answer student questions about painful experiences that some fathers evade. One student asked, "What can you do if your father won't talk about his experiences in the war?" The answers to these types of questions can help families uncover and start to heal hidden bruises.

Potential Problems with *Fallen Angels* and Ways to Address Them

Language

Some of the language may offend readers. However, students find that the potentially offensive words in *Fallen Angels* make the novel real. For example, Scotty, a ball player turned soldier, claims, "Yep, we just shot the shit out of the first platoon" (103) after friendly fire from the fourth platoon of the U.S. Army decimates their counterparts in the first platoon. "Oops, we accidentally shot our own men," just would not realistically fit these situations. The characters' circumstances, age, and background, however, explain the otherwise shocking language. Teachers need not read aloud potentially offensive passages, but they can help students understand how authors use authentic language.

Lack of knowledge about the Vietnam War

If students do not read *Fallen Angels* in conjunction with an American history course covering the Vietnam War, they might lack necessary background knowledge. Consequently, students will need an overview of that period in history.

Point of view

Some parents and community members may believe firmly in the rightness of the United States' involvement in Vietnam. Their perspectives should be included in a unit that also includes *Fallen Angels*. Teachers may invite guest speakers or have students read nonfiction such as Barry Denenberg's *Voices of Vietnam* to gain additional insight into attitudes surrounding the United States' involvement in Vietnam.

Lack of women's experience

Richard Perry's mother and Judy Duncan, a nurse, are two minor characters in *Fallen Angels*. This lack of female presence can alienate female students. Teachers can respond to this exclusion by introducing supplemental materials into the course of study (see Related Works).

References

Walter Dean Myers received the 1994 Margaret A. Edwards Award for four of his young adult novels—*Hoops, Motown and Didi, Fallen Angels,* and *Scorpions*—and has written more than forty books for children and young adults. Myers is also a four-time recipient of the Coretta Scott King Award. He often portrays young black characters positively, but he does not overlook or ignore the negative realities of their lives, and the voices in Myers' *Fallen Angels* are much like the voices of our teenage students. Johannessen writes, "Myers skillfully integrates the themes of innocence, courage, initiation, and mortality in this compelling novel. Readers will emerge feeling that they have experienced 'Nam" (44).

Maria B. Salvadore praised the novel in her review for *School Library Journal*: "This is a compelling, graphic, necessarily gruesome, and wholly plausible novel. It neither condemns nor glorifies the war but certainly causes readers to think about the events. Other difficult issues, such as race and the condition of the Vietnamese people, are sensitively and realistically incorporated into the novel. The soldiers' language is raw, but appropriate to the characters. This is a book which should be read by both young adults and adults" (118).

Writing for *The New York Times Book Review*, Mel Watkins also praised the novel as "a candid young adult novel that engages the Vietnam experience squarely. It deals with violence and death as well as compassion and love, with deception and hypocrisy as well as honesty and virtue. It is a tale that is as thought-provoking as it is entertaining, touching, and, on occasion, humorous" (29).

Myers' message to young adults seems to be this: discover your strengths, be proud of who you are, and be responsible for your actions (Dunan and McLean).

Alternative Works

Books about war will contain realistic language. Thus, there is no true alternative work to *Fallen Angels*.

Related Works

Related works can provide additional perspectives and background information to increase students' understanding.

Kovic, Ron. *Born on the Fourth of July*. New York: Pocket, 1976. *Born on the Fourth of July* is the true story of Ron Kovic's journey from a shy teenager to a courageous marine. Paralyzed from the waist down, Ron had to deal with the daily struggles of being handicapped.

Mason, Bobbie Ann. *In Country*. New York: Harper, 1985. *In Country* portrays the journey of Sam Hughes, an adolescent girl whose father was killed in the Vietnam War the same year that she was born. The repercussions of the war and how it affected the family and friends of the soldiers who never returned is depicted in this poignant novel.

O'Brien, Tim. *The Things They Carried*. New York: Penguin, 1990. Tim O'Brien brings readers into the jungles of the Vietnam War and back home to America in his fictional accounts. O'Brien tells the stories of the brave and not-so-brave soldiers where, in several fictional stories, "the angles of vision are skewed" (78).

Santoli, Al. *Everything We Had*. New York: Ballantine, 1981. *Everything We Had* is a compilation of stories written by several soldiers who fought in the Vietnam War. The soldiers tell their true accounts of their Vietnam experiences, which show the true horrors and fears of war.

White, Ellen Emerson. *The Road Home*. New York: Scholastic, 1995. This novel tells about the effects of the war on a young nurse.

Yedinak, Steven. *Hard to Forget*. New York: Ballantine, 1998. Steven Yedinak showed his courage and determination by his relentless pursuit to become a Green Beret during the Vietnam War. *Hard to Forget* chronicles the horrific and bloody battles of the Green Berets.

Works Cited

Dunan, P. and A. McLean. "Now Is Their Time! Adolescents Learn Skills and Values through Walter Dean Myers' Book." Conf. on College Composition and Communication Convention. San Diego. Mar. 1993.

Johannessen, Larry R. "Young Adult Literature and the Vietnam War." *English Journal* 82.5 (1993): 43–49.

Owens, Sarah. "Treasures in the Attic: Building the Foundation for Literature Circles." *Literature Circles and Response*. Ed. Bonnie Campbell Hill, Nancy J. Johnson, and Katherine L. Schlick Noe. Norwood: Christopher-Gordon, 1995: 1–12.

Salvadore, Maria. Rev. of *Fallen Angels*, by Walter Dean Myers. *School Library Journal* 34.9 (1988): 118.

Watkins, Mel. Rev. of *Fallen Angels*, by Walter Dean Myers. *The New York Times Book Review* 22 Jan. 1989, sec 7: 29.

About Jolene Borgese and Susan A. Ebert

Jolene Borgese recently completed her doctoral work at Widener University. As a twenty-year veteran teacher, she has taught grades 6 through 12 in three different school districts. For fifteen years, she was the codirector of the Pennsylvania Writing Project and has been an active member and presenter for NCTE. She is currently an educational consultant.

Susan A. Ebert graduated from the University of New Hampshire and has an M.Ed. from Widener University. She has taught grades 8 through 12 and currently teaches high school English. She taught *Fallen Angels* to sophomores who were above-average readers and writers and to sophomores who were identified as below-average readers and writers.

IF I SHOULD DIE BEFORE I WAKE

by Han Nolan

We had been riding for perhaps an hour and a half—I with my head resting on Bubbe's shoulder—when I felt Bubbe squeeze my hand again. I knew that this time she was signaling not pleasure but danger. I opened my eyes and standing before me was an old schoolmate, Marila Yankowitz, as fat and hairy as ever.

Her eyes widened as I looked up at her. She pointed a stubby finger at me and said in a booming voice, "Yes, I thought so. I know you!" (161)

Nolan, Han. *If I Should Die Before I Wake.* San Diego: Harcourt Brace & Company, 1994.

Intended Audience

Students in grades 7–12. This is an excellent book to be read by a class as a whole, or as one of several selections for individual reading. If the book is read by a full class, it is best to choose it for upper-grade readers with parental permission. And since this book presumes some knowledge of World War II and the Holocaust, teachers would be wise to use this book as supplementary material to underscore their discussion of this incomprehensible event in human history. Books with harsh language, unremitting violence, and realistic despair demand cautionary action and perceptive teaching when using them with young adults.

Summary

Hilary, a high schooler whose mother is an evangelical Christian, is a mixed-up kid, and the crowd she hangs out with are neo-Nazis, tormenting anyone they suspect is Jewish and worshiping openly at the feet of Hitler. This novel, which explores the dynamics of organized bigotry and violence, begins when Hilary and her boyfriend are in a motorcycle accident. She is taken to a hospital, where she lies in a coma, clinging to her young life. The hospital—a Jewish hospital—provides the setting for what becomes Hilary's transformation. As she slips in and out of a coma, Hilary believes she is a younger version of her hospital roommate, Chana, a Jewish woman who grew up in Poland during the rise of the Nazi regime. This inexplicable change—from gentile to Jew, from today to the onset of World War II—makes for a fascinating story about how Jewish families were persecuted at the hands of Hitler's henchmen. Filled with minute-by-minute detail, the book provides the details of young Chana's life in Poland as the Nazis rise to power. We follow Chana and her family's move to the inhumane conditions of a Jewish ghetto and their subsequent transportation to the hell of all hells, the Nazi concentration camp known as Auschwitz.

There, as she clings to life, Chana loses family and friends to torture and starvation, and manages to survive only through her sheer talent for playing the violin. By becoming a member of the concentration camp orchestra, she escapes unremitting persecution and garners enough strength to remain alive until the Allies can liberate her camp. Along the way, Hilary in a coma learns what it means to be Jewish and how her dream-like alter ego, Chana, has changed her life forever. Awakening from her coma, Hilary points the finger at her neo-Nazi friends, telling family and police where and how her cohorts have tormented Jewish people, particularly a young boy who is being tortured as she speaks.

Relationship of *If I Should Die Before I Wake* to the Program

If I Should Die Before I Wake is a perfect vehicle to be used in a variety of settings to meet a number of established teaching standards. This first-person historical novel is fictionalized in its telling of personal events, but it is all too real in providing a graphic and horrifying picture of what life was like for Polish Jews during the Nazi regime. Nolan's gripping tale of torture and eventual salvation can complement any teacher's desire to have students read and understand a variety of materials, apply critical thinking skills, and recognize literature as a record of human experience. Finally, teachers can emphasize writing standards that address writing for a variety of purposes and conventional formats.

Reading and understanding a variety of materials

Nolan writes in a style that many young adults will find interesting and a touch cinematic. Familiar with television techniques of flashbacks and fade-outs, teenagers will be intrigued as to how Hilary comes in and out of her coma. Fading deeper into her dream state, Hilary transforms into Chana, the young Jewish Polish daughter of a large extended family that becomes, in her dream, closer to Hilary than her real family. Students can explore the different voices that permeate the novel—both surrounding her hospital bed and in her mind's eye—and how the two worlds interact and enhance our understanding of Hilary. Class discussions, journal keeping, and appropriate video presentations can help students become familiar with both time setting and language, and continual teacher assistance can assess students' understanding.

Applying critical thinking skills

Nolan's depiction of character—told in a first-person, semiconscious state—will allow students to explore their understanding of what it means to be in a "near-death state," and how such a horrifying condition could alter a human being's perception. Nolan's graphic depiction of pain and hunger, of anger and despair, and of humility and honor can provoke cautious discussions of what it means to explore the full range of human emotions and how those emotions are often enraged in our most desperate moments. Plagued with self-doubt and self-incriminating information, Hilary becomes a new person—Chana—and students can be guided in her transformation.

Thinking critically about a person's transformation can lend itself to a discussion of how other people change and why they make the choices they do. Nolan's depiction of Hilary's neo-Nazi friends, complete with skinheads and Nazi propaganda, is fascinating for its description of a subculture that is rarely discussed. Students can explore not only this subculture but, more important, why people become intrigued with hatred and violence, and the different steps that individuals must take to become the embodiment of evil. And again, students can explore events in their lives where they have seen parents, relatives, and friends become different people through circumstances that proved to be life-altering.

Finally, thinking critically about language is just as important as thinking analytically about human emotion. Nolan's work is populated by many expressions—some graphically colorful, some in foreign tongues. All contribute to a comprehensive picture of this undefinable and unspeakable period in human events. Explorations of how language and choice of expressions define individuals, and in so doing underscore character and conscience, make for intriguing reads and lessons. Students can look at the language Nolan uses, review any difficulties with comprehension, discuss the reasons Nolan uses the language she does, and explore its importance to telling this story and portraying character identities. Teachers can help their learners draw on their own background and explore how their use of language monitors how they think, behave, and perform. Drawing such parallels provides teenagers with a forum to think critically about how language influences perspective and behavior.

Recognizing literature as a reflection of human experience

Nolan's *If I Should Die Before I Wake* is a perfect vehicle to connect the abstract to students' lives and, more broadly, to the world. Taking an event as incomprehensible and as far-removed as the Holocaust and bringing it to life through the eyes of a young person—an unconventional and angry teenager—invites students to see the world through a recognizable figure, one who haunts the landscape of so many young adult novels and, of course, their own world. Young readers need only turn to their school bus stops, halls, or lunchrooms to find evidence of human cruelty and persecution. Tormenting human beings is nothing new in the course of human events, but when told in a historical context, the nature of this vicious beast of anger and brutality is even more significant.

Taken from a historical perspective, Nolan's novel provides a first-person account of what life meant for European Jews during the Nazi regime. This work can be taught in conjunction with other works that speak of the Holocaust and World War II, and will complement presentations about life in an era that for many students is foreign in context and tone. At the close of the twentieth century, we are approaching an age where few survivors from World War II—Holocaust victims, American soldiers, political leaders, and family members—will be alive to tell the firsthand account of what life was like during the reign of Hitler. Thus, reading Nolan's and similar works becomes all the more necessary.

From a personal perspective, discussion about personal stories—tales of discrimination, persecution, and tragedy—can help students reflect on their lives and the lives of people they know, and it can provide a close look at what it means to face pain and suffering on a very human level. Learning to relate personal tragedies to historical contexts shows students how the line between their lives and the lives of people who lived in a time remote from their own can be strikingly similar. And, naturally, comparing and contrasting stories, novels, poems, and other forms of literature from different countries, time periods, or cultures is one standard teachers can address with this novel.

Impact of the Material on Readers

Learning about the Holocaust can be an eye-opener for young people who have never seen the horrors of war and/or the evils of discrimination. Today, many young adults do not know these horrors unless their relatives have participated in military missions. And even for these children, world events and people become something we just study in history class.

In Nolan's work, though, they will have to confront evangelical Christians, neo-Nazi skinheads, Polish Jews, Nazi soldiers—all in an attempt to bring to life the worlds of today and yesterday. And although they might not identify with specific characters, they will recognize similarities between these individuals and their own lives.

Hilary struggles to come out of a coma and be recognized as a new human being—one who has changed from a neo-Nazi sympathizer to a compassionate, fully realized human being. Her long and carefully drawn transformation will be one that young people will find moving and engaging.

Potential Problems with *If I Should Die Before I Wake* and Ways to Address Them

This book contains many mature themes and literary techniques. Students will have to be introduced to this story gradually. They will need a good background in the historical context of this work in order to help them understand how such events were permitted to happen in a civilized world. Students need to know that the Holocaust was a human tragedy of unprecedented proportions—nearly twelve million people died, six million of whom were Jews—and the United States remained a bystander in saving human lives and destroying the Nazi regime until a few years into the war. Moreover, students need to know why the Jewish people and other minorities—gays, gypsies, and people not of pure German descent—were singled out for persecution and annihilation. In essence, students must have some context for understanding this work or they will be confused.

Students and teachers also need to recognize that Nolan's depiction is stark, real, and vigorous. Opening passages where the teenage neo-Nazi sympathizers express their hatred for Jews—clumsy Jews, dumb Jews, rich Jews, "rich bitch Jews" (4)—include some of the more graphic terms that the novelist employs. The language used to describe how Jews are tortured in the Auschwitz concentration camp must be recognized for its clear, definitive, and yet reserved understatement. Discussion of the language can show how it is a large part of characterization. Tracing the changes in Hilary's language can reveal how Hilary's attitudes change. Nolan's use of realistic language—German and Yiddish expressions, intermittent dialogue, introspective thoughts, and internal dialogue—might prove confusing to readers, but the teacher can help students distinguish among the voices in the novel. The multiple voices are an important element in a work that aims to show several perspectives.

Students who have read only works in which the narrator tells the reader exactly what is happening and why might be put off by the work's structure. Events and characters shift through time and place without notice, and only astute readers will perceive the transitions and how they interweave to make a provocative and cohesive story. Teachers will need to guide students as they make their way from chapter to chapter, and encourage them to outline their reading with a careful consideration about who is saying what to whom and why.

Finally, although the main character makes a positive transformation from Nazi sympathizer to compassionate soul and teenage informant, the journey is populated by many negative characters. Violent, belligerent, vulgar-speaking teenagers appear in the beginning of the story, and vicious, unfeeling, commanding Nazi soldiers figure as the story unfolds. To help their understanding, students can read companion books that show similar stories about life during the Holocaust for both Jews and gentiles. They can also be encouraged to explore their feelings about people who are different from themselves.

Realistic language, overt violence, harsh bigotry, unsavory characters, and unconventional stylistic techniques should not keep students from reading this work. Discussion of the novel's topics—bigotry, racism, war, and survival—are needed for students to confront the realities of a world that often seems maddeningly absurd. As good teachers know, careful, open, and reasonable discussions about rich and involving literature provide a forum for real learning and growth.

References

Han Nolan lives in Connecticut with her husband and children. *If I Should Die Before I Wake* was her first novel, and she wrote it because she believes that the stories of the Holocaust should be told again and again in as many ways as possible, until everyone understands. She has written two other novels, both nominated for the National Book Award—*Send Me Down a Miracle* and *Dancing on the Edge. Send Me Down a Miracle* tells the story of fourteen-year-old Charity's revelation that her preacher father might not be right about everything, and *Dancing on the Edge* is a story of an emotionally disturbed young woman trying to find the truth amid the lies told by her family. Never before in the history of the National Book Award has an author been nominated two years in a row, and in 1997 *Dancing on the Edge* won this prestigious award for young people's literature.

If I Should Die Before I Wake has received many positive reviews. *Kirkus Reviews* calls Nolan's first novel a "deeply felt and compelling work . . . juxtaposing the virulent paranoia of present-day skinheads with their forebears' atrocities" (308). Mary Harris Veeder says that "[w]ithout sensationalizing or blurring, Nolan evokes the physical and emotional crowding of shared living space, the desperate struggle for food each day, and the compromises required for survival" (1436).

Alternative Work

Yolen, Jane. *The Devil's Arithmetic.* New York: Viking Kestrel, 1988. This book, written for slightly younger readers, is also a transformation story. The details, while still realistic, are not as graphic and may be more acceptable to someone who objects to *If I Should Die Before I Wake.*

Related Works

Nonfiction books about the Holocaust

Abells, Chana Byers. *The Children We Remember.* New York: Greenwillow, 1986.

Dwork, Deborah. *Children With a Star: Jewish Youth in Nazi Europe.* New Haven: Yale UP, 1991.

Frank, Anne. *Anne Frank, the Diary of a Young Girl.* New York: Pocket, 1958.

Hurwitz Johanna. *Anne Frank: Life in Hiding.* Philadelphia: Jewish Publication Society, 1988.

Lustig, Arnost, et al. *Children of the Holocaust.* Evanston: Northwestern UP, 1995.

Meltzer, Milton. *The Story of How Gentiles Saved Jews in the Holocaust.* New York: Harper, 1988.

Swiebocka, Teresa, et al. *Auschwitz: A History in Photographs.* Bloomington: published for the Auschwitz-Birkenau State Museum, Oscwiecim, by Indiana UP and Ksiazka i Wiedza, Warsaw, 1993.

Williams, Laura E. *Behind the Bedroom Wall.* New York: Milkweed Editions, 1996.

Books about living in Poland during WWII

Adler, David A. *Child of the Warsaw Ghetto.* New York: Holiday House, 1995.

Fluck, Toby Knobel. *Memories of My Life in a Polish Village, 1939–1949.* New York: Knopf, 1990.

Lukas, Richard C. *The Forgotten Holocaust: The Poles Under German Occupation 1939–1944.* Lexington: UP of Kentucky, 1986.

Books about the Jewish people and religion

Cahill, Thomas. *The Gifts of the Jews: How a Tribe of Desert Nomads Changed the Way Everyone Thinks and Feels.* New York: Nan A. Talese, 1998.

Chaikin, Miriam. *Sound of the Shofar: The Story and Meaning of Rosh Hashanah and Yom Kippur.* New York: Clarion, 1986.

Hertzberg, Arthur. *Jews: The Essence and Character of a People.* San Francisco: HarperSanFrancisco, 1998.

Sussman, Susan. *Hanukkah: Eight Lights Around the World.* Niles: A. Whitman, 1988.

Anti-Semitism

Arnold, Caroline, and Herma Silverstein. *Anti-Semitism: A Modern Perspective.* New York: J. Messner, 1985.

Fictional stories about Jewish life during the Holocaust

Baer, Edith. *A Frost in the Night.* New York: Pantheon, 1980.

Lowry, Lois. *Number the Stars.* Boston: Houghton, 1989.

Fictional stories about being Jewish

These would make excellent additional selections to *If Should Die Before I Wake.* These works are young adult novels that speak to the American Jewish experience.

Arrick, Fran. *Chernowitz*. Scarsdale: Bradbury, 1981.

Blume, Judy. *Are You There God? It's Me Margaret*. Englewood Cliffs: Bradbury, 1970.

Greene, Bette. *Summer of My German Soldier*. New York: Dial, 1973.

Kerr, M. E. *Gentlehands*. New York: Harper, 1978.

Works Cited

Rev. of *If I Should Die Before I Wake*, by Han Nolan. *Kirkus Reviews* 1 March 1994: 308.

Veeder, Mary Harris. Rev. of *If I Should Die Before I Wake*, by Han Nolan. *Booklist* 1 April 1994: 1436.

About Jeffrey S. Kaplan

Jeffrey S. Kaplan is an assistant professor of Educational Foundations at the University of Central Florida, Orlando and Daytona Beach campuses. A previous middle and high school teacher, Kaplan teaches undergraduate and graduate teaching courses in instructional strategies, social foundations, and educational psychology. His research interests include innovative teaching strategies, young adult literature, and fostering positive learning environments. He has published articles in *English Journal*, *The ALAN Review*, *The School Counselor*, and *Virginia English Bulletin*, and chapters in *Adolescent Literature: A Complement to the Classics*, (Joan Kaywell, ed.), *Using Literature to Help Troubled Teenagers Cope with Family Issues* (Joan Kaywell, ed.), and *The Young Adult Writer* (Ted Hipple, ed.). Recently, Kaplan edited *Helping Troubled Teenagers Cope With Identity Issues* (Greenwood Press) and *Teens Around the World* (Greenwood Press).

WHEN SHE HOLLERS

by Cynthia Voigt

She put the survival knife down on the table. It pointed across at him.

She couldn't breathe.

"From now on—" she said. "I'll have this knife." Her knees were watery, and her mouth trembled. "All the time." She sat down.

He was pretending not to hear. He poured milk from the carton into his cereal.

"You better—"

She swallowed.

"—listen—"

She pushed the reluctant words up out of her throat to stand in a row on the table, standing in a straight row facing him.

"You better believe—" (1)

Voigt, Cynthia. *When She Hollers.* New York: Scholastic, 1994.

Intended Audience

When She Hollers should be a choice book for students from 7th through 12th grades because it deals with the sensitive and difficult issue of incest. This novel will be most effective in a thematic unit (perhaps using other literature on survival) or a health unit (dealing with respect for one's body, and the importance of being aware of the choices available for healthy living).

Summary

When Miranda, a childhood friend, commits suicide and it is discovered that she is six months pregnant, Tish, the main character of this book, recognizes with chilling certainty that she could make the same choice. Tish suspects that Miranda was trying to hide a secret just like Tish's. Miranda found one way out; Tish is reasonably sure she wants another way out. The story opens with Tish threatening her stepfather with a knife. Hesitantly, with a mere thread of certainty, Tish stutters out her warning. Her stepfather had better leave her alone.

The book centers on one day in Tish's life. This day unfolds in multiple layers of rage, longing, uncertainty, resolve, and despair. Tish wants to be loved and cherished by her stepfather, not raped. She wants her mother to hear her anguish and protect her, not surreptitiously provide birth control. She wants friends who don't flinch at the possibility of an unpleasant reality, and she wants adults who aren't afraid of disclosure laws.

Tish's flight through her conflicting emotions and relationships culminates in a lawyer's office. Voigt leaves us, at the end of the day, with Tish outside her family home struggling to make the emotional and mental decisions that will keep her alive.

Relationship of *When She Hollers* to the Program

Insight into other people, places, times, and ideas

We want our students to be lifelong learners. Reading books such as *When She Hollers* will allow students to see that literature is not separate from life and real situations. Literature is about us and others; it is about health and wholeness; it is about coping and not coping with the life we have. Using Voigt's book in conjunction with district, state, or national standards in language arts, health, and thinking and reasoning will provide a broad scope of applications.

National statistics and the daily newspaper force us to acknowledge that some children live with incest as a reality. Understanding that reality through Tish's eyes may provide a lens on another world, another reality that is essential, albeit uncomfortable. Literature gives the reader a way to connect to that other world safely.

Family health and individual health

Literature can provide a lens for viewing family health and individual health issues. Students can connect with the compelling story of a protagonist they care about and, in turn, possibly understand the same issues in the lives of families and individuals they might know. Literature will help students see how mental health, social health, and emotional health play out in the lives of characters and in the world of school, dating, and friends, as well as out of the pages of a health textbook.

Problem solving and decision making

Throughout *When She Hollers* Tish is struggling to balance her thinking. Should she just survive as best she can and leave in two months when she turns eighteen? Or should she stab Tonnie (her stepfather) and live with the ramifications of that? Does she have other options? If so, what are they? Is she to blame? She struggles to think clearly; she struggles to make decisions.

This book provides an excellent opportunity to analyze how thinking and reasoning are employed. Students can learn that when our thinking falls apart it is often because we face a decision that is *very* emotional. Thinking through an issue in life is not like writing an argument for debate club. We have to be able to feel the tearing emotions, face the debilitating ambivalence and make a decision anyway. This is a chance for teachers and students to share, through the medium of literature, how people think and make decisions.

If teachers view Voigt's book as providing an understanding of some aspects of life, as providing access to alternative healthy choices, as providing a pattern for thinking, reasoning, or decision making, then assignments and assessments could follow such patterns. Students could analyze the thinking and reasoning processes that Tish uses throughout the story. In addition to exploring their thoughts in writing, students could prepare a thirty-second public service announcement, a story book for younger children, or a speech to inspire and inform.

Students' products should be consistent with Voigt's approach. In *When She Hollers*, Voigt never describes the rapes; yet we know Tish has been abused for years by her stepfather. I find this absence of graphic detail helpful as I think about using this book with secondary youngsters. Thus, in keeping with the author's example, a public service announcement with the emphasis on health and information should provide a window of hope, not fear; a book for young children should be a helpful and hopeful story, not a confusing and scary one.

Impact of the Material on Readers

There is magic in remembering the day that we saw ourselves in literature, or maybe the day we dreamed that we could be the character we'd read about. We imagine we could be the boy or girl that rescued the black stallion, we saw the characters in *Our Town* as our family, or we recognized Sinclair Lewis' *Main Street* as the street where we lived. Students need a chance to find themselves in literature; they need to be able to see ways people deal with untimely death, as in *Our Town.* They need to know that people wrestle with the mundane and the petty, as in *Main Street.* Students can find themselves in literature in painful ways, in powerful ways, or simply in ordinary ways. In literature, characters have a chance to deal with situations.

Not all students should read this book. For some, the issue of incest may be too close. Other students, however, may see hope in this story of survival. If students are facing similar situations then they have a chance to identify and visualize how they might deal with those situations. As the *Horn Book* reviewer notes, "Voigt's remarkable book may give some readers hope and may help others to understand why a victim of abuse might turn to violence" (Knoth 65).

Potential Problems with *When She Hollers* and Ways to Address Them

Uncomfortable topics

The topic of incest is disturbing. Teachers presenting books that deal with tough emotional topics need to make sure that they can present the topic in an unsensational, emotionally neutral way. If a teacher winces every time incest is mentioned, a child who may need some help is going to get the wrong message.

Stereotypes

The portrayal of Tish's stepfather, Tonnie, seems to be a bit stereotypical—new man in mother's life uses his position of trust to abuse a young girl wanting a father's love. Other stereotypes could also be identified. It is important for teachers to help students be cognizant of possible stereotypes—whether they be mother, father, teacher, or teens. People usually are more ambiguous than these stereotypes. Asking students to complete an analysis of one character and then compare their analyses in small groups will allow them to see which characters are multifaceted and which are stereotypes. Class discussion could continue with reasons Voigt chose to portray characters as she did. Discussion of the decision to tell the story from Tish's point of view may help students understand some character portrayals.

In anticipating students' aversion to certain topics I think it is important to choose carefully the words we use to frame the survival situation.

In discussing *When She Hollers* the important issue is survival, not sex. The teacher and the students could brainstorm survival situations, then clarify them. Students will probably note that some situations are more comfortable to discuss than others. As situations emerge from the class, the teacher could ask for some survival strategies. How do people develop the appropriate mental and emotional muscle? Finally, the discussion should turn to how the survival strategies apply in particular situations. An evaluation of their potential effectiveness may help some students understand the reasons for Tish's choices.

References

Cynthia Voigt tackles the tough subjects of child abuse, verbal abuse, racism, and coping with traumas such as amputation. Voigt also writes mystery and fantasy, and has written six books about the Tillerman family. She won the Notable Children's Trade Book Award in the field of social studies for *Homecoming* in 1982, the Newbery Medal in 1983 for *Dicey's Song*, and the Edgar Allan Poe Award in 1984 for *The Callendar Papers*. Among some of her other books, all published by Atheneum, are *A Solitary Blue, The Runner, Seventeen Against the Dealer, Izzy Willy-Nilly, Come a Stranger, Sons From Afar, Tell Me If the Lovers Are Losers,* and *Tree By Leaf.*

By ninth grade Cynthia Voigt had decided she wanted to become a writer. She continued with that dream through college, marriage, a child, divorce, teaching, and remarriage. Says Voigt, "I don't shelter my characters from the world any more than I would keep them from going to the bathroom. The Depression and World War II were experiences that shaped and informed me while I was growing up, just as Vietnam has influenced kids growing up today" ("Cynthia Voigt" 214).

When She Hollers was named a *School Library Journal* Best Book in 1994 and an ALA Best Book for Young Adults in 1995. It has received positive reviews.

Patty Campbell writes in *The Horn Book Magazine*, "Voigt's tightly controlled novel, told through the whirling images and lapses into unreality of Tish's tortured mind, is a small literary masterpiece from this already distinguished author" (94).

Merri Monks praised the book's dramatic realism, calling it a "searing portrait of a teenage incest victim" (420). The reviewer for *Publishers Weekly* called it a "searing new novel" and "an exceptional offering" (246).

Alternative Works

Alternative titles could be chosen to focus on the issue of survival. If students or parents object to the topic of incest, other novels by Voigt could be substituted. All are published by Atheneum.

Solitary Blue (1983). A young man deals with his mother having abandoned him.

Homecoming (1981) and *Dicey's Song* (1982). These books in the Tillerman saga tell of the survival of a family deserted by their father and abandoned by their mentally ill mother.

Izzy, Willy Nilly (1986). Izzy must create a new life for herself after her drunken date causes an accident in which she is seriously injured.

Related Works

Surviving prejudice

Angelou, Maya. *I Know Why the Caged Bird Sings.* New York: Random House, 1970. One of the many struggles Angelou describes is her challenge to survive molestation by her mother's boyfriend.

Taylor, Mildred. *Roll of Thunder, Hear My Cry.* New York: Dial, 1976. A family struggles to survive prejudice in the 1930s South.

Wright, Richard. *Black Boy.* New York: Harper, 1945. A young boy must fight against prejudice and unfair treatment because of his color and economic circumstances.

Surviving natural catastrophes

Mazer, Harry Fox. *Snow Bound.* New York: Delacorte, 1973. A hitchhiker and a runaway are stranded in a blizzard.

O'Dell, Scott. *Island of the Blue Dolphins.* Boston: Houghton, 1960. This is a moving portrayal of a young Native American woman confronting white settlers in the 1800s.

Read, Piers Paul. *Alive: The Story of the Andes Survivors.* New York: Lippincott, 1974. Although many died as a result of a plane crash, sixteen Uruguayans were rescued after two and one-half months in the mountain wilderness.

Works Cited

Campbell, Patty. "The Sand in the Oyster." *The Horn Book Magazine* 71 (1995): 94–98.

"Cynthia Voigt." *Authors and Artists for Young Adults*. Ed. A. Garrett and H. McCue. Vol. 3. Detroit: Gale Research Inc., 1990.

Knoth, Maeve Visser. Rev. of *When She Hollers,* by Cynthia Voigt. *The Horn Book Magazine* 71 (1995): 64–65.

Monks, Merri. Rev. of *When She Hollers,* by Cynthia Voigt. *Booklist* 15 Oct. 1994: 420–421.

Rev. of *When She Hollers,* by Cynthia Voigt. *Publishers Weekly* 18 July 1994: 246.

About Suzanne Lustie

Suzanne Lustie recently received her Ph.D. from the University of Colorado at Denver. She is currently teaching eighth-grade language arts and social studies in Douglas County, a district south of Denver, Colorado. Her writing has appeared in *Thoughtful Communities*, a school district monograph reporting teacher research, and has been accepted for the Winter 1999 issue of *California English*.

MONTANA 1948

by Larry Watson

My father lifted his head and I could tell by his red-rimmed eyes that he had been crying. But that was not what concerned me.

At that moment my father looked so old (he was only thirty-eight at the time), and I knew for the first time how this experience with his brother was ruining him physically. Was that the moment I realized my father would die someday? Perhaps. At any rate I knew that the puffiness around his eyes, the deepening creases of worry across his forehead and around his mouth, his pallor, his slow, stiffening gait were all signs that he was growing weaker. I also knew that to continue to stand up to Grandfather, my father needed all the strength he possessed. And perhaps that would still not be enough.

As if she could read my mind, my mother said, "Your father's just tired, David."

Using his good leg to brace himself, my father pushed himself to his feet. "We're all tired," he said. "Let's hit the hay."

I wasn't tired, and I didn't want to go to bed. I wanted my parents to tell me what happened when Grandfather and Grandmother were there. Though I knew exactly what was said, I wanted my parents to interpret it all for me. I wanted them to explain it so it wasn't as bad as the facts made it seem. (123–124)

Watson, Larry. *Montana 1948*. New York: Washington Square Press, 1993.

Intended Audience

This novel would work best with students in grade 11 or 12 for study as a whole class, as one of a group of selections to be read in small groups, or as part of a reading workshop. It can be part of an American literature course or a combined English/American history course, a contemporary literature course, or a literature of the West course. It is especially relevant for students who are about to enter the world of adults and who are concerned with their own rites of passage. The sensitive issues presented in the novel demand a level of maturity and development that is evident in the upper grade levels.

Summary

During the summer of 1948, David Hayden, a twelve-year-old growing up in Bentrock, Montana, is confronted with issues of justice, family loyalty, violence, abuse, and power as his family goes through a series of traumatic events that tear them apart. David narrates the story as a history teacher looking back at his violent thrust into adolescence and how that made him what he is today.

Gail Hayden, David's mother, informs her husband, Wes, the town sheriff, that Frank, his brother and the town doctor, has been molesting Native American girls during medical exams. The story comes out when Marie Little Soldier, the Haydens' Sioux housekeeper, is bedridden with pneumonia but becomes hysterical when Frank comes in the room to examine her. She will only allow it if Gail stays in the room during the exam. A few days later, while Marie is recovering at the Haydens' house, she dies suddenly. David has to summon the courage to tell his father that he saw his uncle coming from the house the afternoon that she died. Wesley must arrest his brother and bring him to justice, but because of the family's name and power in the town, he brings Frank to their house and locks him in the basement rather than taking him to jail. In the ensuing conflicts that arise between Grandfather Hayden and Wesley and between Wesley and Gail, David learns of his uncle's, father's, and grandfather's racism and of their abuses of power and justice. In spite of all of these troubling issues and events, David also learns about the power of love.

Relationship of *Montana 1948* to the Program

Montana 1948 can be incorporated into a variety of units of study. Depending on how a teacher chooses to teach it, this text might be part of a group of texts that focus on one of the following themes: justice, family relationships and loyalty, abuse of power and the consequences, social and personal responsibility, or rites of passage. It could also be part of a unit of literature that examines the effect of community on the individual and individual on the community, or one that examines the small town in American literature.

Because of the varied possibilities for approaching this novel, the teacher would need to know the makeup of the class before setting up a focus. A mature class could easily deal with the complexities of "doing the right thing" and addressing the theme of justice as David observes his father's struggle with his conscience, his family, his father, his brother, the Native American community, and the community of Bentrock. Students could read this text as a whole class and discuss each event in relation to the theme of justice and how a person determines what is just. Keeping journals of response to the events and the characters' reactions to them, or creating dialogues between characters that David observes and analyzing their motives for actions would help students think critically about the text. Mature students would also understand the conflict between family loyalty and the pursuit of justice, and they could research and discuss the historical background to understand where the racism was coming from and what effect it had on others.

A junior- or senior-level class could examine the family relationships as they study the literary elements of character development and the narrative voice in the novel. They could develop attribute charts of the main characters, using their texts for support in discussing how and why the characters act as they do toward each other. In addition, they could examine Watson's narrative technique and how David tells the story. Students should be able to identify when the narrator is speaking as an adolescent, when he is speaking as a grown man looking back, and why it is necessary to shift back and forth.

Montana 1948 is significant also in a historical sense, and upper-level students can explore the historical precedents for the community's attitude toward the Native Americans as well as their treatment of them. As they discuss the overt racism and the subtle racism that David begins to comprehend, they can relate the text to their experiences and observations in their own community and the world. Frank's abuse of the Native American girls paired with his utter disregard for them as human beings because of their race will stimulate discussion among the students that can be channeled into a debate about how his crimes should be handled and whether his brother, Wesley, is bringing him to justice or not. The power hierarchy that has been set up by Grandfather Hayden in the town of Bentrock, and the repercussions it causes when his own sons are caught up in it, can also be tied in to the development of small towns and the way the class system was perpetuated, keeping those of other races or low economic levels at the bottom. For example, students could compare David's view of Bentrock's class system to Scout's view of Maycomb in *To Kill a Mockingbird* by Harper Lee or Jim's view of Red Cloud in *My Antonia* by Willa Cather.

For teachers who are setting up a comparison or contrast to other cultures or time periods, this novel can be used to show how a sensitive Anglo American writer views racial injustice and what effect it has on him. Students could then read selections by Native American writers, such as Zitkala-Sa (Gertrude Simmons Bonnin), who wrote about how she was treated by the white society and the effect it had on her life. They could read James Welch's *Fools Crow* to examine the colonization of Montana from the perspective of a Native American, or they could read stories by Sherman Alexie to look at the effect racism has on young adults.

To achieve writing objectives teachers can focus on a variety of forms of writing as students work with this novel. Students may be involved in responding to the literature in writing by keeping journals or response logs. For example, they may write in the persona of a character in response to David, analyzing and creating a narrative journal, letter, or monologue. To conclude their reading they might take an analytical stance and develop it in a formal essay.

Finally, to meet oral objectives or standards, teachers might set up dramatic readings or role playing of sections of the text. Students could also set up a mock trial of Uncle Frank and support their arguments for or against him from the text itself.

Impact of the Material on Readers

In setting up the conflict by linking the themes of justice and family loyalty, Watson has raised questions that readers will have to grapple with in the text as well as in their own lives. Students reading this novel will recognize the conflicts Wesley and Gail are faced with and will be able to compare the way that a young boy might perceive them with the way an adult would view them. These are timely themes for students at the junior and senior level who are about to embark on their own lives as adults. As they discuss abuses of power by people in the novel, they can compare them to what they see in their own worlds. As they watch the extended Hayden family fall apart and the nucleus family of Gail, Wesley, and David survive, they will learn of the complexities of human and family relationships as well as the effect of family divisions on both children and adults. They will also see how love can cross family and racial boundaries and what a lasting effect it has on David. Finally, the students will be presented with strengths in the male *and* female characters in the novel, and they will come to recognize those strengths as David does.

Potential Problems with *Montana 1948* and Ways to Address Them

Sexual abuse

Because this book is written from the perspective of a twelve-year-old boy, even though it's narrated by the adult David, the language is direct and clearly understood. The subject of Frank's abuse of the Native American girls is integral to the plot, and students would need to approach this novel as mature and sensitive readers. When David hears his mother talking about how his uncle abused Native American girls, he is shocked, even though Watson has set up foreshadowing. The description is direct, so that the reader can perceive how shattering this information is to David, who idolized his uncle prior to this. To help students work through this subject, they could then look at how Watson sets up David's love for both Marie and his Uncle Frank and then how he feels betrayed. Watson takes care to show how each character reacts to learning about Frank's actions. This would make it easier to discuss his actions because they are related to character development. Frank's almost flippant responses to Wesley's charges reveal more about him to readers than anything else could.

Teachers can also remind students of David's age, innocence, and ignorance at the time he eavesdrops on his parents and also of his statement to us that "if I had gone back into the house . . . I would never have heard the conversation between my father and mother, and perhaps I would have lived out my life with an illusion about my family and perhaps even the human community. Certainly I could not tell this story" (45). They can examine that statement and discuss what he is revealing about the effect of this event so many years later as he tells the story, and the fact that he is still torn between wanting to know and wishing he had never heard about his uncle's actions. The teacher could also point out the effect of this news on David immediately after he hears it: "I may not have been entirely convinced of his guilt, but the story my mother told was too lurid, too frightening, for me to continue thinking of my uncle in the way I always had. Charming, affable Uncle Frank was gone for good" (49).

Prejudice

In addition, the issue of sexual abuse is closely linked to prejudice, which would also be a charged subject. As students move through the novel and learn more about Frank's, Grandfather Hayden's, and even Wesley's prejudices at the same time David is learning about them, they can discuss how prejudice gets way out of control as it is passed from one generation to the next. The counter to this is that Wesley fights to overcome his own prejudices, and that the Native Americans, Marie and Ronnie, are presented as strong characters. Even Ollie Young Bear, who married a white woman and is respected by the whites for his hard work, but who is considered a "sell-out" by the other Native Americans, is portrayed with respect. Students can examine David's mixed feelings about how the town perceives someone like Ollie and his own feelings, colored by his knowledge of his father's prejudice. Ultimately, he must come to terms with what his own attitude is in relation to his father's, uncle's, and grandfather's prejudices.

Students would also need to discuss the time period in which the novel is set and the attitude of the U.S. government toward Native Americans prior to World War II and during the war. Watson presents some of this background in his description of Ronnie Tall Bear and sets up an implied contrast between his return to the community (good enough for the army but not for college) and Frank's return after the war (a hero's welcome). These discussions would help students understand how attitudes were fostered and why some actions, such as Frank's, were allowed to continue by the community.

Suicide

Another issue that must be addressed and discussed is Frank's suicide and David's response to it. If the students have worked through the family relationships and the characters' responses to the events brought up in the novel, the scenes where Gail, Wesley, and David hear Frank's violent outburst at night and then discover what he has actually done to himself will not come as a shock, although the act itself is disturbing. However, they may have trouble understanding David's response:

> No, I took my time climbing the two flights to my mother because I needed time to compose myself, to make certain I could keep concealed my satisfaction over what had happened.
>
> You see, I knew—I knew! I knew! that Uncle Frank's suicide had solved all our problems. (161)

This in itself would be cause for questioning by student readers, but they would need to combine that statement with David's final statement in telling his story:

> What more can I say? I was a child. I believed all these things to be true.
>
> As I climbed the stairs, I felt something for my uncle that I hadn't felt for him in life. It was gratitude, yes, but it was something more. It was very close to love. (162)

With those statements and a discussion of Watson's use of the epilogue to reveal the consequences of Wesley's and Frank's acts, students can discuss the perspective of a twelve-year-old boy compared to his retrospective of the situation as a grown man. In addition, they can look at the impact of Frank's action and how his suicide tore the family apart, which speaks clearly to anyone who might have viewed it as "the only way out" and a solution, as young David thought.

Strong language

Finally, there is some swearing used by the men in the novel, but it is not used gratuitously. Grandfather Hayden uses it in anger. When David uses it at first, he is reprimanded, but by the end of the novel, when the tension among the characters is high, his mother doesn't even look up or comment on David's words. Students should be encouraged to recognize that the effect of strong language should complement Watson's development of the character using it, which it does here.

References

Larry Watson grew up in North Dakota in the 1950s and has a strong sense of place in his own life as well as in the lives of his characters. Watson currently teaches and writes at the University of Wisconsin at Stevens Point. He has published poetry and fiction and has received fellowships from the National Endowment for the Arts. Prior to *Montana 1948* he published a novel, *In a Dark Time*, and in 1995 he published a set of short stories, *Justice*, that involve the Hayden family prior to 1948. This prequel complements the novel and pairs up well with it. In 1996 he published another novel, *White Crosses*.

Montana 1948 has received many awards, including The Milkweed National Fiction Prize, The Mountains and Plains Booksellers Association Regional Book Award, American Library Association Notable Book of the Year, ALA/YALSA Best Book for Young Adults Award, and the New York Public Library's "Books for the Teen Age."

Reviewers have also praised this book. Chris Faatz wrote in *The Nation* that "there's something eminently universal in Watson's ponderings on the human condition, and it's refracted through a nearly perfect life for character, place, and the rhythms of language" (808). Mary Ann Grossman notes that "critics applaud Watson for evoking a clear sense of place, whether he's writing about the endless Plains or the claustrophobic town" (1). *Kirkus Reviews* calls *Montana 1948* "a lean, gaunt narrative rich with implication about a 12-year-old boy who witnesses the anguish of his sheriff father, who is forced to arrest his own brother for rape" and concludes that the novel is "morally complex and satisfying in its careful accumulation of detail and in the use of landscape to reveal character" (816).

Alternative Work

MacLean, Norman. *A River Runs Through It.* Chicago: U of Chicago P, 1976. Two brothers growing up in Montana are influenced in different ways by their minister father, who teaches them about life and fly fishing on the wild rivers of Montana. This novel deals beautifully with family relationships, and the point of view parallels David's in that the narrator is looking back at his youth and the events that shaped him.

Related Works

By Larry Watson with characters from *Montana 1948*

Justice. Minneapolis: Milkweed Editions, 1995. A series of short stories that focus on the Hayden family members in the years before *Montana 1948.* In particular, the story "Out of the Jurisdiction" sets up the personalities and behaviors of Frank and Wesley as teenagers.

Books dealing with the theme of justice

Angelou, Maya. *I Know Why the Caged Bird Sings.* New York: Random House, 1970 [1969]. Angelou's autobiography examines the injustices of growing up as a black girl in a white Southern town. She fights for proving her self-worth throughout this part of her life. This novel is effective for its perspective (female narrator/author), its presentation of the struggle against racism, and the struggle for justice in a time and place where justice is only applied to one class and race.

Borland, Hal. *When the Legends Die*. Philadelphia: Lippincott, 1963. Bear's Brother/Tom Black Bull is forced to leave his native environment and Ute culture behind and adapt to the BIA's "education" of Native American children. He takes out his rage on broncos in rodeos, but Tom must learn how to deal with the issues in his life and come to terms with himself and his culture. This novel deals with governmental injustice as well as injustices by white society.

Lee, Harper. *To Kill A Mockingbird*. Philadelphia: Lippincott, 1960. Scout, the female narrator, looks back at her childhood and tells her story of growing up in a segregated Southern town where justice is not equal when a black person is accused of a crime and brought to trial. This novel also deals with class injustices. Scout's father, Atticus, would make a good comparison to Wesley as a father and upholder of the law.

Books about family relationships and families facing adversity

Cather, Willa. *My Antonia*. Boston: Houghton, 1918. Jim reflects on his relationship with his immigrant friend, Antonia, who arrives in Nebraska from Bohemia at the same time as Jim arrives from the East. Cather details what life was like for immigrants faced with making a life in a hostile environment and how families struggled to survive the climate, the economic conditions, and the class separation in the country and the town.

Lesley, Craig. *The Sky Fisherman*. Boston: Houghton, 1995. Culver's life is overshadowed by the drowning death of his father years ago in the Lost River in Oregon. He and his mother come back to Gateway, where his father died and his uncle Jake still runs the local sporting goods store, and there Culver tries to piece together his father's, mother's, and uncle's lives. Culver's story is intertwined with murders, investigations, a town fire, and the Native American community as he comes of age in this vivid, gripping, and humorous novel.

Sullivan, Faith. *The Cape Ann*. New York: Crown, 1988. Set in Minnesota during the Depression, this novel is told from the perspective of six-year-old Lark, the daughter of a railroad station attendant who lacks ambition and keeps his family in poverty because of his addiction to gambling. Lark observes the injustices in her community toward others of different abilities or classes while she endures injustice in her own family by her father. As she looks back at her life, she realizes that her strong mother helped her come to a better understanding of life.

Books by or about Native Americans

Erdrich, Louise. *Love Medicine.* New York: H. Holt, 1993. The Kashpaw and Lamartine families' lives intertwine on the reservation and in the surrounding towns of North Dakota. This novel portrays the families' secrets, loves, and deaths with great sensitivity and from a Native American's perspective. (Also effective would be Erdrich's *Tracks,* the history of both families a generation before and of the racial prejudice and injustices they faced.)

Welch, James. *Fools Crow.* New York: Viking, 1986. The settling of Montana and the intrusion of whites in Blackfeet territory is told from the perspective of Fools Crow, a Blackfeet warrior whose story parallels that of his tribe at this time in history. The story moves from Fools Crow's entry into the world of adults as a young man to his maturity as an adult who becomes a part of his community.

Works Cited

Faatz, Chris, et al. "*The Nation's* Holiday Picks." *The Nation* 27 Dec. 1993: 808.

Grossman, Mary Ann. "Showtime." *Saint Paul Pioneer Press* 28 Oct. 1993: 1.

Rev. of *Montana 1948,* by Larry Watson. *Kirkus Reviews* 1 July 1993: 816.

About Susan McGinty

Susan McGinty is currently a professor of English at Eastern Washington University in Spokane and Cheney, teaching American literature, women's literature, and secondary English education courses. She is also the Director of Secondary English Education for Eastern Washington University, and she works closely in pairing up her secondary English students with practicing teachers who help them work with the literature curriculum for middle and high schools. She has cochaired the NCTE Assembly on American Literature with Bob Hamm since its inception in 1989. She has taught English at the elementary, middle, and high school level as well as at the college level, and she works with young adults every summer as an instructor for Lake City Writers' Camp in Coeur d'Alene, Idaho.

AFTERWORD: LISTENING TO THE READERS

> I don't much care why Huck and Jim went down the river on a raft. What I really want to know is why someone would want to stop me from reading *The Adventures of Huckleberry Finn.*
>
> —A high school sophomore

Students are interested in controversy. Yet some districts have rules against teachers discussing controversial topics without prior permission from an administrator. Even without such a rule, some teachers prefer not to raise controversial issues in class, especially if they teach in a community where many parents believe that the purpose of schools is to teach the facts only, not interpretations or judgments.

If we do not teach students to deal with controversy, if we do not help them become aware of the issues, we are not doing our job as educators. June Edwards underscores this idea. While admitting that a teacher may not be able to keep a particular book in the curriculum after a challenge, she notes that

> the larger goal for public education is to confront students with a variety of ideas and accurate information, allow them some choices and the opportunity to voice opinions, teach them by precept and example to respect the right of others, have a wide range of reading material readily available, and demonstrate the courage to stand up for what is intellectually challenging, culturally diverse, and democratically sound. (133)

How can we accomplish this goal as we teach literature to young adults? Writing rationales is an important first step. Two other essential elements are listening to what the readers themselves say about controversial materials and teaching *about* controversy, rather than avoiding it.

Listening to Readers

In their rationales, Greg Hamilton and Rene Schillinger provide insights from students reading *Jack* and *Lakota Woman*, respectively. Jolene Borgese and Susan Ebert cite students' reactions to *Fallen Angels.* We wondered what young adults would say about some of the titles in this collection. So we asked. Connie Cushman and Jean Wyrick provided names of teenagers they knew; we contacted the students and their parents, briefly described the books, asked them to select a title, read it, and discuss it with us. The students were chosen because they were available and willing to read and discuss a controversial book. Not all of the students we contacted participated. Neither do we claim that these students who did participate are typical of other young adults or that their comments represent what other teens might say. We do believe that what these young people had to say is worth listening to. Their comments may provide a context or contrast for comments made by the readers in other classrooms. Because the impact on students is an important part of a rationale, these comments may also help teachers support use of a particular title.

We asked the readers to consider the book's strengths and weaknesses and whether they would recommend it to a friend. We also asked them to speculate on what people might object to in the book and what they would say to someone who wanted to stop them from reading it. We have used commas to indicate pauses and ellipses to indicate words we omitted for length or clarity.

The Crazy Horse Electric Game

Kellin Bershinsky is sixteen and a high school sophomore. He enjoys reading but does not have as much time to read as he would like because of sports and homework. He likes Michael Crichton's books and war books like *All Quiet on the Western Front.* He also liked *Crazy Horse.* "I thought the book was pretty good. There were a couple of things like when he popped the acid pills and stuff but we've heard those things tons of times. Fifth grade we had D.A.R.E. and you learned about that stuff all the time. There's a couple of places where he got beat up and stuff and that was pretty graphic but we learn about books like that. Strength and weaknesses . . . it's got a lot of heart and imagination but I didn't really recognize any weaknesses. It's a great book. I enjoyed reading it. I would recommend it to a friend. I recommended it to my mom today."

Kellin does not think that banning books in general is a good idea and he does not see any reason to keep people from reading *The Crazy Horse*

Electric Game. "There's a lot worse stuff out there that I've read in high school already. I think if you were going to put it anywhere it would be in high schools and colleges . . . I don't know about having it mandatory, that you should have to read it, but I think it should be optional. I don't really like it when people try to keep me from reading a book. I like a good selection. I disagree with a lot of the, I like war books and stuff, and I don't like that a lot of them are x-rated and stuff like that."

Overall, he concluded, "it's a great book. . . . It went through a lot of things. It started out calm and it just kept getting things added on . . . the bus driver and everything. . . . It was pretty brilliant that he could think of stuff like that and put it all in a book. . . . It started out with a kid playing baseball and popular and everything, then, poor guy, but in the end it was a kind of happy ending, in a way."

The Ear, the Eye, and the Arm

Kaley Leicester is thirteen and in seventh grade. She had a babysitting job the evening we visited, but her mother watched the children while Kaley talked to us. She enthusiastically summarized the story and then talked about why she liked the book. Our conversation was more like an interview with questions and answers.

What did you think about the book? "I liked it. It was really interesting and it kept you wondering what's going to happen next 'cause they were always just out of like the parents' reach."

Was there anything that you did not like about it? "It went on for awhile, but it all pretty much was worth it."

Could you see it being used in class? "Yeah, I could see it in one of my classes. They'd really like it I know."

Why do you think people would object to it? "I was trying to think about that. There was some witchcraft stuff and I was thinking maybe people wouldn't like that. I don't really see why people wouldn't like it. I don't know."

What would you say to people who did not want you to read this book? "I'd probably tell them that it was an interesting book. . . . I thought it was really creative and it was fun to read . . . I think kids my age would really like it!"

A Lesson Before Dying

Brad Phifer is fourteen and in ninth grade. He had selected Ernest Gaines' book on his own before we even called to ask him to participate in this project. It was a fortunate coincidence. He told us, "I really enjoyed the book. I thought it taught a lot of lessons about life. It just tells you how society is today. I think its strengths were it was great writing, very descriptive, good characters, and it was just an overall great book. It really should be considered a classic. I think its only weakness was the first few chapters were kind of boring. It took awhile to get started, but because it was such a great book I think I would definitely recommend it to a friend."

Brad recommends that high school students read the book but thinks that it may be too mature for younger students. "There's a few instances why I can see why people have objected to this book because there's a few instances of language that would object to a lot of people, I think. And also there's one part where there's, two of the characters have sex. It's not really descriptive, but there's a few lines where it is, so . . . I can see why that could object to some people. People would probably try to prevent teenagers from reading this book because of that . . . because of the language and also it's kind of an adult theme. It deals with the death penalty and just pretty adult themes—murders, stuff like that. . . . It shouldn't be read by younger, probably people under twelve, because they're probably not mature enough to read it just because of the themes and stuff like that."

We asked him to elaborate on the maturity issue. Would younger readers not understand the language and themes or would parents disapprove? "It would be hard to understand for some kids. Also because there are occurrences where they use really bad language just because of what happens in the book. . . . I think for parents that have younger kids I don't think they would want their kids to be reading about sex and stuff like that."

Brad was enthusiastic about *A Lesson Before Dying* for students his age and older. "I think that it should be read by a lot of people because it's just a great book. It taught me a lot of things about life, how people are today, how we treat people, how we're so assuming of people just 'cause of the way they look or how they act even though they may not be like that and I guess overall just a great book."

Shizuko's Daughter

Jeni Bershinsky is thirteen, in the eighth grade, and loves to read. She is very active in sports so she does not have as much time as she would like to read. "I thought the book was really good and I think it would be kind of harder for elementary kids because it was kind of challenging. . . . I thought that with suicide and stuff that elementary kids wouldn't really enjoy books like that. But I liked it because it does talk about life today and what happens. I didn't really see anything wrong with the book. It was kind of sad, and happy at times, but I thought it was good . . . I think that people with little kids would maybe object [to the suicide] but I think if anyone has dealt with a situation like that that it was a good book . . . 'cause it explains how people really feel and like what happens through suicide."

We asked Jeni who she thought should read the book. "If they are young and have problems reading I don't think it would be the great book for them or if they are mentally challenged or something it might scare them. Then I don't think they should read it but people who like books that give them that rush and things like that and people who have dealt with suicide should." We wondered if she thought people might think the book condones suicide. Jeni replied, "I don't think suicide is the answer in any case. . . . I don't think it is saying that suicide is the answer. My school has dealt with suicide before so I think it would be a good book to have out and able to read. I liked it."

Fallen Angels

Ted Cushman is thirteen and in seventh grade. He selected Walter Dean Myers' book because he is interested in war and soldiers. Ted liked the book, saying, "I thought the book was pretty good. I didn't want to put it down. It had really good descriptive words. It's something you can picture." When we asked him if he would recommend it to a friend, he said, "Yeah, in fact, I did. . . . [My friend] read it and it's his favorite book." Ted identified the same potential problems that Borgese and Ebert did in their rationale for *Fallen Angels*: "Some of them cussed a little bit . . . and the violence . . . one of the main characters gets shot in the side. . . . It's not like every page cussing, but once in awhile. They probably wouldn't want their kids to read that. They shouldn't know about it I guess."

We wondered if Ted thought the book would make people violent. He thought it was possible that it could make "some people" violent, "depending on who's reading it." But he would not want anyone to tell him that he could not read it. "I'd get sort of mad at them. I'm pretty mature for my age. It [the violence] doesn't really matter to me. It doesn't affect me." He thought it might be more interesting to learn about the Vietnam War with a book like this one because he found the novels and textbooks they usually read in class to be "boring." *Fallen Angels* was much more realistic and engaging.

If I Should Die Before I Wake

Kate Hall is a high school sophomore and, at the time of the interview, was understudying all of the female roles in the school play. We met her on the one night that she did not have rehearsal. Fortunately, reading the book went quickly for her. "I really liked this book. I got through it in three or four days. . . . I couldn't put it down. It's really good. . . . It was really powerful because it's about the Holocaust. . . . as far as I could tell it was really accurate and a lot of details. . . . I liked the idea because it's like the girl Chana is giving her history to Hilary and I think that's a really cool idea. . . . I can't really think of any weaknesses. It was a good book. . . . It wasn't boring. . . . What I didn't understand was why it was called *If I Should Die Before I Wake*. I mean I can understand it but like that wasn't mentioned and it wasn't a big emphasis . . . but that's OK. . . . I did recommend it to my friend Lisa . . . and she's Jewish and she wanted to read it. . . . But, yeah, I would definitely recommend it to a friend because it's really powerful and it's like honest and good. . . . It's honest about the Holocaust. . . . You can understand what she's going through. They don't just skip over stuff. They go into detail and that's good because you can get into it more and learn more."

Kate was puzzled by why anyone would object to this book. "I don't know why anyone would really object to this because it's not like, it's not, I don't understand why it really should be banned because yeah, it's about the Holocaust but there are tons of books about the Holocaust. And it doesn't go into enough detail where they actually . . . some books we've read go into a lot of details. Yes, there are gas chambers and torture and stuff but nothing that's so bad we shouldn't read it."

We wondered if she thought it was depressing. "Well, no. . . . Hilary goes through this whole transformation. It's good. It comes out good. . . . I don't think it should have been banned." Later in the interview she thought of another possible reason. "I guess maybe the only reason people might want to ban it because Hilary was in that neo-Nazi group. So I guess, but, if they did take that out, it wouldn't be as effective when she changed her ways at the end. But I don't think that's enough to ban it."

Overall, Kate thought the book should be taught in school. "I think this does a good job of portraying the Holocaust because we don't really talk about it at school. It was a huge, huge thing and if you do have history you spend like a day on World War II, just a little portion and this goes through the emotions, you know what happened and I would think people would want people to know how it was. I think this is a good educational tool, assuming they didn't lie about it or anything. . . . I really like this book."

These readers appreciate books that engage their interest from the beginning, although they are willing to be patient for a few chapters. They appreciate good description and books that tell them what life is like now. Young adult readers identified many of the same potential problems as the adult writers of the rationales did. While some of them suggested that a book would be more appropriate for a certain age, they all thought that they were old enough to read it and would not be happy if someone told them they could not. These results are not surprising, but the students' enthusiasm for the books they had chosen was gratifying. The tones of their voices further confirmed that every single reader clearly enjoyed the book he or she chose. Many thought their friends would enjoy the book, too, which is a high recommendation.

If these books were challenged, would readers and their teachers defend them? We did not ask that question directly, but anecdotal reports suggest that some teachers might prefer to avoid the controversy. When we asked readers what they would say to someone who wanted to stop them from reading the book, responses were more puzzled than persuasive.

Teaching About Controversy

If we want students to be able to form and support an opinion, to make informed choices about selecting and evaluating reading material, then we must teach them to do so. We must not only provide students with choices in their reading but we must also help them learn how to discuss and defend their selections. Some teaching suggestions follow.

Pair readings about choice and censorship.

Discussing the topics of choice and censorship may help students understand some of the issues involved in challenges to the materials they want to read. They could read fiction that addresses these two topics. Lois Lowry presents a frightening world in *The Giver.* At first, her world appears idyllic. There is no pain; everything, even sexual desire, is regulated. Of course a world where each person is assigned a particular role in society is not perfect, and Jonas, the young protagonist, must decide what to do about it when given the chance. Teachers could pair this short novel with Kurt Vonnegut's story "Harrison Bergeron." In Harrison's world, equality is legislated. Each person has been given a special handicap. The ballerina must dance with weights so she will not be able to leap any higher than anyone else. Harrison's father, George, has above-average intelligence, so he must wear a radiotransmitter that emits loud noises at regular intervals to keep him from thinking. Harrison plans to overthrow the government and help people realize what has been done to them in the name of equality.

Before assigning these stories, teachers could ask students questions such as these: Would you like to live in a world where everyone was equal so there was no jealousy? How about a world with no pain or sadness? Would you like a world that was safe and comfortable? What would you be willing to give up to get such a world?

After reading the two stories, students could discuss the idea of choice. Lois Lowry addresses this topic in personal correspondence with Marilyn Apseloff:

> *The Giver* is about a world where . . . decisions are made for them [people]. It seems very safe and comfortable. . . . Then it got scary . . because it turned out that it wasn't safe and comfy to live in a world where adhering to rigid rules is the norm. It turned out, in the book, that such a world is very, very dangerous; and that people have to learn to make their own choices. (484)

Censorship eliminates peoples' choices, although it may seem to provide a perfect world where offensive language and ideas no longer exist. Is such a world desirable? What price would we be willing to pay?

Debate challenged books.

Students can understand the issues surrounding controversial materials by engaging in debates of challenged books. Give students a list of frequently challenged books, such as those listed in the Introduction, or lists available from People for the American Way or the American Library Association. Ask students to pair up to read one book. Both students should research reviews and challenges to the book. Then students decide which person in each pair will prepare the arguments against the book and which will prepare the arguments for the book. All students might want to research and prepare more general arguments for and against censorship. Pairs should present their debates in front of the class. Whole-class discussion of issues surrounding book censorship should follow the debates.

Read for multiple interpretations.

Many students and book challengers read books as though they are manuals for living. To people who read only for literal meaning, books may seem dangerous. Literal readers may believe that the characters in novels are models for their own behavior and challengers fear that readers will disobey authority, speak profanely, or act immorally. Teaching that focuses only on the literal meaning of the text and that provides readers with one, "correct" interpretation can perpetuate these beliefs.

Instead of teaching students to ferret out what a text means, we can offer them multiple interpretations and ask them to discuss the merits of each one. Readers who log on to the reviews from readers their age, adults, and professional critics at amazon.com or barnesandnoble.com will find a range of reactions to novels such as *Weetzie Bat.* These reactions are a good place for young adults to start. We will need to help them evaluate the quality of these statements and compare the statements of everyday readers to the statements of professional critics. What makes statements more or less credible? What criteria might professional critics use that other readers do not?

Another way to help students understand multiple interpretations is to show them several approaches. In *Interpreting Young Adult Literature: Literary Theory in the Secondary Classroom,* John Noell Moore offers ways to look at young adult novels. He interprets Walter Dean Myers' *Fallen Angels* through the lens of reader-response theory, tracing the identity theme in Richie Perry's story. Other readers might approach this same novel as a statement about the inhumanity of war and the unfairness of how soldiers are selected for the most dangerous duty. While these two approaches overlap, each provides a different means for interpreting the novel.

As students understand and evaluate the interpretations of others, they also need to form and support their own interpretations. They can present their reading of the text orally, visually, or in writing for other students in the class to discuss.

Reading beyond the literal meaning is essential. Students are able to do so; we must encourage multiple interpretations and informed evaluation. Ken Donelson tells a story that makes this point well. One week Hazel Rochman and Roger Sutton aired a discussion about Harry Mazer's novel *I Love You Stupid* on their Chicago public radio show. During the debate, a conservative adult and a high school student exchanged the following comments:

> CENSOR: You just don't understand how you can be influenced by a bad book.
>
> STUDENT: That's only if you read weak. You've got to read strong. (479)

Listening to readers and encouraging them to listen to each other are essential. Students who read strong will not allow book challengers to stop them from reading.

Works Cited

Apseloff, Marilyn Fain. "Lois Lowry: Facing the Censors." *Para·Doxa* 2.3-4 (1996): 480–485.

Donelson, Ken. "Censorship and Adolescent Literature." *Para·Doxa* 2.3-4 (1996): 472–479.

Edwards, June. *Opposing Censorship in the Public Schools: Religion, Morality, and Literature.* Mahwah: Lawrence Erlbaum, 1998.

Lowry, Lois. *The Giver.* Boston: Houghton, 1993.

Moore, John Noell. *Interpreting Young Adult Literature: Literary Theory in the Secondary Classroom.* Portsmouth: Boynton/Cook, 1997.

Vonnegut, Kurt. "Harrison Bergeron." *Adventures in Appreciation.* Orlando: Harcourt, 1989: 167–171.

TITLES ANNOTATED IN THIS TEXT

SELECTION GUIDES

Intended Audience

A list of books by the grade level of the intended audience can only be approximate at best. Many factors enter into a book recommendation, including your knowledge of the student's interest and abilities, the setting (whole class or individual), and purpose. To provide some guidance, however, we have listed the titles of books in order of the grade levels suggested by the authors of the rationales.

Grades 6 to 8

Memoirs of a Bookbat by Kathryn Lasky (grades 6 to 8 and beyond)

Grades 7 to 9

The Ear, the Eye, and the Arm by Nancy Farmer

Grades 7 to 12

Out of the Dust by Karen Hesse (ages 13 to 80)
Jack by A. M. Homes
Fallen Angels by Walter Dean Myers
If I Should Die Before I Wake by Han Nolan
When She Hollers by Cynthia Voigt

Grades 8 to 12

Spite Fences by Trudy Krisher
Shizuko's Daughter by Kyoko Mori

Grades 9 to 12

Am I Blue? ed. by Marion Dane Bauer
Weetzie Bat by Francesca Lia Block
The Moves Make the Man by Bruce Brooks
Lakota Woman by Mary Crow Dog and Richard Erdoes
The Crazy Horse Electric Game by Chris Crutcher

Grades 10 to 12

Ironman by Chris Crutcher
Annie on My Mind by Nancy Garden
Their Eyes Were Watching God by Zora Neale Hurston
The Bean Trees by Barbara Kingsolver
In Country by Bobbie Ann Mason
Out of Control by Norma Fox Mazer

Grades 11 to 12

A Lesson Before Dying by Ernest Gaines
Montana 1948 by Larry Watson

Thematic Groupings

The rationales in this book can be grouped under a range of topics. We have suggested a few groupings to help you plan your reading list, but others are certainly possible.

Insights into historical events or time periods

Lakota Woman
A Lesson Before Dying
Out of the Dust
Their Eyes Were Watching God
Spite Fences
In Country
If I Should Die Before I Wake

Sexual identity

Am I Blue?
Weetzie Bat
Ironman
Annie on My Mind
Jack

Social issues

A Lesson Before Dying
The Bean Trees
Memoirs of a Bookbat
Out of Control

Shizuko's Daughter
When She Hollers
Montana 1948

Coming-of-age and individual identity

Am I Blue?
Weetzie Bat
The Moves Make the Man
The Crazy Horse Electric Game
Ironman
The Ear, the Eye, and the Arm
A Lesson Before Dying
Annie on My Mind
Out of the Dust
Jack
Their Eyes Were Watching God
The Bean Trees
Spite Fences
In Country
Shizuko's Daughter
Fallen Angels
If I Should Die Before I Wake

Family relationships

The Moves Make the Man
Ironman
The Ear, the Eye, and the Arm
Out of the Dust
Jack
Their Eyes Were Watching God
The Bean Trees
Spite Fences
Memoirs of a Bookbat
In Country
Shizuko's Daughter
If I Should Die Before I Wake
When She Hollers
Montana 1948

CREDITS

The editors and publisher thank those who have generously given permission to reprint material.

From *Am I Blue? Coming Out from the Silence* by Marion Dane Bauer. Copyright © 1994 by Marion Dane Bauer. HarperCollins Publishers Inc.

From *Weetzie Bat* by Francesca Lia Block. Copyright © 1989 by Francesca Lia Block. HarperCollins Publishers Inc.

From *The Moves Make the Man* by Bruce Brooks. Copyright © 1984 by Bruce Brooks. HarperCollins Publishers Inc.

From *Lakota Woman* by Mary Crow Dog. Copyright © 1990 by Mary Crow Dog and Richard Erdoes. Reprinted by permission of Grove/Atlantic, Inc.

From *The Crazy Horse Electric Game* by Chris Crutcher. Copyright © 1987 by Chris Crutcher. By permission of Greenwillow Books, a division of William Morrow and Company, Inc.

From *Ironman* by Chris Crutcher. Copyright © 1995 by Chris Crutcher. By permission of Greenwillow Books, a division of William Morrow and Company, Inc.

From *The Ear, the Eye, and the Arm* by Nancy Farmer. Copyright © 1994 by Nancy Farmer. Used by permission of Orchard Books, New York.

From *A Lesson Before Dying* by Ernest Gaines. Copyright © 1993 by Ernest J. Gaines. Used by permission of Alfred A. Knopf Incorporated.

From *Annie on My Mind* by Nancy Garden. Copyright © 1982 by Nancy Garden. Reprinted by permission of Farrar, Straus & Giroux, Inc.

From *Out of the Dust* by Karen Hesse. Published by Scholastic Press, a division of Scholastic Inc. Copyright © 1997 by Karen Hesse. Reprinted by permission.

From *Jack* by A. M. Homes. Copyright © 1989 by A. M. Homes. Reprinted by permission of Macmillan Publishing Company.

From *Their Eyes Were Watching God* by Zora Neale Hurston. Copyright © 1937 by Zora Neale Hurston. Renewed 1965 by John C. Hurston and Joel Hurston. HarperCollins Publishers Inc.

From *The Bean Trees* by Barbara Kingsolver. Copyright © 1988 by Barbara Kingsolver. HarperCollins Publishers Inc.

From *Spite Fences* by Trudy Krisher. Copyright © 1994 by Trudy Krisher. Delacorte Press. Bantam Doubleday Dell.

Excerpt from *Memoirs of a Bookbat*, copyright © 1994 by Kathryn Lasky Knight, reprinted by permission of Harcourt Brace & Company.

From *In Country* by Bobbie Ann Mason. Copyright © 1985 by Bobbie Ann Mason. HarperCollins Publishers Inc.